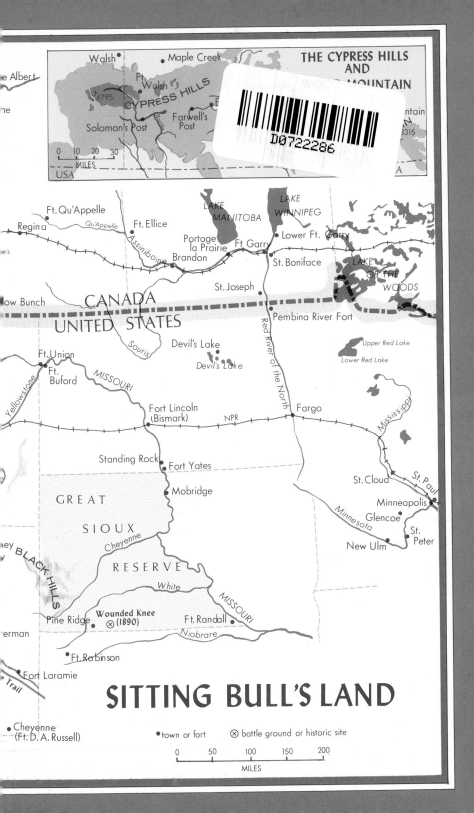

THE CYPRESS HILLS
AND
WOOD MOUNTAIN

Walsh •   • Maple Creek

Ft. Walsh

CYPRESS HILLS

+4795

Solomon's Post

Farwell's Post

0 10 20 30
MILES

USA

Albert

he

e's

Ft. Qu'Appelle

Regina

Qu'Appelle

Ft. Ellice

Assiniboine

Portage la Prairie

Brandon

Ft Garry

Lower Ft. Garry

St. Boniface

LAKE MANITOBA

LAKE WINNIPEG

LAKE OF THE WOODS

St. Joseph

Pembina River Fort

ow Bunch

CANADA
UNITED STATES

Souris

Devil's Lake

Devil's Lake

Upper Red Lake

Lower Red Lake

Ft. Union

Ft. Buford

Yellowstone

MISSOURI

Fort Lincoln (Bismark)

NPR

Fargo

Red River of the North

Mississippi

Standing Rock

Fort Yates

Mobridge

GREAT

SIOUX

Cheyenne

St. Cloud

St. Paul

Minneapolis

Glencoe

St. Peter

Minnesota

New Ulm

ey BLACK HILLS

RESERVE

White

MISSOURI

Pine Ridge

Wounded Knee
⊗ (1890)

Ft. Randall

Niobrare

erman

Ft. Robinson

Fort Laramie

Trail

Cheyenne
(Ft. D. A. Russell)

SITTING BULL'S LAND

• town or fort   ⊗ battle ground or historic site

0   50   100   150   200

MILES

Grant MacEwan
Sitting Bull
The Years in Canada

Hurtig Publishers

Edmonton

Hurtig Publishers
10560–105 Street
Edmonton, Alberta

ISBN
0-88830-073-5

Designed, typeset, printed and bound in Canada

Contents

Foreword/7
Bloody Hands/*9*
The Prairie Neighbourhood/*16*
Massacre in Minnesota/*22*
The Sioux Years in Manitoba/*28*
The Indian Wars/*37*
Violence North of the Line/*45*
Macdonald's Boundary Police/*54*
Custer's Last Stand/*65*
After Little Big Horn/*72*
Walsh Meets Bull/*84*
Laws Must Be Enforced/*90*

Illustrated Section between pages 96/97

The Wood Mountain Scene/*97*
International Complexities/*104*
And Then the Nez Percé/*111*
White Bird's Story/*116*
Bull Faces the Commission/*124*
New Risks and New Dangers/*134*
More Trouble on the Way/*140*
Short Tempers/*147*
Famine in Buffalo Country/*153*
You Can't Continue This Way/*159*
Dissension/*167*
An Old Hat and an Old Horse/*173*
Almost Persuaded/*179*
Qu'Appelle/*184*

The Inglorious Return/*189*
To Whom the Praise and Payment/*196*
What Might Have Been/*201*
Bull's Last Battle / *206*
Notes / 211
Bibliography /217
Index / 219

Credits for Photographic Material
Glenbow-Alberta Institute Archives, Calgary,
1, 6, 14, 15 lower
Manitoba Provincial Archives, 3
Montana Historical Society, Helena, 4
McGill University, Montreal. McCord Museum.
(Notman Photographic Archives), 9
Nebraska State Historical Society, Lincoln, 7, 10
Public Archives of Canada, 11, 15 upper, 16 lower
Royal Canadian Mounted Police, Ottawa, 2
Saskatchewan Archives Board, Regina, 16 upper
Smithsonian Institution, Washington, 12
United States National Archives, Washington, 5,8

Foreword

For many years citizens of both Canada and United States were satisfied to think of the Sioux chief, Sitting Bull, as a treacherous savage, a menace to the white man's design for the development of the country. Newspaper reports made him the most notorious figure on the western frontier. After the Custer affair of 1876 – for which he was held responsible – his reputation was for massacre and murder. At the very mention of his name, settlers cringed and breathed prayers for protection from the terrible Sioux.

That the Chief might have been misjudged seemed to escape most observers. They overlooked the possibility that he might be a thoughtful and conscientious Indian whose actions deserved to be studied in the light of circumstances. Should an Indian leader facing the loss of his land and freedom have done less? What would any good citizen do when his traditional way of life was being uprooted by invaders?

But why the Canadian interest in Sitting Bull? Was he an American or a Canadian Indian – or did it matter? He scoffed at the question until authorities in both countries declared him American; then he insisted that he was at least as much Canadian as American.

Regardless of how the debate should have been resolved, Canada had him and his ferocious followers for a few uneasy and crucial years, and Canadians could not escape concern. He became a symbol of the conflict between the hordes of greedy newcomers and the frustrated native defenders. As most Indians agreed when it was too late, Sitting Bull's leadership offered the best hope for a united stand against the aggressors.

He never lost hope of gaining support from other tribes and conducting a showdown battle for recovery of the buffalo country.

Sitting Bull made an indelible impression upon both Canadian and American history. One can but speculate how the direction of western history might have been changed if he had succeeded during his years in Canada in uniting the prairie tribes and challenging the new authority. Certainly the years of Sioux residence in what is now southern Saskatchewan possessed a special importance in shaping the future of Canada and Canadians would do well to gain a better acquaintance with Sitting Bull and his times. They will likely conclude that the Chief, instead of being a "bad Indian", was actually a good one.

As always, in the development of such a subject, the author has a debt of gratitude to his friends in libraries and archives, and, in this instance, to various Sioux Indians still living in Canada, some of whom claim blood relationships with the great Chief, and all of whom are his ardent admirers.

Grant MacEwan

Bloody Hands

Spare us, O Lord, from the bloody hands of Sitting Bull and his awful Sioux, was a prayer uttered thousands of times on two sides of the International Boundary, both before and after the slaughter known as the Custer Massacre in 1876. That military disaster which saw General George Custer and his entire cavalry unit wiped out at Little Big Horn, Montana, was a United States affair but native tribes refused to recognize boundaries and the feeling of alarm pervaded the plains from Red River to the Rockies and from Fort Edmonton to Texas. The very mention of Sitting Bull – the most fearsome name in all the buffalo country – was enough to produce thoughts of doom.

Nobody escaped the grip of fear when the *Manitoba Daily Free Press* of March 5, 1877, announced that Sitting Bull with a large army of warriors and over a thousand horses and mules had entered Canada at a point near Wood Mountain. As the leader of a big and powerful tribe, this chief was in a position to make good his threats. Settlers made sure their doors were bolted at night and guns handy at all times.

The anxiety of the period lingered like the seven-year itch, giving residents reason to remember those "Sioux Years" very much as they would recall "Drought Years" and "Smallpox Years". For Canadians, the threat of direct attack from several thousand disgruntled Sioux refugees was serious enough; even more frightening was the danger that the Sioux presence on the Canadian plains would precipitate a general Indian uprising. The Mounted Police, the only deterrent, knew the gravity of the situation. An Indian union for the purpose of driving the white man from the plains was Sitting Bull's dream, just as it had been Pontiac's.

Several times the Sioux and others of the native races on the prairie had it in their power to annihilate the whites. With Indian support, Louis Riel's Métis could have uprooted the Europeans in the West. Big Bear of the Crees proposed a similar united effort that would have cost thousands of lives, and, with the calibre of leadership Sitting Bull could have provided in the sparsely settled country, he might have gained a quick victory. All that prevented a massive massacre between 1877 and 1881 was Sitting Bull's failure to unify the tribesmen of the Canadian plains. The modern scholar must find himself torn between admiration for the native leaders who would fight for freedom and rights, and gratitude to those who refused to indulge in a slaughter, even for liberation.

The bloodbath did not materialize, but a chain of related events in the '60s and '70s – the "Sioux Years" – set the course of western development. The Sioux massacres in Minnesota in 1862 signalled the prolonged Indian Wars in western United States and brought Sitting Bull and his people to the Canadian frontier. Inevitably, the events influenced Indian policy in Canada at that time when traditional Indian society on both sides of the border was being destroyed. With Confederation in 1867 and Canada's acquisition of the West in 1869, prairie Indians were fated to accept the hateful restraints of reservation living. It was like trying to transplant old trees to thin soil but destruction of the buffalo herds and the advance of the white man's civilization left the native people no alternative. It was not surprising that the more hostile bands, goaded by their grim prospects, terrorized the frontier.

It was fear of the Sioux, coupled with reports of atrocities committed by traders from Montana, that brought the North West Mounted Police into existence. The new force, in turn, made it possible for workers to pursue the task of railroad construction and settlers to enter upon their land with assurance of at least some organized resistance in the event of Indian rebellion. Adversity was part of the price of progress and experience with the Sioux had its useful as well as its terrifying aspects.

Although the Sioux were regarded as a United States responsibility, the tribesmen crossed the Boundary as if it were of no more account than a buffalo path, arguing that they were Canadian Indians as much as American. But however much the Sioux insisted upon British connections, the permanent residents north of the border – both European and native – wished they would return to Dakota or Montana.

But who could be sure Sitting Bull was not born on the Canadian side? It was easy to presume, as some historians did, that he was born in Dakota Territory, about 1836, where his people were concentrated at the time. He and his fellow tribesmen claimed what is now southern Manitoba and southern Saskatchewan as their traditional hunting ground. Certainly, Sitting Bull was no stranger to the Canadian prairies. Perhaps his claim to British connections was couched in wishful thinking but on various occasions he paraded medals given to his grandfather by King George III in gratitude for support during the American Revolution and insisted that British North America was his original home territory. "This is my land," he proclaimed in the presence of General Terry at Fort Walsh in 1877. Moreover, members of his tribe who remained in Canada after fleeing the United States insisted that the old Chief was indeed born on the plains of what became southern Saskatchewan, probably close to Wood Mountain.

Every now and again someone repeated reports that Sitting Bull was a Métis from Fort Garry, who had been educated at St. John's School and then rejected by the local half-breeds. It made a good story but, like many good stories, had no basis in fact. He was an Indian, an Unkpapa Sioux. His father was Jumping Buffalo, killed in a hand-to-hand battle with a Crow. When the fierce struggle ended, both adversaries were dead.

As a boy, Sitting Bull was known as Hunkeshnee, meaning "slow". But if there was reason for the name, it did not remain with him long. He became Sitting Bull when, as a growing boy, he was attacked by a young buffalo caught in a pound. In self defence, the boy seized the animal by its horns, wrestled it to the ground the way he had thrown young Indians in wrestling matches, and then jocularly set the bull on its buttocks. Or was the new name acquired because of a squatting posture in which the young man had been seen many times, probably a pose for meditation? If the latter explanation is accepted, the young Sioux was simply "The Bull Who Squats".

The North West Mounted Police who met him in 1877

agreed that he was an outstanding personality. Standing about five feet, ten inches in moccasins, he was shorter than most adult males of his tribe but more muscular than the majority. He weighed a hundred and seventy-five pounds, mostly bone and sinew, and was obviously powerful. He was not handsome but he had a mischievous twinkle in his eye and, even with the marks of smallpox etched permanently on his brown face, he was strikingly attractive. Men in his company said they had the feeling of being in the presence of a Napoleon. His dark brown hair hung in two heavy braids in front of his shoulders, a double challenge to enemies who might have considered themselves smart enought to take his scalp. His nose was slightly hooked and the gaze of his black eyes seemed to penetrate like a powerful ray. After much youthful riding, his legs were bowed to fit the contour of a horse and, in the best Indian fashion, he walked with toes turned inward. There was a slight trace of lameness resulting from an early war wound. Scars on his bronzed body told of other battles and the deep lines of his weather-beaten brow came from the unending stress and strife in his life.

Some critics argued that he was a medicine man more than a warrior, a schemer more than a fighter. He was indeed a medicine man but that fact did not prevent him from being a warrior in the best Indian tradition. Long before the usual age for boys to join the fighting men, he stole away to be with the braves in their battles against the Crees and Crows. In due course, he submitted to the cruel sun dance tests to demonstrate a Spartan-like capacity to endure pain and thus qualify to become a brave. Late in life, Sitting Bull was induced to record the story of his life in sketches. The pictures, drawn roughly, show him fighting against Assiniboines when he was only sixteen years old. It was probably his first fight after qualifying as a brave. On that occasion, he captured one prisoner. Perhaps this captive was the young Assiniboine known as Hohay, later adopted by Sitting Bull. The captor's treatment of his prisoner denies the allegations of needless cruelty on the part of the Sioux. The Assiniboine acknowledged the benevolent treatment and became devoted to the man who captured and befriended him.

On yet another occasion when engaged in a battle with the

Crows, Sitting Bull emerged with the best record for bravery. He called for a charge and led the way, expecting the other Sioux warriors to follow him. He was surprised to discover he was alone. But he continued and encountered a single Crow Indian in a protected position. There was an exchange of shots. Then the Crow was out of ammunition and at the mercy of the Sioux. But Sitting Bull, rather than take unfair advantage of his enemy, threw him some powder and balls and challenged him to fight on. As the battle progressed, Sitting Bull was wounded by one of his own bullets, but finally the Crow was killed and the Sioux returned with another scalp.

Sitting Bull had three wives in his tipi, although this was not "as many as his brother-in-law had". Nonetheless, he was a good husband and patient father, which is probably more than could be said of some of the critics who called him a savage. And if he was satisfied to support three squaws and they were happy about the arrangement, there was no particular reason for others to complain.

About ten years before his meeting with the North West Mounted Police in 1877, Sitting Bull was elevated from the rank of medicine chief to that of war chief over all the Unkpapa Sioux. From the beginning, he left no doubt about the quality of his leadership. He could be friendly or, if occasion demanded, he could be brutally tough. He knew that rumours of gold in the Black Hills would bring white men rushing to his area, molesting and trying to displace his people. This, he believed, was a time to be firm and he ordered that any Indian disclosing information about gold to white men would have to die. And any white who found gold in the Indian territory could expect the same treatment.

That writers of his time chose to call him "the typical savage" did not bother him. He answered to his own conscience and to that alone. When he believed there was cause, he could fight like a fiend but he was not cruel and murderous. Unschooled in the conventional sense, he was wise in the ways of nature. He regretted even the necessity of killing animals for food. He was kind to children, polite to women, and loyal to all who earned his loyalty. He was known to treat prisoners of Indian wars with compassion and he appeared to be no more vengeful than most humans. Speaking about the Indian reputation for barbarous revenge, he gave it as his opinion that the spirit of inhuman revenge came to the native people only after association with the white race.

True, a large part of Sitting Bull's life was devoted to war against the white man, but this was not war for the sake of war. He could say with Chief Crowfoot of the Blackfoot that before going to war there must be a reason. He saw the highest moral purpose in resisting the advance of the white man and the displacement of his people and was prepared to give his life fighting for it. Quite convinced that he was ordained to be the saviour of the Indians on both sides of the "Big Road", he saw it as his task to liberate his people from the invaders and to lead them back to the freedom of the buffalo ranges.

In the course of wars with American forces, he developed an unyielding hatred for soldiers in uniform, and other white men had difficulty in escaping the stigma. After coming to Canada, he viewed the men of the Mounted Police with deep suspicion and respect for them did not come rapidly. Gradually he discovered that he could trust these Canadian law officers. For the favourable relationship which existed ultimately between the Mounted Police and the Chief, much of the credit was due to the understanding, tact, and firmness displayed by Major James Morrow Walsh, one of the Mounted Police "originals". Between the Major and Bull, as Walsh called the Sioux leader, a fine friendship developed but it did not mean that the Chief was abandoning his hope to annihilate the whites in the West or at least all who were not friendly toward the Indian cause. He made displays of peaceful intent but never lost the conviction that there could be neither freedom nor justice for his people until the last white man was removed from Indian country. After being insulted, robbed, attacked, and starved on his own hunting ground, he would have found it easy to carry out the extermination of all who had any part in destroying the wild herds and degrading his people. He had confidence; he knew that if the fierce and angry prairie tribes could be welded into a single fighting force – with himself as the supreme leader – it would have both the numerical strength and the battlefield skills to kill to the last white man.

And why should he have been so condemned? To the great Sioux Chief, nothing was more precious than freedom and no criminal was worse that the one who would rob him of his liberty. Patrick Henry was applauded when he proclaimed: "Give me liberty or give me death." Sitting Bull, with no less right, was saying the same, but received only disparaging epithets.

The struggle, however, was more than a simple two-party conflict. Involved were the United States forces who had been at war with the prairie natives for many years, the North West Mounted Police who carried the authority of the Government of Canada, the clusters of frightened and relatively helpless traders and settlers on both sides of the International Boundary and, of course, the Indians of various antagonistic tribes who were reluctant to band together, even for survival. It was a complex situation with distinct international overtones. With an increasing concentration of both Canadian and United States Indians in the vicinity of the Cypress Hills, the prairie seemed like a sputtering volcano, ready to erupt. American editors warned of an explosive situation developing on the British side. Indeed, the western prairie came closer than Canadians realized to a bloodbath which would have made the Custer massacre appear trivial.

At that crucial period in Western Canadian history, while the fate of nearly half a continent seemed to hang in a balance, the course of history was determined very largely by the discussions between Major James Walsh and Chief Sitting Bull. Two of the most daring and uncompromising figures in Canadian history, they talked again and again, sometimes bluffing, sometimes cajoling, sometimes bullying. Sometimes the reactions were tense and bordering on violence. But the awful explosion which had been prophesied did not occur and the two men came to the end of their prairie sojourn as loyal friends.

The Prairie Neighbourhood

Sitting Bull's Sioux, as indigenous to the prairie as the buffalo and almost as far-ranging, gained a reputation for evil and a lack of remorse. Neighbouring tribesmen knew them as fierce and uncompromising warriors, and settlers in both the northwestern States and parts of prairie Canada feared them. "Be ready to shoot first," was the admonition from a Portage la Prairie pioneer speaking from experience; and mothers disciplined naughty children with: "You behave or the Sioux will get you." On the United States side, with a growing list of atrocities marked against them, the Sioux became the "Ishmaels" of the plains, "their hands against every man and every man's hand against them".

Even in their tribal name they were defamed. Although they preferred to be called "Dakotas" meaning "friends", the Ojibways called them "Nadowessioux" – "snakes" or "enemies" – and this latter word was abbreviated to "Sioux". The linguistic family was Siouan, a large and complex but not necessarily friendly federation. Sioux and Assiniboine were the two best known western tribes and were rarely on good terms. The Sioux embraced several subtribes: Santee, Sisseton, Yankton, Yanktonnai, Wahpeton and Teton. And the Tetons could be further divided into the Sans Arc, Brule Sioux, Ogalala, and the Unkpapa, to which Sitting Bull belonged. Minor tribes were found as far east as Virginia and as far south as Mississippi. But the biggest and most powerful group was that which hunted the buffalo ranges of the West, from the Mississippi River to the headwaters of the Missouri and as far north as the North Saskatchewan River. It was an area embraced ultimately by the states of Minnesota, North and South Dakota, Montana, Wisconsin, Nebraska, Iowa, Kansas and Missouri, and the southern sections of the provinces of Manitoba and Saskatchewan. With license drawn from strength, members of the tribe did not hesitate to penetrate deep into hunting territory claimed by neighbouring tribes. Hence, many of the explorers and traders in the Canadian West encountered parties of the Sioux.

Alexander Henry[1] mentioned them in his journal frequently. His Saulteaux Indians, when travelling along the Red River warned about the constant danger of attack from their ancient enemies. On August 17, 1800, Henry recorded a Sioux attack upon Crees camping near the mouth of the Red River and on September 15, 1806, he wrote that a party of "our Indians" was attacked by a war party of fifty Sioux near Portage la Prairie. Another day, December 29, 1807, a large band of Sioux fell upon "our principal body of Saulteaux" and killed "our great Chief Tabashaw, his eldest son and an old woman". Still later, on March 4, 1808, his Indians at the Pembina River Fort were "in such a state of consternation from the Sioux having fallen upon them that they have given over hunting for the season."

The Selkirk Settlers were on good terms with the Saulteaux Indians. With the Sioux, it was different; the less the settlers saw of those Indians blamed for the murder of La Vérendrye's oldest son, the happier they were. But the Sioux came again and again and the settlers found it difficult to avoid them. Over the years, Sioux and Saulteaux clashed many times on ground which was uncomfortably close to the settlement.

The Red River half-breeds found it difficult to be neutral and generally sided with the Saulteaux. Recognizing the folly of such fighting, however, the Métis took the initiative and negotiated a peace for a few years at least. "A peace," according to Robert Hill, "was effected between the half-breeds and the Sioux in the fall of 1844, on the strength of which the hunters returned to the plains, smoked the peace pipe, and passed the summer amongst the Dacotahs. Shortly after, a number of Sioux returned the compliment by making a friendly visit to the whites in the settlement."[2] The gesture was noble but peace did not last and the old bitterness flared again, intensely enough to stop the Fort Garry and Red River hunters from venturing into Sioux country on annual expeditions for buffalo meat.

The Selkirk Settlers heard stories about the fate of hunters and travellers who encountered the Sioux or "Scalping Dakotas". Robert Hill reported a trader named Hess who, after pursuing buffalo, returned to his camp to find his companions and a daughter murdered and a second daughter missing, evidently taken captive by the attackers. A short time later a Red River blacksmith, his wife and child, were reputedly murdered by Sioux on the warpath. Perhaps the Sioux were guilty but it must be admitted that almost any atrocity for which there was no clear proof of guilt was blamed on them and they may have been blamed beyond their deserving.

The Sioux were, like other prairie Indians, children of the plains, nomads, followers of the buffalo herds. For thousands of years the prairie was buffalo country, vast, virgin and unchanging, and the Indian was the monarch. There the tribesmen moved with the herds, battled with enemy bands, stole horses whenever there was opportunity, and lived as free men without imposing any serious threat to the natural environment. Fixed boundaries did not exist although tribesmen laying claim to a hunting ground of their choice fought furiously to protect it from intruders. Tribal territory, roughly defined as it was, could change from day to day depending upon the fortunes of war, but was unlikely to shift substantially or often. The Blackfoot Indians, who at one time occupied the eastern prairies, fought their way westward and came, ultimately, to possess some of the best buffalo range. Their one-time allies, the Gros Ventres or Big Bellies – the name having come from a tribal sign suggesting an abdominal protrusion – were on the Canadian side of the forty-ninth parallel until gradually forced south. The Crees living in moose and beaver country, the first of western Indians to acquire guns, easily forced an extension westward of their hunting ground. And the main body of Sioux was shifted westward by Ojibway pressure when the latter obtained guns from the French.

Culturally, the western Indians were similar. Adapting to their surroundings, they were nomadic. As long as buffalo herds were present for the killing, they felt no urge to settle down and make permanent homes. The chief was the undisputed head of the community but his rank entitled him to no better fare than the lowliest. The people were religious in their own way. In spite of what churchmen said, they were not pagans. The Great Spirit was very real to them and they believed that no human could tell them more about that deity than they could discover for themselves. It was for each one to search for the truth and hope to win the favour of the Great One.

All the prairie tribes had sun dances or something resembling them. Basically a religious exercise, for the Blackfoot and Sioux it included the making of braves. A good warrior had to be able to endure suffering without flinching. The whites might be horrified at the demonstrations in which young men tugged against skewers and leather ropes inserted under skin and flesh of breasts and stoically ignored the awful pain, but in their condemnation were showing a lamentable intolerance of a religion they did not understand. The best concept of the Great Spirit came with many years of searching. Finding nature's great truths was likely to be a lifetime task. The Sioux told missionaries that they had more confidence in what the Great Spirit revealed to them than in what the churchmen related from human experience and human prejudice.

All the western tribes suffered from smallpox, one of "the white man's gifts". With no knowledge of prevention or cure, some bands were almost wiped out in early epidemics. The disease appeared first among the Montagnais of Eastern Canada in 1635, and spread to weaken or decimate tribes right across the continent. During the epidemic of 1781, more than half of the natives in many bands died. The Sioux suffered too and, as the pock marks on his face showed so clearly, Sitting Bull was among those who felt the agonizing affliction.

Indian reaction to the immigrant whites varied from tribe to tribe, depending upon local circumstances; where the natives sensed immediate benefit in their association with the newcomers, they found it easy to be friendly. Otherwise, they were likely to be angry. The Saulteaux, a western branch of the Ojibway, welcomed the white man's trade goods and adopted a benevolent attitude. The great Saulteaux chief, Peguis, came voluntarily to help the Selkirk Settlers when the colony was threatened with destruction in 1815 and 1816.

The Crees, first western Indians to make contact with the new race, became steady trading customers and remained loyal.

There were other circumstances favouring lasting harmony: many Cree women were shapely and pretty, and traders, enjoying the absence of marriage laws, took them as wives. They were experts at making moccasins and pemmican and erecting tipis. The unions did not necessarily last long but they were sufficient to place the Crees in a position of preferment among the whites. In some respects, the responsible Crees could have put their white friends to shame. To their credit was a conscientious concern for the protection of fur-bearing animals. While white trappers and some Indians were guilty of plundering and taking all the beaver in a lodge or on a stream, Crees were inclined to leave the young ones, at least a pair in every house. And it was told that Cree women, with admirable scorn for needless killing, refused to cook buffalo tongues when they outnumbered the hides brought in for tanning.

It was when they occupied wooded country around James Bay that the Crees made contact with the first Europeans to penetrate that far westward, notably the Frenchmen, Radisson and Groseilliers. Then, with the guns they were able to obtain, the Crees forced their way westward as far as the Peace River. Eager for all possible advantages in dealing with the white traders, they tried to gain a monopoly by robbing the Chippewa and others from the far Northwest who might be taking furs to Hudson Bay. The Crees then discovered that prairie buffalo offered easier and surer sources of food than the northern moose and successfully fought their way southward to establish a claim upon northern prairies, eventually dividing into two branches of the tribe, Plains Crees and Swampy Crees.

The Assiniboine Indians, a branch of the Sioux tribe which broke away from the main body following a quarrel about four hundred years ago, occupied prairie territory in what was destined to be southern Saskatchewan and southern Manitoba and accepted the Plains Crees as neighbours. The tribes of the Blackfoot group, on the other hand, chose to regard the Crees as perpetual enemies. Crees and Blackfoot fought at every meeting for generations. The last major battle between the rival tribes was fought in the river coulees below the present site of the city of Lethbridge in 1870, while Louis Riel and his Métis followers were holding out at Fort Garry and Sitting Bull and his Sioux were trying to resist the pressures on their Black Hills hunting ground. The Crees, hearing that their old enemies had been weakened by smallpox, went on the warpath primarily for scalps. Chiefs Piapot and Big Bear made a successful attack upon a small and relatively defenceless camp beside the Belly River. But a message pleading for help reached bigger camps of Blackfoot, Blood and Piegan warriors and the response was immediate. With half-breed Jerry Potts, later a scout for the North West Mounted Police, as leader on the Blackfoot side, the Crees were forced to fall back to the river and then into the river to swim for their lives. The Piegans had repeating rifles and continued the killing while the retreating Crees tried to reach the opposite side. It was supposed that the Crees lost almost half of their warriors that day.

Members of the powerful Sioux tribe, many of whom became at least temporary residents on Canadian soil. were almost always on fighting terms with their neighbours, the Crows and Gros Ventres on their western flank, the Blackfoot tribes to the northwest, and even their distant blood relations, the Assiniboines, to the north. Occasionally, the Sioux travelled far to engage the Crees in battle and were even known to carry a fight to the Kootenays. No tribe was more feared than the Sioux. Whether they deserved it or not, they had a reputation for treachery. But in addition to bravery and fighting skill, the Sioux possessed many fine features. Generally, they were tall people with high cheekbones, rather oval faces, Roman noses and strong features. They held their heads high and moved with a proud bearing. At least one writer called them "the finest natives to be found on the plains". Although the opinion was in direct contradiction to popularly accepted views of the period, it was one with which Major James Walsh of the North West Mounted Police would have agreed heartily. As quoted in the *Winnipeg Weekly Times*, July 25, 1879, he spoke in the most glowing terms: "I have found them [the Sioux] the most noble, moral, hospitable, truthful and tractable red men I have ever come in contact with. The character of their women would be a credit to any nation. As a people they are affectionate, and family ties among them are stronger than they are among white people."

Massacre in Minnesota

Sitting Bull, recalling boyhood years, said his people held no bitterness for the palefaces. At that point in time, Indian reaction to the newcomers was one of curiosity and amusement more than anger, and the Sioux laughed at these human oddities with sickly white skins and strange ways. Perhaps they were smart fellows, these whites, but they were amusingly inconsistent. Although clever enough to create wheels and guns and gunpowder, they were hopelessly awkward at fashioning bows and arrows; apparently well-meaning in sharing their religion with Indians, they had no conscience about selling firewater. Even the unbelievable greed of these people who walked with an air of superiority seemed funny at first.

As long as the whites were few in number, Indians could afford to laugh at them. The earliest parties could cross the plains to the California Gold Rush without bringing alarm to the Indians, and the Sioux in 1851 could cede their rights to land in the Territory of Minnesota, west of the Mississippi River, without realizing the implications. But with another rush after gold was discovered at the present site of Boulder, Colorado, in 1859, and a growing migration of landseekers after the Union Pacific Railway reached Kansas, the Indians became first alarmed and then angered. As the whites grew more numerous, their domineering and possessive ways became less entertaining. Their true motives made them dangerous and Indians were beginning to understand. The invaders tried to placate the native people with presents, treaties, and promises of better living. But it was not long before the promises were broken. To the whites, nothing was more important than profit and they saw no sin in robbing Indians who were obstructing their purposes.

From 1851, United States policy was to force prairie Indians to settle on reserves. The idea of being fenced in was abhorrent to the free spirits of native people and they resisted. But resistance and rebellion brought only bigger military forces. Ownership and control of land was imperative; if Indians refused to submit, force would have to be used. The whites were practical people and nothing, not even treaty promises, could be allowed to deter them when they saw gold or the necessity of building a railroad across a reserve.

The Sioux in the Territory of Minnesota saw themselves becoming pawns in the hands of the new tyrants and ultimately struck back with savage fury. The Minnesota massacre gave the attackers a bad name but they had only two choices: they could acquiesce to the loss of everything they believed in or they could strike back. They rebelled and in so doing fired the opening shots in the prolonged and costly Indian Wars of the American Northwest. It was in mid-August, 1862, when Indian patience and endurance were reaching a breaking point, that "all Hell seemed to break loose" in Minnesota. Settlers on both sides of the International Boundary wondered where the killers would strike next and when. Red River residents on the Canadian side made better locks for their doors.

The trouble started at New Ulm, where the Cottonwood joins the Minnesota River, about seventy-five miles southwest of St. Paul. There, many of the Indians were hungry; some may have been on the verge of starvation. One of the Sioux chiefs, Little Crow, presented himself at a supply depot, begging for food. Story has it that the agent behind the counter refused with the comment that hungry Indians should learn to eat grass. Chief Little Crow prepared for the warpath.

The suddenness and scale of the revolt indicates that it was premeditated. Except for a few isolated murders, there was no warning. When the first report reached the outside world, several hundred whites at New Ulm and nearby communities in southern Minnesota were dead. The village, named by German immigrants eight years earlier to honour Germany's cathedral city of Ulm, was devastated. The attack, on August 17, 1862, was ruthless. And the man who would have hungry

Indians "learn to eat grass", among the first to be murdered, was found with his mouth stuffed with dry grass.

The attackers killed as though their purpose was complete annihilation. Gruesome stories were told about the Indian savagery. Even allowing for exaggeration, they were still shocking: a farmer returned from his fields to find his wife and children murdered; an entire family was wiped out during the night while still in bed; a stage coach travelling between Fort Garry and St. Paul was attacked and its passengers killed and scalped.[1]

The revolt spread to widely scattered parts of the Territory of Minnesota and frightening rumours reached the Fort Garry community almost daily. Dr. John C. Schultz, later Lieutenant-Governor of Manitoba, was in St. Paul at the time of the outbreak and preparing to return to his Fort Garry home. Warned of the danger of travel in any part of the Sioux country, he made a wide detour, avoided campfires and travelled only at night, reaching his home without mishap.

Citizens in the East were horrified at what they heard and read. The *New York Tribune* of Saturday, August 23, 1862, announced:

On Monday night the light from burning buildings and grain stacks were seen in all directions. Escaped citizens came into the [fort] during the night, giving accounts of horror too terrible for imagination to conceive. Mothers came in rags, barefooted, whose husbands and children were slaughtered before their eyes. ... The roads in all directions to New Ulm are lined with murdered men, women and children.

Two days later, the eastern press reported that all missionaries had been killed and total deaths were being estimated at five hundred. If as feared, other bands were to join the Minnesota Sioux, this could represent but the beginning of slaughter on a much larger scale. The villages of Redwood, St. Peter, Henderson, and Glencoe were attacked and the light of burning homes continued to illuminate the Minnesota night.

The Sioux, if united, would have been able to field close to 10,000 warriors. That was one fear; what the Chippewa or Saulteaux Indians living in northern Minnesota and the southern part of what was to become Manitoba, might elect to do was another. Sioux and Chippewa were long-time enemies but they might well forget their differences in a war against the intruders. Less than a week after the outbreak at New Ulm, the influential Chippewa, Chief Hole-In-The-Day, issued an ultimatum to the authorities to negotiate an acceptable treaty at once. If the demand were not met, he warned, he would not be responsible for the conduct of his Indians "after Tuesday"; all whites would be well advised to leave the country in the meantime.[2]

It was to Chief Hole-In-The-Day that editors William Buckingham and William Coldwell of the *Nor'-Wester* – first newspaper to be published in Western Canada – paid a visit when coming to Fort Garry with their printing press in 1859. In one of the earliest issues of the pioneer paper, February 28, 1860, they reported a visit at Crow Wing on the Mississippi where they saw the Chief living in a luxurious house where he had six wives, seventeen rocking chairs, and eight portraits on the walls – seven of himself. Of the six wives, the editors noted, three were old like the Chief and three were young and beautiful.

Government agents believed they could still reason with Hole-In-The-Day. Their chance to reason with the Sioux seemed to have passed. Nearby Fort Ridgely was under heavy attack and facing grave danger. The besieged occupants watched their resources for survival being drained away. "We can hold this position but little longer unless we are reinforced," a message from the post revealed. "We are being attacked almost every hour and unless assistance is rendered us, we cannot hold out much longer. Our little [water] tank is becoming exhausted."[3]

The Indians knew they would be marked for punishment. Attempts at revenge took many forms; poisoned cakes were deliberately left behind by fleeing settlers. The most vigorous reprisals came on government instructions from the army forces. Judge Flandreau, commanding a hundred volunteers, marched to New Ulm and routed the Indians. President Abraham Lincoln authorized the transfer of several thousand men being trained for combat in the Civil War, who were rushed to Minnesota for emergency service under ex-Governor H.H. Sibley. The new force impressed the Sioux and reassured the Minnesota people who had been fleeing to the larger centres of St. Paul, Minneapolis, St. Peter, and Hastings. Chief Little Crow sent word to Colonel Sibley that he would be willing to discuss a settlement. After a running fight for weeks, a battle at Wood Lake brought that first round of the wars of the American Northwest to an end.

As the trouble subsided, eastern writers looked for the reasons of the Minnesota rebellion. Some presumed that Confederate agitators had stirred the Sioux to violence. Others reasoned that the Indians were simply seizing upon United States involvement in Civil War to strike their blow for freedom. The practical advantages of attacking when the country was engaged in war on other fronts was not overlooked, but in the main, the uprising reflected the mounting frustration and the inevitable rupture of Indian patience. Broken treaty promises, deception by government agents, theft of land, scandalous treatment from traders, and debauchery of Indian women were more than Indians could stand.

A correspondent using pen-name "Chippewa", writing from St. Anthony, Minnesota, to the *New York Tribune*, confidently blamed the administration for much of the Sioux trouble.

The fraud and deception practised by Government agents and officials generally, in making treaties with the Indians, are the result of the baneful system of money annuities paid by the Government to the Indians. This collects around them a number of 'Indian Traders' who get licenses from the Government to reside among them and trade with them. From these men and their employees, the Indians soon learn all the vices, with very few or none of the virtues of civilized society. Licentiousness, fraud and profanity are the first fruits of intercourse with these traders ... firewater is the greatest hindrance in the way of their civilization.

Promises of great benefit are often made to the Indians by commissioners at the time of making treaties. The whole system of dealing with the Indians, from the Government officials to the traders, has been not only tainted but rotten with fraud and robbery.

Now, as to the Sioux who have taken many lives of the innocent women and children on our frontier, they have been grievously wronged and outraged, and have a thousand griev-

ances or causes of complaint against us to one which our fathers had at the commencement of the Revolution. Their women and children have been seduced by white men, have had children by them and these unnatural fathers have left their offspring to starve or be taken care of by the poor Indian mothers and her friends. The Indians never forsake their offspring.[4]

It took more than a year for the United States administration to count the cost of the Minnesota trouble. Facing numerous claims in connection with the uprising, the authorities appointed a three-man committee to make adjustments. The committee was in session at St. Peter for five months and dealt with 2,940 claims for a total of $2,450,000. The actual awards amounted to $1,370,450, with much of the amount being paid to 1,400 people who were made widows or orphans by the Indians. It was the commission's conclusion that over eight hundred men, women and children had been murdered. Thousands more abandoned farms and homes and some of these did not return.

In the meantime, a tenuous peace settled over Minnesota. The Sioux were neither beaten nor appeased. Some of the leading offenders were captured, tried for murder and hanged; some escaped to fight another day, and some were hunted refugees who took shelter in territory soon to be declared the Province of Manitoba. And by withholding Sioux annuities, the United States authorities did nothing to dispel the hatred.

Sitting Bull, less than thirty years old at the time, was not directly involved. But when the Minnesota Sioux came into Dakota Territory looking for support, Sitting Bull announced that he was ready to serve anywhere. When the Sioux warriors were skirmishing with United States forces the next year, the young brave was there.

27

The Sioux Years in Manitoba

For several years after the Minnesota tragedies, Fort Garry and Portage la Prairie seemed to be at the heart of the Sioux country. Residents were both worried and bewildered – worried at the thought of an extension of the recent killing spree across the border and bewildered about how to get rid of the Indians. To furnish the food and ammunition the Sioux wanted would encourage them to stay; to refuse their requests could anger them. The early Manitoba attempts at diplomacy were not very successful and, in desperation, citizens came to favour an invitation to United States army forces to cross the International Boundary and get their Indians. From 1857 to 1861, a detachment of Royal Canadian Rifles was stationed at Fort Garry as a safeguard against border trouble but now, when the need for military support seemed greater, the soldiers were not there.

The refugee Sioux, seeking escape from punishment the American army command intended to administer on account of the Minnesota crimes, argued that they were really British Indians who merely hunted in the United States but considered their first loyalty to be to the Queen. They could refer, quite correctly, to Sioux support for the British cause in both the Revolutionary War and the War of 1812, but Fort Garry and Portage la Prairie people refused to be impressed. They opposed anything that would induce the Indians to remain on the Canadian side.

News travelled slowly during that period and residents of Fort Garry received the first clear indication of the New Ulm disaster when they read their local paper, the *Nor'-Wester*, on September 11, 1862. The Minnesota Sioux were on the warpath and communication with St. Paul had been severed. "The mail carrier arrived from Pembina last night, without any mail." All travel between St. Cloud and Georgetown was suspended. Merchandise intended for delivery at Fort Garry had been plundered at Grand Forks. And to make matters worse, the Saulteaux Indians in eastern and northeastern Minnesota and some Minnesota half-breeds were threatening to join with the Sioux. The latter were said to have offered the Saulteaux or Red Lake Ojibway a thousand horses in return for their aid.

Chief Little Crow, whose name was associated with the beginning of the massacre and who knew he was being pursued by Colonel H.H. Silbey, wrote from Iron Village enquiring what he could do to "make peace for my people", adding that the prisoners he was holding were receiving good care and were getting the same fare as themselves. Colonel Sibley communicated his willingness to talk with the Chief but made no promises of pardon and continued his pursuit, coming closer and closer to the Canadian border. While the fugitive Chief, with eight hundred lodges, was at Devil's Lake, he confessed to his friends that if the Americans continued to press, he would move across the boundary into Rupert's Land where his loyalty to the British Crown during earlier wars would, he was confident, ensure him a friendly reception.

At Christmas time, the first group of Sioux crossed the boundary and advanced toward Fort Garry. Hearing of the movement, Bishop Taché, A.G. Dallas, who succeeded Sir George Simpson as Governor of Rupert's Land, and a large body of Red River Métis, rode out to meet the weary Indians, about one hundred of them, at the River Sale. But the attempt to persuade them to turn back was unsuccessful. Having come this far, the Sioux were determined to continue. At Fort Garry they found further proof that they were not wanted. The Hudson's Bay Company officials, anxious to retain Sioux good will, provided meat rations for a few days and in so doing, invited criticism from the *Nor'-Wester*'s editors who opposed any form of welcome to "these wretches" fresh from butchering innocent families in Minnesota. "One Sioux actually boasted of having killed thirteen whites," the editor noted. The refugees were still at Fort Garry when the *Nor'-*

Wester of February 9, 1863 reported: "Thirty-eight Sioux were hanged on the 26th December at Mankato, Minnesota, but this dreadful punishment, instead of striking terror into the braves, seems only to kindle a more bitter animosity and rouse a fiercer spirit of revenge."

The United States authorities wanted Little Crow but were not having much success in taking him. Perhaps they were more interested in keeping him moving than in actually capturing him. If they took him prisoner, they would be obliged to place him on trial and probably hang him, and that would infuriate the Sioux more than ever. Certainly, the Chief made no attempt to hide. In February he was at Devil's Lake and making no secret of it. In April he was at St. Joseph, a short distance west of Pembina. And in the *Nor'-Wester* of June 2, 1863, it was reported that "Little Crow and some sixty of his braves, together with some women, arrived in the settlement last Friday and left again on Sunday."

It was a short visit but long enough for him to discover that his King George III medals had lost their magic. It was also long enough for the local editor to make a superficial study of this notorious fellow. "He is about fifty years of age," the *Nor'-Wester* of August 5, 1863, reported, "of medium height and spare in figure. Of course he has high cheek bones. His face is thin and cadaverous, and he has suffered much from sickness." His attire was as striking as his features. When he visited Governor Dallas, he was, indeed, the well-dressed Indian, wearing a black coat with velvet collar – a garment which might have been taken from one of his victims – a blue breech-cloth, and a costly shawl instead of a sash around his middle. Deerskin leggings and the usual moccasins completed the incongruous outfit.

Little Crow's arms were withered but the deformity did not weaken his power in the tribe. "His matchless eloquence" more than compensated for any physical defects and no one who knew him questioned his authority, certainly not his three wives, all of whom, according to the editor, "he beats in approved Indian style". But Little Crow was not one to inflict needless cruelty and the white prisoners taken by his warriors were treated compassionately.

At Fort Garry, Little Crow invited Governor Dallas to write to Colonel Sibley, assuring him that if the United States forces would release the Indian prisoners, his warriors would stop fighting. The Governor agreed to write the letter but to the Chief's request for a grant of land and permission to settle in British North America, the Governor offered no encouragement. Obviously disappointed, the Chief accepted the necessity of returning to the South and had some parting advice for the Governor: if the people of Fort Garry found it necessary to travel in the Territory of Minnesota during the season, they should carry British flags which would safeguard them against attack by the Indians.

Little Crow returned to join his main band and Fort Garry did not see him again. On July 2, an unidentified Indian was shot six miles north of Hutchinson, Minnesota. The slain man, as it was discovered, had withered arms. It was Little Crow. Fort Garry, while not wanting him as a neighbour, had come to think of him as a man with honourable ideals.

But Fort Garry had not seen the last of the Sioux. The most troublesome and biggest bands were yet to come. Two chiefs not to be forgotten were Standing Buffalo and the objectionable Little Six. Accompanying Standing Buffalo to Portage la Prairie were 3,000 Sioux refugees, all hoping to remain under the "Great White Mother's flag". Standing Buffalo, leaving his tribesmen behind, went to Fort Garry to confer with the Governor and make the customary requests for food and permission to stay in Rupert's Land. Again there were gifts of bread and meat and again a refusal to furnish land for a reservation. Standing Buffalo, like Little Crow, went back to the United States but some of his followers squatted and never returned. In time, some settled near Griswold; some moved to make homes on the Whitecap Reserve, south of Saskatoon.

At Portage la Prairie, the Sioux far outnumbered the white residents. But most of the stout-hearted pioneers like John McLean, first farmer on the Portage plains, refused to be intimidated. More practical than diplomatic, McLean was frequently on the verge of trouble and occasionally exchanged gunfire with the visitors. But he knew when to yield; in 1864, while carrying the Queen's mail from Fort Garry to Portage la Prairie, he came face to face with Standing Buffalo and several hundred warriors. McLean had a load of provisions along with the mail and the Indians were hungry. McLean did not want to lose his supplies but knew it was no place for an argument. He threw the Indians a bag of bread and biscuits and while they were devouring this morsel, he drove away as fast as his horses could travel and saved the rest of his cargo.

Little Six, who, quite different from Little Crow and Standing Buffalo, had the distinction of being the most unpopular Sioux of all was finally ejected forcibly from British territory. Early in 1864[1] Little Six and eight of his followers made the mistake, when visiting Fort Garry, of terrifying some local people. The stopped at the Silver Heights home of Charles Curtis when he was away on a trip to Pembina. When Mrs. Curtis opened her door, the Sioux rushed in. The Chief invited his men to relax on chairs while he washed and prepared himself for lunch. He then spread his blanket on the floor and smoked his pipe while urging Mrs. Curtis to place food before her guests. He fancied the fine table cloth and told Mrs. Curtis that he would take it. The lady seized an opportunity to signal for help to a passing neighbour and when he responded to her call, the Indians left.

The woman and her children moved to her father's house at once. When Curtis arrived home, he found the entire community in a state of excitement. A meeting was called and a plan was drawn. The troublesome Indians were to be invited to dine at Bannatyne's where they would be given all the liquor they could drink. Then, when drunk, they would be drugged with chloroform, shackled, and removed southward to Pembina. The plot worked exactly according to the plan; the Indians were simply kidnapped – all nine of them – and transported by sleigh to the United States side of the border where a sadder fate awaited the treacherous Little Six, "said to be the ringleader in most of the Minnesota Massacres."[2] The Fort Garry paper of October 12, 1865, reported that Little Six was charged with the murder of thirty-six people in the Minnesota massacre, and the issue of December 11, 1865, told that he had been hanged.

Another Sioux to gain fame around Portage la Prairie was Wolverine and even the Sioux called him a "bad Indian". He was more of a nuisance than a criminal. Then there was the Sioux, more industrious than most of his race, who prospered by selling "moose meat". His racket was to steal horses from the settlers, slaughter them and sell the carcasses as moose meat. A jury found him guilty and sentenced him to be hanged. But John Garrioch claimed that the sentence was excessive and the Indian was sent to Fort Garry for a new trial. His first attempt to escape from jail was unsuccessful but he did better the second time and returned to Portage la Prairie. An order was issued for re-arrest but by this time the enterprising dealer in "moose meat" had disappeared.[3]

As long as the large bands of Sioux remained in Manitoba, they were prime topics for conversation. But they furnished more anxiety than entertainment and when they fought with the Manitoba Saulteaux, the settlers wished that they would go elsewhere. A United States batallion set up headquarters at Pembina, just below the Rupert's Land boundary. Major E.A.C. Hatch, who was in command, was eager to engage the Sioux camping at Fort Garry, White Horse Plains, and Portage la Prairie. The Council of Assiniboia, essentially the voice of the Hudson's Bay Company, invited Major Hatch to cross the border and take the Sioux away. But an American officer could not do this without violating international law and some other solution had to be found. The Métis living at White Horse Plains sent a message to the Fort Garry people proposing joint action involving force if necessary.

A public meeting was called at the Fort Garry Court House on February 15, 1864, for the express purpose of considering the White Horse Plains suggestion, presented by Pascal Breland. The meeting adopted resolutions recognizing "the great distress occasioned by the presence of the Sioux." [4] There seemed but small chance that a locally organized campaign to drive them out would succeed but the men of the two communities agreed to co-operate in a continuing operation, seizing them, a few at a time, and hauling them by sleigh to the boundary where they would be handed over to Major Hatch. This would be more acceptable to the United States authorities than driving the Indians to the American plains. Red River men attending the meeting were reminded that if there was evidence of co-operation at the boundary, the United States authorities would be more likely to allow Red River and White Horse Plains hunters to continue to conduct their seasonal buffalo hunts on the Dakota plains. With some United States officials in Washington accusing the Métis of furnishing ammunition to the American Sioux, there was added reason for making a public display of support in the hope of regaining American good will.

The plan to seize and transport the unwanted Indians was not carried out and just a few weeks after the meeting, Fort Garry people learned to their sorrow that Major Hatch and his batallion were being withdrawn from Pembina for service at Fort Abercrombie, thereby removing the only protection available to southbound travellers.

Still new bands of Sioux came to Portage la Prairie and Fort Garry. The year 1865 saw more than any previous twelve-month period. Standing Buffalo and his horde came again, repeating that they had nothing to do with the Minnesota massacre. Closely supervised by the able chief, the 3,000 Indians demonstrated nigh perfect behaviour. "They were very careful neither to steal anything, nor indeed, to do anything to give offence."[5] Obviously, it was another attempt on the part of the Chief and his advisers to win public approval and permission to remain in British territory. Carefully, he displayed the sixteen British medals given to men of his band by fathers and grandfathers who received them after the War of 1812 and the Revolutionary War. "And now," said he, "we bring them back to the place where our people got them long ago. They told us that whenever we wanted anything, we must come and show these medals.... We are very anxious to hear from our Mother, the Queen. We want to know if she has any words for us and whether she can help us now that we have been driven from our hunting ground."[6]

Editorial praise was brief and it was not long before the same writer was insisting that the time had come for citizens to organize and arm themselves to repel the invaders. "We must make a display of force when they are next coming into the settlement, and treat them in a way far different from what we have hitherto done – such a style as shall cause them to fear and respect us."

But how did it happen that Standing Buffalo, making another visit to British North America, was able to bring such skill to his attempt to create a good impression, and how was it that one Sioux Chief was in possession of sixteen British medals? Surely this was part of a carefully conceived design. If such were so, who was the clever planner? Was he the young Sioux medicine man, Sitting Bull? Proof is difficult but there is circumstantial evidence. When Sitting Bull moved into Canadian territory in 1877, he was carrying about the same number of medals and his people appeared to be following similar rules of conduct. Moreover, some of the Sioux remaining in Canada insisted that Sitting Bull was not only born close to Wood Mountain but was actually with Standing Buffalo in Manitoba.

Sitting Bull, by this time in his thirties, was gaining tribal fame as a medicine man. "Making medicine" was not for everybody. To be successful, a man needed special gifts conferred by the Great Spirit as well as practical instruction from older Indians who understood the mysteries of illness and the best ways of effecting cures. The basis was a principle to which most Indians subscribed: Nature, the source of all wisdom, could furnish a remedy for every disorder. It was for humans to discover and use the proper one. The medicine man was the specialist, never allowing his fellow tribesmen to forget that part of his imposing qualifications came from study and part by divine gift.

The native people in the period before the white man brought smallpox and various other diseases were rarely ill. They had not heard about the microbe and virus and, as children of Nature, they survived very well. Roots, leaves, bark and blossoms held Nature's specifics in the case of disorder. When they failed, the medicine man could resort to his witchcraft. The squaws knew much about herbs but left the mystical arts to the medicine man. The medicine man did not work for nothing any more than modern doctors. They took payment in dogs, horses, robes or anything they might fancy. For a herbal cure, the payment could be one horse or dog; where it was necessary to resort to magic, the payment would be doubled. Perhaps, if the truth were known, what the medicine man needed most was imagination and good judgment.

Members of Sitting Bull's tribe living at Griswold, Wood Mountain, and Saskatoon – some of whom claimed relationship – insisted that he was always a great warrior but his most outstanding success was as strategist and tactician. Gradually he emerged as the wise man of his tribe. When the Sioux were at war Sitting Bull, as medicine man, was sought out for guidance and advice. He became a sort of roving commission by which he was expected to bring advice – both mystical and practical – to his fighting fellows. In later years, much of the Sioux success in keeping the United States forces confused was due to his planning. It is easy to suppose that when Standing Buffalo appeared at Portage la Prairie and Fort Garry in 1865, Sitting Bull was with him, serving as a one-man brain trust.

The Indian Wars

The new Northwest was in for a long spell of troubled times. The Indian position was becoming increasingly intolerable and, with leaders like Red Cloud and Sitting Bull, the tribesmen were in no mood to suffer further affront. The Indians of all tribes were now disillusioned. The whites they had befriended on arrival in the country had turned out to be treacherous, wanting nothing less than the Indian lands. To the newcomers, the natives had become mere obstacles to their plains for development. English and French in Newfoundland, Spanish and Dutch in more southerly regions, and now people of mixed races in the West were known to shoot Indians like wild animals and even to offer rewards for their scalps.

An offer of bounties in Minnesota was reported by the *Nor'-Wester*:

We learn from the Mankato Record *that the County Commissioners of the Blue Earth County have appropriated the sum of $500 or as much thereof as may be necessary to purchase blood hounds to be used in tracking Indian murderers and horse thieves prowling around frontier settlements.... The following resolution was also adopted: Resolved, that the County of Blue Earth will pay the sum of two hundred dollars for each and every Sioux Indian hereafter killed within the limits of the county, until this resolution shall be rescinded; said sum or sums to be paid to the person or persons killing same...upon production to the board of county commissioners of said county at any meeting thereof the scalp of said*

Indian and proof to the satisfaction of said board that such Sioux Indian was killed by the person or persons claiming pay thereof within the limits of this county, and after the passage of the resolution.[1]

In a few instances, the whites, with benevolent concern for Indian souls, attempted to convert the natives to the white man's religion before murdering them. This was supposed to assure for the victims a place in Heaven, even if there was no place remaining for them in the earthly scheme of things.

It was a frustrating time for the native people who suddenly found themselves outnumbered and outmanoeuvred. The new civilization, like a steam roller, was squeezing them off their traditional home and hunting ground. Some of the smaller tribes, realizing they had no choice, accepted without protest; the Sioux and their allies, the Cheyennes – a powerful combination – refused to submit peaceably. With the buffalo country, the very source of their livelihood, at stake, these tribesmen were ready to fight to the death. It was a fight to survive and a fight for the right to live as they chose on land they could rightfully call their own, Sitting Bull told his people in the Black Hills.

Trickery and broken promises had brought the Sioux to violence in Minnesota in 1862; the same factors brought them to war farther west. The Indians seemed to win most of the battles but the United States ultimately won the war. When the whites suffered losses as they did at Little Big Horn, they called it massacre; when they imposed heavy losses as at Fort Union in 1864 where 2,000 Indians were slain, they described it as a fair fight and great victory. There was no remorse on the part of the forces when General Sully's expedition met Medicine Bear's band of Sioux on the Missouri River in that same year. The Indians, it was reported:

had concluded a peace with the troops and pitched their camp close to the American camp, when, for some cause or other, unknown to our informant, the soldiers fired into the Sioux and a fight of some six hours duration commenced. The Indians, taken by surprise, fell in heaps, until five hundred— including men, women and children—were slaughtered. The troops sustained very little injury.[2]

Treaties were made and broken when it suited the paleface invaders. One such treaty in 1865 assigned the country north of the Bighorn Mountains in Wyoming to the Sioux and produced a temporary lull in the fighting. But when settlers and gold-seekers were moving into Montana, they demanded governmental protection and Brigadier-General H.B. Carrington was instructed to advance through Wyoming by the Bozeman Trail and help the immigrants, most of whom were travelling with Conestoga wagons hauled by mules or oxen. The Indians might have accepted the coming of the settlers but they rebelled at the prospect of soldiers and forts becoming permanently attached to the trail that cut across the best of the buffalo range. The great Oglala Chief, Red Cloud, with the young chief, Sitting Bull at his side, led the resistance. Intercepting the first detachment of troops, Red Cloud took them prisoner and refused to meet the United States officers sent to parley with him.

In June, 1866, government men attempted again to secure Red Cloud's permission to build a road from Fort Laramie via Powder River to the gold fields in Montana and punctuate it with military posts. Again the proud and defiant leader with straight back and fine physical features refused, declaring that such a road would drive the buffalo far away and leave his people without food. But even before the discussions ended, United States troops were penetrating the Powder River country and Red Cloud prepared at once to meet the soldiers with force.

Carrington, commanding soldiers with the very latest muzzle-loading muskets, set out for Fort Reno in May, 1866, intending to build another fortification forty miles farther west on the trail, as well as posts on the Bighorn and Yellowstone Rivers. Arriving at Reno on June 28, 1866, he decided against closing that post. Instead, he left a small garrison of men there and pushed on to start building the ill-fated Fort Phil Kearney. The new post was harrassed from the beginning. Red Cloud's scouts spied constantly, stole horses, killed cattle, shot hunting parties and wood crews, and made direct attacks on the fort. Freight, wood and hunting parties never left the fort without armed escorts. A lookout had to be maintained constantly.

Carrington was criticized by subordinate officers for being overcautious. Captain William J. Fetterman favoured an early showdown with the Indian marauders. His chance for direct confrontation came soon enough. With eighty-one men, he marched out to engage the Sioux who were molesting wood-cutting crews. The teams and teamsters on that December day were having more trouble than usual but Fetterman was advised by his superior to act judiciously and avoid another incident. Nonetheless, he resolved to teach the Indians a lesson. The opposing force was bigger than expected and he was soon in serious trouble. The Indian fire proved deadly and Fetterman's men were falling. Carrington sent reinforcements but the Indians were still too strong, forty-nine of the Fort Phil Kearney men, including Fetterman, were killed, still more wounded or missing. It was Red Cloud's victory, although it appears that he had Sitting Bull with him. The older chief received a thigh wound from a bullet that day.

Throughout the next year, Red Cloud kept up the attacks and in 1868, just two years after construction had commenced, marked victory with the closing of the Bozeman Trail. Fort Phil Kearney was abandoned and the Indians lost no time in burning it to the ground. Clearly, it was a year of reverses for the American forces. Authorities in Kansas attributed one hundred and fifty murders to the Indians. Children were kidnapped, horses and cattle were stolen, homes were burned, and coaches and wagons overtaken on the trails were destroyed. Men in government, embarrassed by defeat, were eager to discuss a new treaty. But Red Cloud and Sitting Bull were in no hurry to meet the white officials until there was complete abandonment of the military forts on the Montana route. As the victors, they could practically dictate the terms and the Treaty of 1868 promised a large Sioux reservation in which Indian rights would be respected forever. Here was the hope for peace on the frontier. Indian rights would be inviolate.

Government men breathed more easily at seeing the trouble-some Sioux accepting the Black Hills in Dakota, where they could enjoy isolation from white people and still have opportunity to roam and hunt over wild country. It was not valuable land but, as the United States negotiators concluded, it was good enough for Indian purposes and unattractive to whites. There was now a show of congeniality on the part of government. Soon after the Treaty was concluded, Red Cloud, Sitting Bull, and Spotted Tail were brought to Washington as guests of President Grant. Officials were pleased with the prospect of better relations; the Chiefs were impressed but probably largely unchanged in their convictions; public opinion was mixed. Commenting about a gift from President Grant to Sitting Bull, a fine rifle enclosed in a leather case and engraved: "Sitting Bull, from the President. For bravery and friendship", the editor of the *Fort Benton Record* said:

Had Grant securely locked the case so that Sitting Bull could not have removed its contents, we should have no comment to offer. Who is this Sitting Bull? He is the blood thirsty villain who has committed more murders than any one Indian since the days of the Wyoming massacre. He is the treacherous scoundrel who has made life-long threats against the white race and sworn to kill every U.S. soldier that crossed his path, provided he could do so without danger to his own cowardly carcass. He is the Indian whom Major Anderson sets down in his report as the mischief maker of his race in the vicinity of the agency, and we all know that much worse could truthfully be said concerning him. This is the man to whom the President presented a rifle, 'for bravery and friendship'.[3]

Having gained his purpose and signed the Fort Laramie Treaty, Chief Red Cloud agreed to quit fighting and accepted for himself a place on the reservation at Red Cloud Agency in Nebraska, and later at Pine Ridge in South Dakota where he remained for the rest of his life. His agreement to lay down his arms drew criticism from leaders like Crazy Horse who believed that there could be no end to the war until the white race was dislodged. But Red Cloud, a man of his word, retired without losing the respect of most of his people. Until the time of his death in 1909, he was the Grand Old Man of the Oglalas.

The war, however, was not over. Although Red Cloud was out of it, others were ready to fight on. The Indian territory described in 1868 as "inviolable", did not remain that way. The Sioux were to have the Black Hills forever but as one writer stated: "Forever lasted six years". In 1871, surveyors searching for a route for the Northern Pacific Railway westward from the Missouri, asked for military protection and received it while working in Sioux territory. It was only the first of a series of treaty violations. When the engineers came again in 1872 and more settlers were seen on the trail, the Sioux attacked. A bigger military force was needed in 1873 when miners and settlers came in ever increasing numbers. General Stanley and 1,700 United States soldiers were sent to the field.

Accompanying General Stanley that year was Lieutenant-Colonel George Custer. Thirty-four years of age, Custer already had an impressive military record and was gaining a new reputation as an Indian fighter. A graduate of the United States Military Academy, he saw action at Bull Run in the Civil War, at Aldie, Yellow Tavern, Winchester, Woodstock, Cedar Creek and Waynesboro, and had grown accustomed to praise for gallantry. After the Civil War, he had signal successes in the campaign against the Cheyenne Indians in the Southwest. He appeared to love war, particularly the adulation accompanying victory.

But Custer's experience included reverses as well. One incident involved Secretary of War Belknap for whom he had a strong dislike. Custer had implied that he had pertinent information about irregularities in the appointment of traders at military posts on the Upper Missouri. It was the prerogative of the Secretary of War to make these appointments to monopolistic and profitable positions and the Custer inference was that Belknap had accepted payment for them. In this, Custer was probably in error; in all likelihood, Belknap did no more than pass the privilege of naming traders to politicians who in turn gave the appointment to their friends. Anyway, when Custer was called to Washington for questioning, it became evident that he had nothing more than hearsay on which to base his statements. His sin was simply in talking too much. But President Grant took a dim view of the man's conduct and suggested to General Sherman that Custer be removed from his command. He was to be left behind to suffer the mortification of seeing his regiment march away without him. The order, however, was reversed and Custer was reunited with the Seventh Cavalry to serve under General Terry. Before the season was far advanced, he engaged Sitting Bull and his warriors in minor skirmishes. Custer had lost none of his military skill and the next summer, 1874, he was carrying out quite a different assignment in the Black Hills, right at the heart of the Sioux country.

White men knew they were not supposed to enter the Black Hills without Indian consent. With rumours of gold being discovered there, they were not too inclined to dwell upon rules and regulations. Government officials tried to suppress the reports of gold discoveries but it was impossible, and more and more prospectors and miners ventured into the forbidden hills. Those who eluded the Sioux and returned related stories about easy fortunes in gold. By 1874, there was public demand for a geological report on the Black Hills resources. There had been tales about a Sioux squaw bringing "a nugget of pure gold as large as a hen's egg"[4] into one of the forts and revealing that she found it in the Black Hills. "It's a perfect Eldorado," according to another published report, but anybody going there "is liable to be massacred by the wily savages. . . . Indeed, several parties have already been murdered".

Reluctantly, the government, yielding to the pressure, violated its own treaty with the Sioux, and in July sent Custer with a force of 1,200 soldiers, four Gatling guns, sixty scouts, a great wagon train of provisions and a few experienced miners to establish once and for all whether the rumours had any basis in fact. Custer's report confirmed the presence of gold and impulsively he invited interested people to "come and get it", a shocking defiance of the treaty which was supposed to bar all whites. Indian anger mounted. The Sioux, who had been remarkably docile while Custer's investigation was being conducted, prepared for the resumption of war. Military officers knew now that they had to crush Sitting Bull and Rain-In-The-Face.

Rain-In-The-Face was at Standing Rock where he boasted of killing two well known white citizens. The report was carried back to Custer, who with a hundred men, including his brother, Captain T.W. Custer, set out to capture the Indian leader. The arrest was made amid great excitement and prompted a threat from Rain-In-The-Face that he would have revenge and, when the opportunity came, he would eat Captain Custer's heart. The prisoner was taken to Lincoln jail where he was charged with murder. He promptly escaped and rejoined Sitting Bull, to become a bigger menace than ever.

After it was known that there was gold in the Hills, thousands of prospectors ignored the warnings and converged to seek their fortunes. When the authorities failed to halt the rush, the frustrated Indians took matters into their own hands. Many of the Sioux left their reservations, stole horses, killed cattle, burned houses and shot settlers. In December, 1875, a government communication ordered all Sioux to return to their reserves before the end of January or be declared "hostiles" and face the consequences. Many of the wayward Indians returned; others like Sitting Bull and Crazy Horse made ready to fight. Crazy Horse was attacked by General George Crook and when routed, he and his followers hastened to join Sitting Bull's camp on the Rosebud River. Most of the dissidents followed, swelling Sitting Bull's warrior army to several thousands. It became obvious that a major battle was imminent.

Violence North of the Line

On the Canadian side, with only the shelter of an imaginary boundary line, there was reason for uneasiness. Canadian tribesmen had been relatively peaceful but there was no guarantee that Indian wars in the United States could be isolated there any more than the whiskey traders could be kept out of the Northwest Territories. Birds, buffalo herds, criminals and Indians crossed the boundary as though it did not exist. Two major dangers were present: the first, of Canadian Indians becoming involved on the American side and, second, of United States Indians bringing their wars northward. Americans everywhere repeated the words of General Philip Henry Sheridan at Fort Cobb, January, 1869: "The only good Indians I ever saw were dead".

Canadian Indians and Métis were becoming bolder. Intertribal rivalry prevented unified native attacks against the white population, but the Métis, traditionally bitter enemies of the Sioux since the Red River insurrection of 1870, were showing interest in co-operating with Sitting Bull's people. The new Province of Manitoba had, for a short time, a Dominion force consisting of about 340 officers and men, mainly a safeguard against Fenian raiders from the South. But the big country farther west had no constituted means whatever of dealing with crime such as the Cypress Hills atrocity of 1873.

Reverend John McDougall, visiting at Fort Whoop-Up in 1874, was impressed by the casual manner in which murder was discussed. In conversation with Joe Healy, he was told that there was no need for government intervention because

Healy and his friends knew exactly how to solve the problem. "For instance, there was So-and-So. He came in and was going to run things. He lies under the sod at Standoff. And there was So-and-So. He went wild and we laid him out at Freezeout, and some more at Slideout. These bad men could not live in this country. We simply could not allow it".[1] The Cypress Hills killings were clearly criminal but the perpetrators managed to escape penalty. The episode did much to injure the image of the white man in the eyes of all the natives. Indeed, it did not escape the attention of Sitting Bull and he used it to support his case for the destruction of the palefaces.

Whoop-Up was the earliest and most notorious of the whiskey forts built by Americans on Canadian soil. It was situated at the junction of St. Mary and Oldman Rivers, a few miles southwest of Lethbridge. The first of the trading posts operated from Montana, it was the biggest, the most costly and probably the most lawless. The original fort on this site, known as Hamilton, was burned to the ground in the first year of operation. But, more than ever convinced of the rich opportunities in unobstructed trade with Blood and Blackfoot Indians, owners J.J. Healy and A.B. Hamilton ordered immediate rebuilding. The new structure, much larger than the first, was ready late in 1870 and took the name, Fort Whoop-Up. Success there led to the building of other trading posts, also with novel names: Standoff, Kipp, Slideout, Spitzie and Robbers' Roost.

Why this invasion by Montana traders? First there were the buffalo skins which had become readily marketable. At the same time, with growing conflict between the western tribes and the United States Cavalry, traders found the natives on the Canadian side to be more amenable. There was still another reason, an important one: United States law prohibited the sale of alcoholic liquors to American Indians but did not attempt to restrain traders from operations beyond the borders. These new merchants carried a variety of trade goods but found firewater the source of biggest profits. There was no prescribed formula. The recipe depended mainly upon the ingredients at hand. Generally there was some alcohol but there could be any combination of chewing tobacco, black pepper, vinegar, pain-killer, laudenum and red ink, along with liberal amounts of water from the nearest slough for bulk.

Whoop-Up was probably the second structure with more permanency than a tipi to be erected in that part of Alberta lying south of the Bow River. The only other habitation of record when Whoop-Up was built was Kootenai Brown's cabin beside Waterton Lake. The Mounted Police, trekking westward in 1874 expected trouble at Whoop-Up and approached with guns ready, but, to their surprise, they found the post almost deserted. Assistant Commissioner James Macleod considered buying the abandoned structure for use as a police base but the price quoted was exorbitant and the weary Mounties continued on until they reached the site beside the Oldman River where they built the fort which was to carry the Macleod name. A monument unveiled on September 18, 1870, marked the site of Whoop-Up and reminded Canadians of the lawlessness prevailing in that section of the Territories before the coming of the Mounted Police.

The most important single misdeed to be laid at the door of those traders from the South and the one which aroused the Government of Canada to action was what became known as the Cypress Hills Massacre, perpetrated on or about May 1, 1873. Which side started the shooting was very much in doubt, depending entirely upon whose story was accepted. As Canadians heard it, the action was indeed a massacre. The Montana men insisted that they were fighting a defensive battle at the beginning and finished as overwhelming victors. In any case, the action took place close to Abel Farwell's trading post on Battle Creek, near the spot on which Fort Walsh was constructed two years later, and not far from where Sitting Bull and his angry fellow-chiefs met General Alfred H. Terry of the United States Army in one of the most delicate confrontations of the decade. Altogether, it is enough to identify the scene of the killings on that spring day in 1873 as one of the important focal points in Canadian history.

Farwell, an eye-witness to the slayings, was the first of the Benton-based traders to locate in the Cypress Hills. It may be presumed that his trading activities were no more respectable than those of his colleagues but because he assisted the Canadian authorities when they tried to bring the alleged culprits to justice, he simultaneously improved his Canadian standing and ruined his Montana reputation.

It all began as a group of traders and wolfers returning

homeward from a winter at Whoop-Up camped on the Teton River, about ten miles from Fort Benton. When they awakened they discovered that their horses were missing. Theft by Indians was the easy conclusion. The same sort of misfortune had overtaken them before and, finding themselves horseless and comparatively helpless with carts loaded with furs, they were angry enough to shoot every last native. As they trudged the remaining miles to Fort Benton they vowed revenge. The season for good wolf pelts had passed and the wolfers had time for some diversion; after recovering their carts and spending a night at the Benton saloons, they obtained fresh horses and a supply of ammunition and returned to the camp site. There was no positive proof that the horses had been stolen by Indians but no one considered the alternatives. The horses could have strayed or they might have been taken by a rival gang of wolfers but the Benton men chose to blame the Indians and pursue them.

By general consent, the leader was Thomas Hardwick, a one-time sheriff and a man known as a hard character. Sometimes called "the Green River Renegade", he had served the I.G. Baker Company. With him as second-in-command was John Evans who had been captain of the notorious Spitzie Cavalry, a body that maintained a fort on the Highwood River and had tried to bring gangland rule to the plains. There were other well known Bentonites, Trevanion Hale, Charlie Harper, Jeff Devereaux and Sam Vincent, altogether about fifteen tough fellows.

After several days, the tracks made by the lost horses were no longer discernible but for at least fifty miles they had pointed northward in the general direction of the Cypress Hills and it was logical to suppose the thieves were Canadian natives heading for that favourite Indian rendezvous. From this point in time, stories of events that followed differ even more. No doubt the men involved preferred to avoid the truth as much as possible. But Canadians elected to accept the evidence of Abel Farwell who witnessed the crucial events and the following account is generally consistent with opinions formed by the former Mounted Police Commissioner, S.T. Wood, who summered for some years in Cypress Hills and tried through personal research to separate the truth from fiction.

The angry men travelled deep into the Hills and camped

beside Battle Creek, three or four miles below Farwell's post. While the others made camp, Hardwick rode on as far as the post to visit Farwell and enquire if he could furnish any clues to the whereabouts of the horses and the thieves. Farwell had no information. He explained that Little Chief and his band of Assiniboines were at that moment occupying about forty lodges nearby but insisted upon clearing them of guilt. They had just come from the north and were weakened by the combination of severe winter cold and a shortage of food. Hardwick either was not convinced about the Assiniboine innocence or did not want to be convinced, and in the morning he returned with the other members of the gang, guns in hand.

At Farwell's post the Benton men were joined by three others from the trading fort belonging to Moses Solomon, just across the creek – George Hammond, John McFarland and George Bell – who had similar complaints about Indians lifting their horses. Hammond was particularly incensed about a recent experience. One of his horses, strayed or stolen, was returned by Assiniboines who demanded as a reward a jug of firewater. While the Indians were celebrating with the brew, two more of Hammond's horses disappeared. He readily agreed that the time had come for a showdown with horse thieves. Everybody except Farwell was eager to get started; he continued to argue that the thieves were Crees. Certainly, the Assiniboines who were Farwell's customers had not recently seen Montana and could not have taken the horses from the Teton.

Hoping to prevent a battle beside his post, Farwell went directly to the Indian camp to seek verification of his views and ascertain the truth about Hammond's lost stock. Before he was able to complete his mission, the traders, displaying an alcoholic impulsiveness, warned him from their seclusion in a coulee to leave the camp before the shooting started. The call was repeated and when it was issued the third time, he realized the seriousness of the threat and fled for cover. Indians began to scatter and somebody began to shoot. According to Farwell, a Benton man fired the first shot and it was followed by a volley from the coulee. This the traders denied, saying the Assiniboines sent a message to the effect that Crees took the horses but if the white men wanted a fight, they could have it then and there and followed the challenge with a burst of gunfire. But if, as Farwell contended, the Indians were only

49

recovering from a season of extreme privation and were practically out of arms and ammunition, it seems improbable that they would choose to start a battle.

The traders had some of the newest Henry repeating rifles. Indians fell in shocked confusion. Only one of the whites, Ed Grace, was killed. If the Indians had been prepared for battle, it is most likely that the toll in the ranks of the traders would have been much higher. But the Montana men persisted, killing men, women and children. The Chief was among the victims and it appeared that only a few of the camp residents escaped to the hills. Exactly how many were slaughtered will never be known. Some authorities placed the deaths at twenty, some as high as a hundred and twenty. The dead white man, Ed Grace, was buried under the floor of Solomon's store and after the post's contents were loaded on carts, the building was set afire by the traders who then returned by way of Whoop-Up to Fort Benton.

Back in Montana, the unabashed killers told different stories. As one member of the gang later related the exploits to the editor of the *Fort Benton Record* (June 26, 1875), the entire operation was a good neighbour act:

We went to the camp for the purpose of assisting a neighbour in the peaceable recovery of a horse. We had no other object in going there, our own property was not in the camp and we could have no motive in commencing the fight. Four or five shots were fired at us before we pulled a trigger, and then the odds were so much against us that we acted only on the defensive, until one of our party was killed, when through sheer desperation we changed from the defensive to the attack and routed the whole five or six hundred warriors, killing some thirty or forty.

They were indeed smart fellows if nineteen routed five or six hundred warriors, killing thirty or forty and losing only one of their own men. There were contrary reports that most of the Indians in the camp were women and children and only three or four of the males had guns and ammunition. The latter story seems more plausible.

At first, the Montana men thought they had nothing to fear because the killings were on foreign soil where law enforcement was still unknown. But reports of the slaughter reached Winnipeg, then Ottawa, to prick the public conscience. On October 18, 1873, Sir John A. Macdonald, as Prime Minister, sent a message to Lieutenant-Governor Morris at Winnipeg, instructing him to have information laid and warrants issued against Hardwick, Devereaux, Harper, Vincent and other "murderers of Indians at Cypress Hills" and to secure all evidence possible for purposes of extradition. But hopes of bringing the accused to justice in Canada proved futile. Washington authorities were co-operative but sentiment in Montana was so strong on the side of the gang that when arrests were made prior to the examination for extradition, the federal authorities believed it necessary as a precautionary measure to first ring the Town of Benton with United States cavalry.

It was almost two years after the killings and almost one year after the Mounted Police had come to the West that five of the accused men were brought to the extradition proceedings at Helena. The Canadian case was handled by lawyer M.C. Page. Assistant Commissioner James Macleod presented the evidence. The Canadians had no criticism of the American judge but they did have for their own legal representative who appeared to have trouble hiding his sympathy for the accused. The hearing lasted three weeks and became something of a farce. Instead of winning the request for extradition, Assistant Commissioner Macleod experienced the added indignity of a countercharge lodged by Jeff Devereaux, alleging false imprisonment and actually spent a few days in a Montana jail before the charge was dismissed.

After the judge heard the contradictory evidence and could find no positive proof of premeditated intent to kill, the Bentonites were discharged as free men. They were greeted by some of the wildest scenes of celebration the western frontier had experienced. Bonfires lit the streets of Helena all night and citizens danced and drank and sang. And back at Benton, preparations were being made for the arrival of the discharged men. As reported by the *Fort Benton Record* on July 31, 1875:

At 2 o'clock the firing of a cannon notified the people that the procession which was to escort the prisoners into town was about to form.... The party passed up Third Street to the old fort, then down Main Street to the Overland Hotel, amid the roar of cannon and cheers of welcome. . . . At 8 o'clock a meeting was held in the hall of Mr. Solomon to deliver an address of welcome and substantial proof of friendship to the ex-prisoners. The hall was tastefully decorated. On the American flag were the words: 'Home once more. Didn't extradite,' and beneath a drawing of the British Lion in full speed with an American Eagle biting his tail. Mr. John W. Tattan was called to the chair. A deputation was then appointed to escort Messrs. Hale, Evans, Devereaux, Harper and Hardwick to the hall. On their entrance the feeling of the meeting was evinced in hearty cheers. Col. J.J. Donnelly was introduced and read the address. Mr. Hale responded in a neat little speech. A purse of money was then handed to Mr. Hale for the benefit of the ex-prisoners. Mr. Hardwick responded in a well-delivered oration.

There was much in the trial which people on both sides of the boundary would not forget. The case produced obvious tension between the governments of the two countries. It brought together the greatest array of legal talent ever seen in the area and succeeded in arousing a new Montana loyalty. The accused were elevated to the status of heroes and Abel Farwell, upon whose eyewitness evidence the Canadian case was based, was made the villain. He was the one who would stoop to testify that Indian-shooting Bentonites were in the wrong. As recalled in the *Calgary Herald* of September 13, 1902, one lawyer for the defence, in presenting his summary, declared: "If your honor please, you are certainly not going to turn over to the tender mercies of the Canadian government these brave and hardy citizens of Montana upon the evidence of Abe Farwell, an informer who will hereafter be known as a man to whom the woods will deny shelter, the earth a grave and Heaven a God".

The Montana people were happy to collect Canadian government money spent on the case: payments for the witnesses, for guarding the arrested men, for feed for the horses owned by the witnesses, food for arrested men, fees charged by the U.S. Marshal, interpreter's fees, livery stable services, road tolls and $2,500 for the attorney.

But the matter was not settled. A short time later, three men, Vogel, Hughes and Bell, were arrested on the Canadian side and brought to trial at Winnipeg. Again Abel Farwell and his interpreter, Alexis Lebombarde, were the principal witnesses for the prosecution and again the evidence was so contradictory that there was no conviction. The three accused men were discharged. Farwell returned to the Cypress Hills and was engaged by the Mounted Police to carry mail to and from Fort Benton. But there were many threats against his life and he retired to trade again in the Hills. The Winnipeg trial was the concluding act in the story of a crime which, more than anything else, emphasized the necessity of a law enforcement body in the developing West.

Macdonald's Boundary Police

Standing beside his desk in the House of Commons on April 28, 1873, Sir John A. Macdonald answered impatiently. He had listened on various occasions to Dr. John Schultz and Donald Smith making long speeches about western Indians and the attendant dangers and may have wished that the Hudson's Bay Company had kept Rupert's Land which he had never been more than moderately eager to acquire. He was now well aware of the mounting troubles; the Indian wars south of the border, the lingering Métis discontent north of the border, and the whiskey trade across the border. The West at the time of the take-over from the Hudson's Bay Company inherited Canadian law but did not have the means to enforce it. The need for a police arm was obvious and Sir John did not argue the point. He was familiar with the recommendations about policing the plains made by responsible men like Butler and Ross.

William Francis Butler, a young Irishman who came west with the Wolseley Expedition and then accepted an assignment from the infant Province of Manitoba to report on police needs, recommended a force of between a hundred and a hundred and fifty men, one-third of whom would be mounted. Colonel Robertson Ross, in the next year, reported to the Canadian Government on the lawlessness among border country traders and the debauchery among Indians. Seventy-eight Blackfoot people had been murdered in the course of drunken brawls in a single year, 1871. He advised a mounted constabulary. Both men recommended immediate action.

On this occasion, Sir John was replying to a fellow Member of Parliament who wanted to know the Government's position for bringing law and order to the west and, according to the official record: "Sir John replied that it was the intention of the Government to ask Parliament for an appropriation for the purpose of organizing a boundary police".[1]

*

A few days later, May 3, 1873, Sir John introduced the bill described as "An Act Respecting the Administration of Justice and the Establishment of a Police Force in the Northwest Territories". The bill advanced quickly and received final approval twenty days later. Then there was a further delay.

The Order-In-Council directing recruitment of men for the North West Mounted Police was passed on August 30, 1873. Instructions were issued to select officers and men with the utmost of care to ensure the very highest possible standards of integrity and courage in the force. As provided in the Act, the new force would be structured to a maximum three hundred men. To qualify for acceptance, applicants were required to be "of a sound constitution, able to ride, active and able-bodied, of good character and between the ages of eighteen and forty, and able to read and write either in French or English." Enlisted men would be committed to three years and were unlikely to become rich during that time. Constables would receive a maximum of one dollar a day in addition to board; sub-constables would get not less than fifty cents and not more than one dollar per day. The highest ranking officer, the Commissioner, would qualify for a salary between $2,000 and $2,600 per year. And upon retirement, a man would be entitled to a hundred and sixty acres of Crown land in Manitoba or the Territories.

Colonel Osborne Smith who was commanding the Manitoba Military District, was named Acting Commissioner of the Mounted Police and recruiting started at once for three troops, A, B, and C, to be sent to Manitoba before the end of the autumn. Major James Morrow Walsh directed the recruiting. His splendid figure and character ideally represented the type of manhood needed for the service. He was thirty-one years old, with fine posture and a spirit of iron. Determination was written on his face and yet it was not an unfriendly face. His ideals reflected a rural Ontario upbringing and a military training. He was medium in size, with proud bearing, broad shoulders, and trim buttocks. The oldest son of Louis Walsh and his wife, Margaret Morrow Walsh, he was commonly at the bottom of his school class but the undisputed leader in all outdoor activities. When boys played at Indian wars in back lanes, "Bub" Walsh was either the white man's general or the Indian chief. He could outrun, outswim and outfight any boy of his size. He was captain of the Prescott Lacrosse Team when in 1869 it was acknowledged the champion of the world. Three members of the Walsh family played on that team which, after winning against nearby towns, defeated teams in Montreal, Kingston, Ottawa, Toronto and Buffalo. A writer of the time rated James Morrow Walsh of Prescott and Dr. Beers of Montreal as the leading lacrosse personalities of the period.

"Bub" Walsh was the versatile athlete, a good runner, an enthusiastic cricketer, an expert canoeist, and a formidable soccer player. Active in just about every outdoor pastime, he was a natural leader. Even in the Prescott Volunteer Fire Brigade, he was the captain. But in making a career for himself, he was scarcely as successful and his father worried because his athletic son was slow in settling down. The young fellow had tried his hand at various things. For a while he was engaged in a local store selling dry goods. His next venture was in a machine shop; then he set about to become an engineer on the railroad. None of these activities suited him.

Walsh reacted quickly to the call for volunteers to help stop the Fenian Raiders in 1866, and discovered army life. There was a family tradition for it, Irish Walsh ancestors having served with the Duke of Wellington. Now the army seemed to be claiming its own. James attended and graduated from Royal Military College at Kingston. He was twenty-four years of age at graduation; for the next few years his fortunes were those of a soldier. He was posted to the 156th Grenville Regiment (Lisgar Rifles) where he gained the rank of captain. Eager for experience beyond the infantry, he enrolled in the Toronto Cavalry School and won high commendation. In the opinion of the commanding officer, he was "the best drilled Canadian" to graduate and one of the best anywhere in action against those wild Irishmen known as Fenians.

In 1870, he married Mary Elizabeth, a daughter of John Mowat of Brockville, and he began operating the North American Hotel at Prescott. The business was moderately successful but Walsh did not withdraw completely from military activities. He organized the Prescott Cavalry Troop which he commanded until the autumn of 1873 when he gave up all business connections in order to join the North West Mounted Police.

It may have been his unusual success with the Prescott Cavalry Troop – winning praise from Lord Dufferin, the Governor General – that brought him to prominence. When the new force was organized, he was recognized at once as a man who by training, reputation and personality, was right for the job. By the latter part of September, he was engrossed with recruiting, hoping to see the first police troops in the West before the onset of winter. The Government knew there would be practical advantages in having a body of police stationed in the West as quickly as possible. Not even waiting for uniforms, A Troop was ordered to travel.

Fortunately, it is possible to draw upon Walsh's own account of events: "The detachment of Mounted Police consisting of one officer, one non-commissioned officer, and 32 privates proceeded from Ottawa by train at 9:30 p.m. on the 1st October, 1873, arriving at Prescott Junction at 1:10 a.m., 2nd instant."[2]

As fresh recuits without uniforms, the men must have looked more like an off-duty gang of lumberjacks than police personnel and they had much to learn about discipline. They had, however, an efficient teacher. Even before the men were instructed on marching, they were told that good behaviour was a prime requirement. This lesson was reinforced when, less than twenty-four hours after leaving Ottawa, one of the recruits, "T. O'Neil, trumpeter, was discharged and sent back to Ottawa for being drunk and riotous". Next day, when ready to leave Toronto, one of the recruits was missing and Walsh went without him. Then, at Collingwood, while waiting for the boat to take the group across the Great Lakes, another rookie policeman, "Todd, accidently shot himself in the forearm with his revolver while practising on the shore".

Walsh must have wondered if he would have any men left by the time he arrived at Fort Garry. But before leaving Collingwood, the troop benefited by an addition; William Walsh took the oath of allegiance before Mayor Moberly, and the man left behind at Toronto caught up with his fellows in time to receive his issue of blankets, greatcoat, towel, soap, tin plate, cup, knife, fork and spoon. While waiting for the steamer, Walsh took the opportunity to instruct his men on conduct and discipline. To avoid misunderstanding, one order was written: the men should avoid taking "too much liquor. While he [the O.C.] is no advocate of wholly abstaining, still it will be his duty to report to the Commissioner on his arrival at the Fort any cases of drunkenness." But Major Walsh wanted co-operation as well as obedience and the further memo was appended: "The C.O. wishes it to be distinctly understood that this is intended more as a request than a warning."

The boat left Collingwood late in the afternoon of October 4 and arrived at Thunder Bay early in the morning of October 8. The men were still far from Fort Garry and the most difficult part of the journey lay ahead. Travel over the Dawson Route, by this time well marked, was made by wagon, small lake boat, canoe, and on foot. The men left Thunder Bay only a few hours after their arrival. The country was displaying its autumn colours. Migrating birds were in southerly flight and beavers were reinforcing their mud and log houses for winter. Evenings were becoming colder as the men sleeping in tents soon discovered. Everyone was concerned to reach Fort Garry before being caught by winter and no objection was heard to the early morning starting hours. On October 10, according to Walsh's record, the men were starting at 2 A.M. Leaving Lake of the Woods on October 17, they faced the first snowstorm of the season but four days later they were at St. Boniface, across the river from Fort Garry. There remained but one more night of camping and then, on October 22, the travellers completed their journey by Steamboat Alpha on the Red River. They reached Lower Fort Garry exactly three weeks after leaving Ottawa.

Troops B and C, under the command of Colonel James Macleod, followed a week later and encountered storms and delays. The weather turned so bad that baggage and supplies had to be left at Lake of the Woods, and remained there until the following spring. By November 3, the three troops were united at the Lower Fort. Lieutenant-Colonel Osborne Smith, Acting Commissioner of the new force, came down from the Upper Fort and administered the oath of the North West Mounted Police to all enlisted men. All promised that during their period of service, they would "well and faithfully, diligently and impartially, execute and perform such duties as may from time to time be allotted to us, and submit to such penalties as may at any time be imposed on us by law, and will well and truly obey and perform all lawful orders and instructions given to or imposed upon us".

The police were now in business, despite an annoying delay in the delivery of uniforms. Western horses were purchased for riding practice. Superintendent W.D. Jarvis became the Officer Commanding and Superintendent Walsh was appointed Acting Adjutant, Riding Master, and Acting Veterinarian. Lieutenant-Colonel George A. French, formerly of the Imperial Army in Canada, was appointed Commissioner of the North West Mounted Police by Order-in-Council, October 16, 1873.

The force's first demonstration of authority was a raid on a whiskey peddler's cabin on the west side of Lake Winnipeg. Four men made the trip by dog-team and snowshoe in temperatures of thirty degrees below zero. After several days on the trail the men approached the secluded cabin with guns loaded. Taken by surprise, the suspects surrendered and watched the policemen empty the liquor on the snow. Then the officer, exercising his commission as a Justice of the Peace, proclaimed court in the cabin, tried the six prisoners, convicted them and imposed fines.

For the new policemen, strangers in Manitoba, the winter seemed long and one day was annoyingly like another. Under orders from Acting Adjutant Walsh, the rising call was at 6:30; stable duty was from 7 to 8; breakfast at 8:15, routine at 10; parade at 10:30; stable duty at 11:30; dinner at 1:00; parade at 2; afternoon tea at 4:30; stable duty at 4:45; evening meal at 6; last post at 10 and lights out at 10:15. But the men made the most of their visits to Winnipeg, especially after being issued uniforms consisting of red jackets, dark grey breeches, blue trousers with white stripes, dark blue great coats, blue "pillbox" hats with white bands, and either high brown boots for use with breeches or black wellingtons for wear with trousers.

On November 8, only five days after the Mounted Police took their oath of service, Winnipeg was incorporated as a city. Winnipeg citizens, now numbering close to 2,000 had seen police officers before but not all their recollections were favourable. This time they would wait and see, as the editor of the *Manitoban* suggested:

In our little Province we have had various experiences with respect to our police....We have seen the Town of Winnipeg in the hands of a riotous mob, and we have seen our police when informed that in the hands of that mob, property was being destroyed and lives endangered, hidden away in their little office, quivering and shaking and refusing to do their duty....Now we have a new one headed by Captain Walsh....When the force arrives we trust that they will show themselves as police.[3]

Three weeks later, the same editor reported the arrival of the first troop and was reassured.

The first detachment of Mounted Police consisting of forty-three men arrived here on Tuesday, in charge of Sub-Inspector Walsh. They encamped on the other side of the river near the Rifle Range and on Wednesday left for the Stone Fort by the steamer Alpha....Judging from the first detachment, the Mounted Police are a fine body of men.

As first officer, Walsh's public relations were important. He won the respect of Winnipeg from the start. At once the newcomers entered into the social life of the community. "The Police are making things lively," an editor wrote. At Christmas there was the ball at Government House where Lieutenant-Governor Morris and Mrs. Morris welcomed Winnipeg's leaders and a month later, January 30, while the young city was recovering from the excesses of its first civic election – 388 names on the voter's list and 562 votes cast – the Mounted Police were the hosts at a ball held in the Canadian Pacific Hotel. It was said to have set a new social tone for the community. The editor of the *Manitoban*[4] reported sales of thirty-nine lots "on the Magnus Brown property and a number of lots on the Portage road" to members of the force "during the past week".

*

By midsummer, 1874, men on Winnipeg streets heard at least one fresh and blood-curdling rumour concerning the Sioux every day. It was known that Lieutenant-Colonel George Custer was leading a large military force into the Black Hills to answer popular questions about the gold to be found there. Sure enough, he discovered the precious treasure and the *Manitoba Daily Free Press*, noting the rich gold and silver resources, concluded that "the immediate section bids fair to be the Eldorado of America."[5] The Custer expedition only infuriated the Sioux more than ever and killings were accelerated. Some of the stories of murder committed by the frustrated natives were true; many were completely false; all were frightening. The rumour mill was at peak production about the time the Mounted Police were preparing for the great westward advance.

The *Manitoba Daily Free Press*, making its first appearance as a daily paper just two days before the Mounted Police march began, reported "intense excitement" in the Pembina district following "the extermination of two half-breed families" near St. Joe, close to the Canadian border.[6] It was the work of Sioux and fear was being expressed that they might launch an attack on working parties with the Boundary Commission. Some of the Indians seen near the boundary were observed to be riding shod horses, suggesting that these animals had been stolen from a working party or were police horses recovered following a wild stampede induced by a summer storm.

Commissioner French soon concluded that the hundred and fifty men who wintered at the Lower Fort were not enough for the challenges likely to face the force in the country to the West. By this time, there was a change of administration at Ottawa. In the face of the Pacific scandal, Sir John A. Macdonald had resigned. Alexander Mackenzie and his Liberals won the election of January, 1874. The change gave French an opportunity to request an increase in strength. It was approved and recruiting began again. French and Walsh went east to direct the new programme and on June 6, 1874, sixteen officers, 201 men and 244 horses left Toronto by special train, to travel by rail as far as Fargo, North Dakota. From there they marched to Fort Dufferin on the Manitoba side of the boundary.

By this time, the Commissioner and Assistant Commissioner were anticipating direct conflict with the Sioux. On the day prior to the beginning of the big march, Sioux Indians under Chiefs Grizzly Bear and Young Chief paid a visit to the Lieutenant-Governor in Winnipeg. They were noisy but peaceful. However, Winnipeg became conscious of its helplessness should a visiting band prove warlike. The *Manitoba Daily Free Press*, on the very day the police march began, related that "36 men of the Boundary Commission, including some people well known here, have been scalped by the Sioux."[7] Happily, the editor could add that it was just a rumour and totally without basis in fact. But another report printed on the same day appeared correct and told of an outbreak in Nebraska which left fifty Sioux dead.

The fear of war with the Sioux was given as the reason for the sudden increase in desertions from Mounted Police ranks and Winnipeg papers carried several references to it. Travellers coming from the south were saying "that the North West Mounted Police are deserting in large numbers."[8] Two days later, departure day from Dufferin, the same paper denied a rumour that the Mounted Police had been attacked by Sioux and, at the same time, informed readers that Commissioner French had just left with four troops of the police, "the fifth having nearly all deserted; he follows the boundary line and expects to have a brush with the Sioux band that massacred the Half-Breeds at St. Joe."[9] The desertions were not as numerous as the reports indicated but they did reveal the state of mind at that time.

After months of preparation, the great cavalcade moved out of Fort Dufferin. In addition to the 297 officers and men, an observer might have counted 308 horses, 142 oxen, 93 cattle, 114 Red River carts, 73 wagons, 20 Métis drivers, and farm implements. Strung out in marching order, the parade stretched for more than two miles on the prairie trail. Unfortunately, there was scarcely a spectator and not a press photographer present. Under the circumstances, the officers might have relaxed discipline for the sake of comfort but the Commissioners believed that good policemen should look like good policemen even when they were not under observation. It was to be a parade all the way and the column was as orderly as it was possible to make it. As one of the officers reported it:

First came A Division with splendid dark bays and thirteen wagons. Then B with dark browns. Next c with bright chestnuts drawing the guns and ammunition. Next D with greys, then E with black horses, the rear being brought up with F with light bays. Then a motley string of ox carts, ox wagons, cattle for slaughter, cows, calves, mowing machines, etc."

To a stranger, it would have appeared an astonishing cavalcade. Armed men and guns looked as if fighting was to be done. What could ploughs, harrows, mowing machines, cows, calves, etc., be for? But that little force had a double duty to perform: to fight if necessary but in any case, to establish posts in the far West.

Before long, however, the troop lost much of its glamour when the horses and oxen became fatigued and weakened. The loads were too heavy and the watering places too far apart. The oxen, able to live off the land, survived better than the horses. After travelling two hundred and seventy miles from Fort Dufferin, the Commissioners directed Inspector W.D. Jarvis to take Troop A along with unessential horses and cattle and swing toward Fort Ellis and Fort Edmonton. The other troops continued toward the Rocky Mountains.

The Commissioners had the good fortune to obtain the services of an unimposing Métis guide, Jerry Potts, whose help throughout the balance of the expedition and in the years ahead proved invaluable to the force. With the qualities of a homing pigeon, little Jerry became the eyes and ears of the force. He directed the police to Fort Whoop-Up where a battle was expected. But the Mounties found the notorious fort almost deserted and drove on to the Oldman River where they camped and began to build Fort Macleod. Assistant Commissioner Macleod estimated they had travelled 781 miles and after the first eighteen, they had not seen a single human habitation except for Indian tipis. Nor had they encountered any Sioux. Macleod decided to send sixty-four horses, twenty oxen and ten young cattle to winter at Sun River, Montana, where they would have a better chance of enjoying winter grazing. That called for an additional journey of two hundred miles, and Inspector Walsh and thirteen men, including Jerry Potts, were assigned the task. Constable Cochrane of B Troop was to remain in Montana with the animals for the winter.

Shortly before Christmas, men of the North West Mounted Police were settled in at their new but crudely constructed fort on the Oldman. Walsh made a second trip to Montana during that winter to purchase better horses for the heavy demands of police patrol. And early in the spring, he left Fort Macleod for the Cypress Hills to select a site for an outpost close to the scene of the Indian massacre of two years earlier. Police attention seemed to be needed in that area where Indians and Métis loved to congregate and hunt. The spot chosen was in a broad valley, close to the headwaters of Battle Creek. Indians of many tribes, including some unfriendly Sioux, called to inspect the buildings and gaze at the man who would be the "White Chief". The new post was given the name Fort Walsh.

Custer's Last Stand

George Armstrong Custer, sitting tall in the saddle, rode boldly at the head of twelve companies of the Seventh Cavalry on that fateful morning of June 25, 1876. The irrepressible officer who had attained the rank of brigadier-general of Volunteers in the Civil War and reverted to that of lieutenant-colonel in the postwar force, gave his usual impression of confidence bordering on arrogance. If he did believe with the late Captain William Fetterman that with eighty good men he could "ride through the whole Sioux nation", at least he was convinced that the Seventh Cavalry, with himself in command, could rout any band of Indian warriors foolish enough to challenge.

The sun shone pleasantly and the park-like setting did not seem a battlefield. The Little Big Horn River, flowing northward from the mountains bearing the same name to join first the Big Horn River and then the Yellowstone and Missouri, cut a twisted course through the broad valley. Beyond the cutbanks and tree-covered slopes the countryside was marked by grassy hills, tipi-rings and bleaching buffalo bones.

The Yellowstone expedition of 1876 was to be a pincer-like thrust with three military columns converging upon the troublesome natives believed to be concentrated near the Little Big Horn River and other nearby streams – the Powder, Rosebud and Tongue. According to the plan, the three columns were to move simultaneously, one from the north, one from the south and one from the east, leaving no way for escape. There could be no leniency in dealing with these recalcitrant people. A government order had given them until the end of

January in 1876 to return to their reserves. It was now June and the order had to be enforced. General George Crook with 1,300 men started north from Fort Laramie. General John Gibbon marched eastward from Fort Ellis in Montana with four hundred men to join General Alfred Terry's force of a thousand men coming from Fort Lincoln in Dakota.

It may have been a well-conceived plan but it was not a well-kept secret. Newspaper reporters seemed to know all about it. Even the Canadian papers related the plan. The *Manitoba Daily Free Press* of Winnipeg reported that:

General Crook has started with a force from Fort Laramie, and General Custer with troops from Fort Lincoln to be joined by a detachment from Montana, to operate against Sitting Bull at the mouth of the Powder River in the Yellowstone country. Sitting Bull has 1,500 warriors and sets at defiance the treaty which requires his people to remain on the reservations. The number of United States troops in the expedition is about 2,000.[1]

With the publication of such information, there was no chance of taking the enemy by surprise. In April, Sitting Bull called a council of the bands to discuss war. The meeting was held beside the Tongue River and at it he established himself unquestionably as the tribal leader. At the same time, he vowed to perform a sun dance, thereby seeking approval and guidance from the Great Spirit. Sitting Bull gave as a sacrifice a hundred pieces of skin from his body and while still bleeding, danced continuously for a day and a night. The vision he sought came very clear and he was reassured. The Great Spirit would help him in the war soon to break.

General Crook moved up the Bozeman Trail to the Tongue River and on June 17 encountered Chief Crazy Horse and about 1,200 Oglala Sioux who seemed to be waiting for him. The ensuing battle beside the Rosebud sent the American general into retreat to spend the following weeks waiting for reinforcements. It was the second time Crook had tasted defeat at the hand of Crazy Horse.

Unaware of the battle of the Rosebud, Generals Gibbon and Terry continued with their plans although the Dakota column marching from Fort Lincoln, near Bismark, was delayed because of Custer's involvement in the Washington investigations of alleged graft at army posts. Custer was to have commanded the column, but having incurred presidential displeasure, he saw General Terry get the appointment while he had to be satisfied with the lesser responsibility of commanding the Seventh Cavalry.

General Gibbon with his four-hundred-man regiment marched eastward to meet the Dakota column and made joint camp on the south side of the Yellowstone River at the beginning of June. There Terry, Gibbon, and Custer met in council on the riverboat, Far West, and drafted plans for their thrust toward Wolf Mountain where they believed Sitting Bull was camping. In guessing the chief's whereabouts, they were fairly accurate but nobody suspected that as many as 3,000 or 4,000 warriors had rallied to him – a formidable army.

Major Marcus Reno returned from a scouting trip on the Rosebud and reported a fresh Indian trail leading to the Little Big Horn. From this information, the commanding officers concluded that the main encampment would be found there. They agreed to divide the force and attempt to strike the Indians from two sides. Custer and his 655 men of the Seventh Cavalry would march up the Rosebud and then swing west toward the Little Big Horn. Contingency plans included supplies for fifteen days as well as extra salt in case they had to eat their horses before returning. Terry and Gibbon, with the remainder of the two original columns, would travel west to the mouth of the Big Horn River and then south to the Little Big Horn. Custer's men would have the shorter distance to travel but he was advised to avoid the direct approach which might bring him in contact with the Indians before the infantry had time to come up. If the two groups reached the river about the same time on June 26, there could be a co-ordinated attack with better chance of success.

The Seventh Cavalry started south at noon on June 22 and followed the Rosebud River for two and one-half days. The advance was hasty, even though Custer had been advised not to reach the Indians before Terry and Gibbon. It is said that Custer confessed to his subordinate officers his intention to follow the Indian trial westward. This was later interpreted as a deliberate disobedience of Terry's instructions. Perhaps Custer was nursing the idea of a sweeping victory, unaided, to restore his popularity with Washington officials.

The men of the Seventh rode twenty-eight miles on June 24, and then mentioning the increasing danger of being discovered by Sitting Bull's Indians, Custer ordered preparations for a night march. Leaving at 11:30 A.M., the men rode for three hours and made camp when only it was found necessary to have daylight for crossing the height of land between the Rosebud and Little Big Horn. After resting for three hours, the regiment was moving again and by 8 A.M. the men of the Seventh were in the valley of the Little Big Horn. Their presence was no longer a secret. They could see Indians and Indians could see them.

Custer knew he must attack or be attacked. Any thought of waiting for Terry and Gibbon vanished. He still believed that Sitting Bull had fewer than 1,500 warriors and victory for his troops would be quick and easy. Around noon on that day, Sunday, June 25, 1876, he instructed his officers. Conferring briefly with Major Marcus Reno and Captain Frederick Benteen, both of whom were on less than friendly terms with him, he explained his decision to divide the regiment into three commands. Captain Benteen with three companies – about 120 men – was to patrol to the east and "pitch into anything he came across". Reno, also with three companies, was to attack the south of the Indian village while Custer with five companies – 240 men – would advance on the east side of the river to strike the encampment from a more northerly angle. The one remaining company, under the direction of Captain McDougall, was charged with the responsibility for the packtrain.

Benteen, on patrol where he might intercept fleeing Indians, saw none. The Indians were not fleeing. Reno, advancing in a central position down the valley on the west side of the stream, was forced into early action. Chiefs Crazy Horse, Gall and Crow King hurled what seemed like a thousand warriors against his cavalrymen and brought them to a brutal halt. As Reno's left flank fell back, so did the rest of his line. He tried for a new stand, ordered his men to dismount and fight but this was no better and after a desperate struggle and severe losses, he shouted an order to "Mount and get back to the bluffs."[2] Retreating in wild disorder, the troops crossed to the east side of the river and collected in a wooded coulee. There they regrouped and were joined by Benteen's companies. They were still seriously outnumbered, with but slight chance of fighting their way out of the pocket.

Meanwhile Custer, with the major part of the Seventh, was advancing in downstream on the river's right. From the high banks, he could hardly fail to see Reno's distress. But Custer's gaze was upon the Sioux encampment spreading far out in the valley to his left. He was probably surprised at the immense size of the camp, but he was an optimist. He had not heard of Crook's defeat of some days earlier[3] and may have supposed that the main body of Indians had taken flight at his appearance. As he tried to cross the river to make a direct thrust at the village, warriors appeared and he was driven back. He continued on the high ground for another mile or two, which gave the Sioux time to inflict further damage to Reno's troops and to rally for a charge against Custer.

If the Sioux recognized Custer – Long Yellow Hair they called him – they would be especially eager for revenge. After his mission to the Black Hills, the Indians accused him on two counts: failing to keep his promises, and doing bad things to Indian girls taken as prisoners. Chief Gall took his painted and seminaked fighters across the river to strike Custer's left flank, while Crazy Horse crossed farther down for a frontal attack. As Custer and his companies crossed a ravine and came out on high ground, warriors appeared suddenly both in front and behind. From the wooded depressions they came in hordes and practically surrounded the troopers. Custer knew now that the main body of Sioux had not taken flight. He sent an urgent message to Captain Benteen: "Benteen, come on. Big village. Be quick. Bring packs. p.s. Bring packs." The two heavy volleys heard by Reno's party was probably a signal for help. Reno, by this time, had rallied his men and might have ordered an advance in the hope of joining his superior officer, but for reasons best known to himself, he did not leave his wooded refuge. Later in the day, Captain McDougall and the pack-train joined Reno and at about 5 p.m. they attempted to move in the direction of Custer's battleground. But the Indians drove the cavalrymen back to the shelter of the trees where they fought defensively until nightfall.

Exactly what Custer did remains a mystery. In the heat of battle, his men dismounted in the hope of being more effective defensively. Ammunition was running low. Guns were jamming. Horses stampeded, taking munition supplies with them. Custer looked hopefully for Reno to come. Late in the afternoon, Chiefs Gall, Crazy Horse and Rain-In-The-Face led another vicious attack, completely surrounding the force and killing to the last man. No one survived except a Crow scout called Curley who, blanketed as a Sioux, got away early in the afternoon.

It was Custer's last stand. Found two days later, his body had two bullets, one of them in the temple. Many of the bodies were stripped and mutilated. Some were scalped. Lieutenant-Colonel Custer's scalp was not taken. Although the Indians disliked him, they admired bravery. The body of his younger brother, Captain Tom Custer, was slashed and visceral organs were protruding. Rain-In-The-Face had vowed to eat the younger Custer's heart. The vengeful fellow shot the captain with his revolver and as he bragged later, cut out "Little Hair's" heart, "bit a piece of it and spit it in his face."[4]

The dead numbered two hundred and twenty-five. Among them was *New York Herald* correspondent, Mark Kellog, whom Custer had brought along to tell the world of the glorious triumph he expected. Adding the losses among Reno's men, the total would be about two hundred and sixty-five. Most of the bodies were buried on the hillside which was to become part of the Custer Battlefield National Monument and where, exactly seventy-five years later, 7,000 people gathered for the anniversary and to speculate again about what had happened.

The American troops were, indeed, hopelessly overwhelmed in fighting strength. Nobody could be sure about the Sioux numbers but the United States leaders should have known that the defeat of General Crook would inspire hundreds of nonbelligerent Indians to join the hostiles. Estimates varied widely but there was reason to believe that Sitting Bull could have counted at least 3,000 warriors that day. It was a reverse so complete, according to a Canadian assessment at the time "as to imply that someone blundered."[5] Custer was criticized for ignoring General Terry's instructions to wait for the infantry before striking. He was criticized, too, for failing to cross the river to help Reno when the latter was being forced into retreat. And Reno was criticized for indecisive leadership and failing to join Custer.

As in most wars, there was nothing conclusive about the outcome. It was striking defeat for the American army and the nation was shocked. But the men in uniform knew they had to fight until the hostiles were crushed. And Sitting Bull and his fellow chiefs knew their apparent victory might instead be a tragedy; it could trigger the beginning of a campaign to completely destroy Indian freedom and even the race.

After Little Big Horn

News travelled slowly in the prairies and several weeks passed before the Mounted Police at Fort Macleod and Fort Walsh heard about the battle at Little Big Horn. Eleven days after Custer's last battle Colonel Irvine, Assistant Commissioner, wrote from Fort Macleod to share certain confidential information with the commanding officer at Fort Walsh.

Confidential   FORT MACLEOD, *5th July, 1876*
SIR,

I have received a confidential communication which indicates the possibility of the United States operations against the hostile Indians of Dakota and Montana on the Yellowstone and Bighorn Rivers, resulting in their being driven for shelter into the Territories and using Canadian soil as a base for predatory and hostile operations.

The place for which these escaping parties (should the suspicions expressed prove correct) would make might be somehwere in the vicinity of Wood Mountain.

I wish you not only to keep a strict watch in the vicinity of your post but to keep a sharp look out towards Wood Mountain and on the slightest indication of what has been anticipated taking place you are to have it communicated to me by special messenger at once.

I have thought it advisable to strengthen your post for the present by fifteen men. Sub-Inspector Antrobus with eleven men leaves here in the morning for Fort Walsh. I have instructed Mr. Antrobus to report to you and place himself under

your orders. I will leave here myself for your post on the 15th inst., bringing the other four men with me. . . .
I have the honour to be, sir,
Your obedient servant

A.G.Irvine[1]

Irvine was prepared for all contingencies.

People across the United States were shocked and angry. To them what happened at the Little Big Horn River was nothing short of bloody murder and the murderers had to be punished or destroyed. The Chief who masterminded the victorious battle was not surprised. He knew the risks his tribesmen were taking for freedom and birthright. He knew there would be retaliation and the full force of the United States would now be brought against him. He warned his warriors to be ready to fight again and the women and children to be ready on short notice to flee.

Sitting Bull's leadership was now generally recognized although, like other leaders in history, he had his critics and enemies within as well as without. One of those was Chief Gall who was critical of Sitting Bull for making medicine when the other chiefs were fighting. Gall, taller than Sitting Bull and more refined in appearance, was a great warrior; he believed that every chief should be in the thick of battle with his followers. Sitting Bull had his own views on leadership. He was a seasoned warrior and had the battle scars to prove many skirmishes. No man could say his courage had ever failed. But now he was both medicine man and fighter and, having faith in the rare gifts he possessed, he was anxious to bring all his resources to the struggle against the enemy. His resources as a strategist could be used to better advantage than his talents as a fighter. After all, the Sioux had plenty of warriors but no other with all the qualifications for co-ordinating the fighting effort.

Gall was jealous and prejudiced. When he accused Sitting Bull of being absent from the Little Big Horn affair, he was wrong. According to the record published by the Bureau of Indian Affairs,[2] Sitting Bull was an active leader in the fighting which repulsed Major Marcus Reno in the latter's initial thrust on the west side of Little Big Horn River. It was only when Sitting Bull saw Custer's troops advancing on the opposite side that he withdrew from the front in order to co-ordinate and direct the entire Sioux operation. Be that as it may, victory was decisive and a big Indian feast marked the end of the battle. Sitting Bull attributed the success to his "good medicine", which had made his warriors unusually brave and made him wise in leadership. Gall objected, insisting that victory was due entirely to the Sioux warriors who did the fighting, not to the Chief who took time to "make medicine".

When news of the Custer disaster reached Fort Leavenworth, General Miles and the Fifth Infantry were ordered to the scene of the trouble. He overtook the Sioux at Cedar Creek on October 21 and gave Sitting Bull an opportunity for an interview. A conference was arranged and Sitting Bull, in the company of a few warriors, admitted that he wanted peace on what he regarded as fair terms; that meant the right to keep his guns and hunt at will rather than be fenced in on a reserve. Miles, on the other hand, could only repeat the demand that the Sioux must surrender their guns and accept life at the agencies. Neither side could or would accept middle ground.

Sitting Bull, described by Miles as a fine, dignified, powerful and intelligent man, began the conference quietly and courteously but grew first impatient and then defiant. The Great Spirit, he said, made him an Indian, not an agency Indian. Raising himself to his greatest stature, he fixed Miles with a stare. There was a threat of assault but Miles adjourned the meeting, suggesting that discussions resume the following day. But the next day was no more productive. Sitting Bull, as noted by a Canadian paper at the time, was "anxious for peace but not on the terms which would be imposed upon him."[3]

Miles, seeing no hope of the Chief yielding in his demands, informed him that if he remained adamant, the only alternative was to settle the dispute on the battlefield. He announced that the truce would last only fifteen more minutes which would give Sitting Bull time to get back to his camp and give the warning for war.

The two leaders moved quickly and after Miles checked off the specified minutes, he ordered an advance toward the Indian lines. The Sioux by this time had fired the dry grass and the ensuing battle was fought amid flame and smoke. But the Indians were driven back, to attack again and again without much success. The Sioux lost heavily and some surrendered. Others scattered. Sitting Bull and Gall with about four hundred followers were soon joined by Rain-In-The-Face and Iron Horn and their warriors. Dispersion was part of Sioux defence tactics but the beleaguered people could find few avenues of escape. There was still a hopeful alternative, to flee across the boundary and into Canada. The most likely point of crossing was southeast of the Cypress Hills, which would make the unwelcome visitors a Fort Walsh responsibility.

As it happened, the post's commander, Superintendent James Walsh, was at that time on sick leave at Hot Springs, Arkansas.[4] A telegram from the Department of Interior, Ottawa, informed him of the Custer defeat and the possibility of a Sioux movement to the Canadian border. Walsh left immediately for Ottawa and, a few days later, resumed his command at the Cypress Hills post. Arriving at Fort Walsh about the beginning of August, he dispatched scouts to watch the boundary for a distance of two hundred and fifty miles. For the next month all was quiet; then Walsh received word that a big band of Indians had crossed the Missouri River and was moving toward the border. After another week, the Sioux were at Rock Creek, only forty miles south of the border and were reported to be planning attacks upon trading posts and Indian agencies along the river. Walsh sent his best scout, Louis Lavallie, to inform the Americans. The United States authorities were grateful and took immediate steps to protect those who might have been victims.

Lavallie, a French-Cree Métis, six feet tall and spare, had become the police superintendent's constant travelling companionion. He was, said Walsh, "the best scout I ever saw, faithful and efficient". He was an expert shot and "with a good horse and Henry rifle, would kill in a run nine or ten buffalo". The two men made a notable combination. The Walsh brand of daring became a frontier legend: regardless of the danger, the faithful Lavallie was always at his side. Walsh told of an occasion beside Frenchman's River (Whitemud Creek) when he was riding far ahead of his troop. A band of strange Indians appeared suddenly and, Lavallie, seeing it, knew he should be close to Walsh. He knew, also, that the other scout had the faster horse. Not waiting to ask for his companion's horse, Lavallie knocked him off his mount and left him lying on the ground while he, Lavallie, dashed off to Walsh's side.

After sending Lavallie to the Missouri River, Walsh rode south to the place where Rock Creek flows from Canada into the United States. But the Indians were running buffalo and nobody could be sure when, if ever, they would attempt to cross northward. Making sure he had sufficient men patrolling the boundary area, he returned to Fort Walsh.

In November, as winter was beginning to tighten its grip on the prairies, members of the same Sioux group – about a thousand men, women and children – crossed to the Canadian side and began making camp in a sheltered valley near Wood Mountain. Walsh sent Sub-Inspector Edmund Frechette and several constables to visit the camp and bring back a report. But the weather became severely cold and stormy and Frechette had not returned. Taking twelve policemen and three scouts, Walsh set out on December 13, intending to go first to Louis Legaré's trading post at Wood Mountain. En route, he passed Frechette moving homeward slowly on exhausted horses. After eight days of difficult winter travel, Walsh arrived at Legaré's post and then presented himself at the encampment of Chief White Eagle who, with his Sisseton Sioux followers, had been living in Canada since the Sioux massacres in Minnesota fourteen years earlier. The Chief proved especially helpful to Walsh as he went on to visit the most recent arrivals, Black Moon, Long Dog, Spotted Eagle and their following, who had arrived only two days before and were camping close to White Eagle. Walsh told Black Moon and his friends at once how they would have to conduct themselves if they were to find asylum on the British side. The newcomers were hungry and made a plea for ammunition with which to shoot buffalo. Having spent what gunpowder they had in fighting the United States troops, they had none for the hunt and were reduced to killing buffalo with bows and arrows and trying to lasso the animals with ropes. Walsh hesitated. He would give them no ammunition for fighting either United States forces or other Indians but, with a promise of good behaviour, there would be a minimum for hunting.

Scouts kept Walsh well informed. He seemed to know more than the American authorities about the movements of Indians in the northern parts of the United States. In March, 1877, when the prairie was still blanketed with snow, he was informed that Sitting Bull had crossed the Missouri River and was likely to continue his journey into Canada. With yet another report of a large band of Sioux following Rock Creek toward the border, Walsh with three scouts, Lavallie, Morin and Daniels, and several constables, again left his Cypress Hills post to ride the long winter trail to Wood Mountain. "We established our headquarters", he wrote, "about midway between the Pinto Horse Butte and the Wood Mountain, about 120 miles east of Fort Walsh and 40 miles north of the international line."[5]

There was still no sign of Sitting Bull and Walsh resolved to remain near the border and help with the scouting. The new grass was changing the colour of the plains which had been burnt over in the previous autumn. Trees in Wood Mountain ravines were attracting nesting birds like a buffalo carcass attracts coyotes and the landmark, Indian Cliff, at the west side of the hilly range stood out sharply as if trying to supervise all the springtime activity. It was beside Indian Cliff, later in the season, that the Sioux held a huge council and celebration that saw forty young men lacerating themselves and enduring the torture which would qualify them as braves.

Walsh and his scouts rode south to Frenchman's River (Whitemud Creek) badlands where the little party divided; Daniels and Lavallie followed the east bank of the river while Walsh and Morin, a Sioux Métis, scouted the west side. "We had not travelled more than seven miles when we struck a large new Indian trail", Walsh wrote. "We were satisfied they were the people we were looking for and we followed the trail back." The marks of hoofprints and travois pointed to the Mud House, a dugout beside the river, used previously as a shelter by buffalo hunters. "Passing around the base of the butte and near the stone piles that mark the International line, [we] came upon the main body making camp on the opposite side of the stream." The sudden appearance of white men surprised and alarmed the Indians who

supposed we were Americans, the advance party, perhaps, of a

77

large force following their trail from the Missouri. The women and children broke into a panic, screeching, yelling and pulling down the lodges that were partly up. Horses were rushed into the camp and a regular stampede of the women and children for the hills on the north bank of the river took place. The Indians formed up at the ford on the opposite side to us to forbid our crossing. The stream was narrow – not over 50 yards wide – so we could easily speak with each other. The Indians charged us with being Americans and the advance of a large force.

At this tense moment, the other scouts, Lavallie and Daniels came racing up, fearing that Walsh might be in some trouble.

This gave the Indians a second scare and many of them took to the hills.... These poor people had suffered so much from treachery and raids upon their camps that the women and children did not have for a year a comfortable night's rest. When the boundary line was reached, they supposed that at last, here was a haven of safety but...when every heart was filled with joy and every soul most thankful for the Great Spirit's protection, they were thrown into alarm. They had our sympathy and hard did we plead with them to have no fear – that we were not messengers of evil as they supposed.... We made an attempt to cross [but] the Indians guarding drew their guns. Lavallie got very indignant...and drew his gun in return. Lavallie was instructed to desist and be patient. We conversed further with the Indians, answering a good many questions and informing [them] that we were determined to remain with the camp until we convinced them. We crossed and persuaded them to put their lodges up and have no fear. After some time we succeeded in getting them pacified. We then asked who was chief of the camp and Four Horns, an old man about six feet in height and 70 years of age was presented. We offered our hand and he took it. [We] asked what tribe he belonged to. He replied: 'We are Tetons, Unkpapa branch, and followers of my adopted son, Sitting Bull, who is still south of the Missouri, but looking this way.'

We informed who we were and now that he was on British soil, he and his followers must be instructed in the line of conduct they would have to pursue while north of the 49th parallel; we asked that his sub-chiefs and warriors would be called to hear what we had to communicate.[6]

By this time a number of lodges had been erected and Walsh was invited to enter a large one made with new skins. He was impressed. The lodge was clean and neat and the people occupying it appeared refined and handsome, especially the young ladies, two of them daughters of the owner, Little Saulteaux. The host was not a chief but obviously a man of considerable influence in the tribe. He was about fifty years of age, clean and well dressed in blankets and feathers. The lodge was laid out in compartments around the outside. The first section next to the entrance belonged to the owner's two wives, "good looking and well dressed women"; the next two sections were claimed by the two daughters, "about 16 and 18 years of age, very beautifully dressed and clean in person". The girls were busily engaged in beadwork. On the other side of the lodge was the owner's section, and then that of a young lady known as White Tooth, a niece of Little Saulteaux who had been visiting from the Red Cloud Agency when the United States troops struck and put all occupants of the camp to flight, preventing her return home. Walsh's eyes were fixed upon the girl, "picturesquely dressed in garments of fine texture and becoming to her". With black hair, beautiful features, dark and mild eyes, hands and feet delicately small and well shaped, tall and just slender enought to make her graceful, she was in the officer's own words, the "most handsome woman I ever saw of any colour".

Sensing that Walsh was tired, Little Saulteaux invited him to rest. Stretching out on the buffalo robes spread for him, he was almost immediately sound asleep. Such an incongruous situation the Indian spectators had never witnessed before. Here was a white man in uniform who, just minutes before, was being treated as an enemy and now was seen to be fearless enough and trusting enough to sleep in a Sioux lodge. Could it be that these Canadian police officers were really so different from the uniformed officers the Indians had come to know on the other side? For Walsh, the moments of sleep were all too brief. Daniels awakened his boss to tell him that Four Horns and his men had assembled to hear him in front of the lodge. Indeed, the entire population of the camp – men, women and children – had gathered in wonder to see and hear a man who was so unusual and who just might have a genuine message of peace.

Without ceremony, Walsh asked the listeners if they knew they were now on British soil. Four Horns answered for all, saying they knew. "All right," said Walsh, "you must know there are laws here and everybody – whites, reds and blacks – must obey. You and your people will have to obey or you cannot remain. . . . The laws you must observe are made with the consent of three hundred million Britishers. They govern the conduct of every person who stands on British ground and every Britisher defends them with his life. What they demand of you is that you will not kill either man, woman or child, no matter what their colour or tribe may be. You will not steal. . . . You will not do injury of any kind to either persons or property. . . . Horses, oxen, wagons, tents, lodges, guns, robes or any article whatsoever must not be removed by any person but the owner [unless] with his permission. That the person of a woman or female child must not be violated and it is the duty of every man to protect them. This, of all our laws, is the most sacred. Men must not cross the International line to·commit depredations. . . . We shall exercise patience and do all we can to educate you in the line of conduct you must follow and in return we expect to obtain from you that respect. If you obey these laws you and your families can sleep soundly here. You are as safe as if walled around by 10,000 warriors, but if you think you cannot conform to these laws, return whence you came for you cannot live upon British soil any more than fish can live without water."

Four Horns advanced, shook hands with Walsh and said, "We are tired. Our women and children are crying for rest. We want peace. We only ask to be allowed to hunt for buffalo. Your words we take into our hearts. We will obey them."

Suddenly the meeting was disrupted. An Indian courier arrived from the Missouri and breathlessly presented himself before the assembled group. He shook hands with Four Horns and seated himself in the inner circle, immediately opposite Walsh. He eyed the officer accusingly. Walsh tried to ignore his staring. But the fellow would not be ignored. He addressed Walsh as though he had rehearsed his speech, "The first time I met you was on the Missouri River, at Buford. The last time was on the Yellowstone at the camp of Bear Coat. You are a Long Knife American."[7]

The runner got to his feet, gestured to the four winds and called upon the Indians to heed his advice. "This man is nothing more than an American spy who would gladly murder all these people while they were sleeping. He should not be allowed to leave the camp".

Walsh tried to treat the matter with a smile but the accusation could not be dismissed so easily. He knew he had to answer the wild charges. "Who is this man?" he asked scathingly. "Does he belong to your tribe? Are you sure he is a friend and not a traitor?" Then turning to the accuser, he asked, "What is your purpose in trying to deceive these people? They have crossed to this land to seek rest from war, to let the smile return to the cheeks of their women, to let their children learn again how to play and amuse themselves. Are you so sorry to see them reach this condition? Do you want to encourage these people to commit some crime so that they may be refused shelter here and placed between two fires? Man, if you are not a devil, look upon these poor women and little children. If you have a heart, pity their tired and worn faces."

The runner interjected, "I know you know me."

Walsh grew bolder and pointing his finger, said, "Your words are false. You are a traitor and an enemy of these people."

Noticeably distressed by the change in events, Four Horns expressed disappointment that hearts were again beating fast from fear. Walsh nodded to express his own disappointment and then asked the Chief if it would relieve the fears any if he and his little party were to remain in the camp over night. Four Horns replied that it would be helpful.

"Very well," said Walsh, "I shall remain if you will see to it that this man will not be allowed to leave until tomorrow when I shall show you a rascal."

Four Horns agreed and Walsh made another request. "Four Horns, I want to hire two or three of your young men to carry a message and I shall pay them. Seventy miles southeast of here in the United States, at a place known as Burned Timbers, Medicine Bear and Black Horn and their people are camping. I want your young men to tell them that you have in your camp as a prisoner the White Forehead, Chief of the country north of the Big Road."

Four Horns did not want the word prisoner to be used but Walsh answered: "I am a prisoner. If I were to leave the camp, your warriors would attempt to stop me."

Some of the young men of the band said they would go and Walsh asked Four Horns to have the police horses turned in with the Indian animals to be herded and cared for until the next day. This the Chief was glad to do and after an evening meal of dried buffalo meat, Walsh and his men rolled up in buffalo blankets spread for them in the big lodge belonging to Little Saulteaux. Four Horns took the precaution of having the lodge guarded all night.

If Walsh was worried, he did not show it and in the morning he became quite romantic about the vista.

Nature appeared to be in her best form – thousands of horses feeding on the green spring grass, Indian warriors sitting in groups on the little hill tops, handsomely dressed maidens moving about with all the grace of fairies, women arranging their lodges, children amusing themselves with bows and arrows, old men lounging in the shade discussing the situation, the whole a picture as beautiful as it is possible for words to paint.[8]

Then, from far down the valley was heard an Indian war whoop. There were Medicine Bear and Black Horn and with them were two hundred warriors and the four young men who had gone as messengers at Walsh's request. It was a pretty sight with warriors in gay dress, their "eagle plumes nodding in the air like those of conquering heroes".

No one was more pleased to see the visitors than Walsh. The messengers had informed the two Yankton chiefs of what had happened beside Frenchman's River (Whitemud Creek) and after describing the red-coated officer's appearance, the chiefs said: "That is White Forehead. We will come and greet him."

Now, as the Yanktons approached, Black Horn recognized Walsh, dismounted from his horse and rushed forward to embrace him. Turning to Four Horns, Black Horn asked in anger, "Where is the man who says White Forehead is a Long Knife? Let him come forward." The accuser, realizing his mistake, managed to make an escape from the camp. "It is well that he is not here", said Black Horn and then, confronting Four Horns and taking his hand, said: "My friend, this is the Chief of the land on this side of the Big Road. His word is the law. You can depend on him."

Medicine Bear added his agreement, saying for all to hear: "If you want to live north of that line you must obey the law, just as White Forehead tells you." Black Horn had more to say: "My friends, I came here prepared for war but I am glad to find no cause. My heart is glad, for had one hair of his head been injured, this camp would not be standing now. Listen to his words. His tongue is not crooked."

Four Horns promised to obey the Canadian laws and apologized for doubting White Forehead's words. Walsh had only one complaint: the Chief had broken a pledge in allowing the accuser to escape. "But," he added, "think no more of that fellow."

Walsh and his guides left the camp late in the afternoon to return to the Cypress Hills, pleased with their success in winning the hearts of the much-feared Sioux. There remained, however, the biggest challenge of all, that of dealing with and winning Sitting Bull if he decided to cross the border.

Walsh Meets Bull

If the powerful Sioux tribe with 40,000 or more adherents across the country had a chief of chiefs, he was Sitting Bull, the warrior, orator, medicine man and prophet. The muscular, slightly lame and unsmiling leader was acknowledged by Indians and whites as having been the mastermind in the Indian victory at Little Big Horn. He was now the most fear-inspiring man on the continent. Relentlessly pursued by United States forces, he moved northward, aiming at the Canadian buffalo country to which he laid at least some moral claim. Mounted police feared that he would try to use the Canadian territories as a base from which to raid the United States.

Superintendent James Morrow Walsh was just back from the meeting with Chief Four Horns when scouts reported that Sitting Bull and another thousand refugees might not be far behind. They had crossed the Missouri River intending to cross the Boundary and escape from the Long Knives who, as the Sioux realized, were not supposed to step over the "Medicine Line" or "Big Road". The police lost no time in starting out toward Pinto Horse Butte which marked the westerly end of the low, sprawling Wood Mountains. With Walsh were four members of the force and two guides, Louis Lavallie and Gabriel Solomon. It was May, travel was easy, and night camps on the open prairie were pleasant.

Reaching Frenchman's River (Whitemud Creek), Walsh discovered a fresh trail and beside it a new grave. The trail, he suspected, was made by the newcomers he wanted to meet and the grave, as he learned later, was the burial place of an

Indian who died from wounds suffered in the Custer engagement and whose body was carried for days for the sake of interment in friendly Canadian soil. The force first spotted the Indians camping in the Frenchman's River (Whitemud Creek) valley on June 2, 1877. The border crossing, according to Father Chabot, was "along the Frenchman River," below the present villages of Val Marie and Mankota. "Their first camp was established in the ravines of Pinto Horse Hills."[1]

A minor chief, Spotted Eagle of the Sans Arc, rode forward to warn the strangers that they were approaching the camp of the highest ranking chief and that they approached at their own peril. The officer received the message courteously, but responded by asking the Sioux emissary to point out Sitting Bull's tipi. Walsh rode straight to his goal with neither halt nor change of pace. Nothing like this had ever happened before: a white man riding unannounced and apparently unafraid into the presence of the most feared native leader on the continent. The war-weary Chief gazed in astonishment as this mounted man in immaculate police uniform led his little group to the tipi entrance at a bold gait.

The Indian had a reputation as a ruthless killer and the police officer was making a reputation as one of the most fearless figures of his time. It was a tense moment, a crucial confrontation in Canadian history. As defenseless traders and settlers scattered across the prairie country knew very well, any act of violence could have explosive repercussions. The Indian held all the physical advantages. Behind him, within mere minutes travelling time, were more than 5,000 unhappy Sioux, including a thousand warriors. Immediately behind the police officer were six supporters. The officer halted a few paces from the Chief's tent, bringing the Indian to his feet. For an instant, both men remained motionless, gazing at each other like bulls measuring each other for a fight. Superintendent Walsh broke the spell by dismounting and passing his reins to one of his constables. Striding confidently toward the Chief, he offered his hand in greeting. With surprise bordering on shock, the Chief responded and the two shook hands.

"You and I must have a conversation," the officer began. "You know you are now on British soil." Walsh beckoned to his faithful interpreter and guide, Louis Lavallie, who translated. The Chief nodded reluctantly and at once laughed at the ridiculousness of this situation – a man with six followers telling a powerful chief with a thousand braves what he must do. Walsh asked that the lesser chiefs and head men be brought together so that he might instruct them on how they must conduct themselves if they were to remain on the Canadian side. Still visibly surprised, Sitting Bull condescended to call his Council.

The scene was one worthy of an artist's attention. Scouts on the nearby hill held dutifully to their posts. Leather-covered tipis with poles projecting at their tops filled the valley beside the slow-moving stream, just a short distance north of the International Boundary. Other Indians, becoming bolder as they became relaxed, crowded around, their eyes fixed upon the splendid figure of Major Walsh. The thirty-five-year-old officer, well built, athletic, agile and the ideal personification of the spirit of the new force, was studied intently. His thick brown curly hair showed clearly below his cap and his heavy mustache and well-trimmed imperial whisker fascinated the Indians. His expression was sober; nothing escaped his sharp eyes. If Walsh's fine physical presence was not enough to captivate the Indians, his colourful uniform would have done it. In the selection of police clothing he departed often from the prescribed styles. He demanded perfect fit but had no objection to individual colours and styles. With his riding breeches he wore cavalry boots extending above his knees. His cap bore a heavy gold band and his crimson coat was like nothing the Indians had seen before.

Facing Sitting Bull and all the assembled chiefs, Walsh spoke slowly. It was important for the Sioux to understand. He assured them that General Miles of the United States army who had followed them to the boundary, would not be continuing any farther. And the Sioux must not, under any circumstances, conduct acts of warfare across the border and hope to use the Canadian side as a refuge. To this Sitting Bull showed surprise and disappointment.

"If you cross," said Walsh, emphatically, "you will not be permitted to return to this side. You are now in another country and you must live by the laws of this country. People who break the laws of this land, whether they be whites, blacks or browns, will not escape punishment. There is no place here for lawless men who think it fun to shoot and kill Indians. And Indians must learn to respect the property of other people. There must be an end to the widespread practice of stealing horses or stealing anything belonging to others. Canadian law will be enforced uniformly for people of all races. If you are prepared to obey these Canadian laws, the police will protect you. If you are not prepared to obey, you can expect to be jailed or forced to leave the country."

Sitting Bull liked the idea of justice for all but found it hard to understand why he should be prevented from raiding south across the "Big Road". He became oratorical, told of treaties broken by United States officers, about attacks on Indian women and children, about Indians being hunted like wild animals. While loathe to give up all thought of striking back to square some old accounts with the Long Knives, he admitted most of his people wanted peace. Perhaps his people would find that peace in Canada where he had a hereditary right. He brought out the old medals. He might have added that the Sioux knew something about diplomacy as well as warfare. After the fall of New France, the Sioux gave their friendship to the British conquerors. Their loyalty persisted and in both the Revolutionary War and the War of 1812 they sided with the British. Whenever it suited his convenience, Sitting Bull declared himself a British Indian and displayed the George III medals given to his grandfather.

"Yesterday," he said, "I was fleeing from them [the white men] and cursing them as I moved. Today they plant their lodge by the side of mine and defy me. Have I fallen? Is my reign at an end?"[2]

Walsh and his men, to demonstrate their good faith, remained in camp overnight. Before departure the next day, there occured an episode which served to show the great Chief how the "law he had just promised to respect was maintained". Just as the Mounties were about to leave three Indians leading five horses rode in. One of the police scouts, Gabriel Solomon, identified the Indians as United States Assiniboines from the Missouri district. One in particular, White Dog, had a bad reputation. He had been a great warrior, so great that Sitting Bull was said to have offered him three hundred horses as payment if he would join in the Sioux war campaigns. The police scouts recognized three of the horses as those belonging to a Catholic priest, Father De Corby, serving in the Cypress Hills.

The scouts told Walsh of their discovery. The Superintendent instructed them to go again and examine the horses. They reported their confidence about the proper ownership of at least three of the animals. "Then," said Walsh, "we must act at once and demonstrate to the Sioux how we deal with horse thieves." Walsh ordered Sergeant Robert McCutcheon to arrest White Dog and his two companions who were at that moment boasting to the Sioux. Boldly, the Sergeant and two constables marched into the milling body of Indians and made the arrests. White Dog screamed in anger, demanding to know why he was being arrested. He was told that he had property that did not belong to him. He denied the imputation, saying: "These horses are mine and I will not give them up. Neither will you get away with arresting me".

At this stage, Walsh strode forward and confronted White Dog, ordering that the arrested man be disarmed. The order was carried out and White Dog grew even more hostile. Walsh addressed him: "You say you will not surrender the horses and will not be arrested? Well, we shall see. You are being charged with theft and you are now under arrest."

Thereupon, the officer called for the shackles. The Indians became excited. Some were ready to fight for White Dog. Some were moved by the display of police courage. Some appeared electrified. Walsh remained cool and looking at White Dog, said, "Tell me where you got these horses and what you intend to do with them, or I shall put these leg irons on you and take you to Fort Walsh to face trial."

White Dog wilted and made a stumbling statement. He had been travelling over the plains east of Cypress Hills when he saw the horses wandering and took them. He did not know he was doing wrong, he said, because his friends had always taken loose horses when they found them on the Milk River. Walsh doubted some of White Dog's statements but warned him of the consequences if he did such a thing again on the Canadian side and the let him go.

Nor was that the end of the lesson, as Walsh related later: "When White Dog was about to withdraw, he looked at me and said 'I shall meet you again'. I caught his words and ordered him to halt, called for the interpreter, and told him to now repeat what he had said as I did not wish to misunderstand him. He would not repeat." But after Walsh warned that he might still take the man to Fort Walsh to explain his conduct, White Dog yielded and said he did not mean to make a threat. Walsh accepted this. Having forced White Dog to abandon his defiance of Canadian law, he had accomplished his purpose, Best of all, this success had been won with the great Sitting Bull as a witness.

"White Dog was disgraced in the presence of the Sioux," Walsh wrote "and felt his position severely but the lesson was long remembered by Bull and his followers. Within 24 hours after entering Canada, they witnessed British law at work."[3]

Before Walsh and his party left the camp, Sitting Bull asked the officer for additional information concerning the laws he and his people would have to obey while north of the boundary. It was evident that the White Dog affair had made a strong impression. Finally, having won the confidence of Sitting Bull and most of the people in the camp, the Mounties departed.

Laws Must Be Enforced

During the months of June and July, 1877, wrote the Major, "Fort Walsh was visited by large bands of Indians – Crees, Assiniboines, Sioux and South Piegans – each hostile to the other. Consequently, our forces were kept in quite an uneasy state."[1]

Why this sudden concentration of population in the Cypress Hills? Two reasons may be offered. First, United States Indians were coming north to escape pursuit, and second, tribesmen, both Canadian and American, finding it harder to obtain buffalo meat on the prairies, knew the Cypress Hills reputation for good hunting. Those hills, rising like an island in the vast prairie sea, seemed unfailing in their game resources and skilled hunters could always find food and shelter. Surely, this was the closest approach to a "happy hunting ground" on earth. There was no reason to think, however, that the uneasy state mentioned by Walsh worried him very much. The Cypress Hills command suited him well because of the challenge it presented. And, far removed from supervision, he could conduct his administration precisely as he thought best. He could stride over the hills as though he owned them and direct operations without the necessity of compromise.

Clearly, the arrival of large numbers of Sioux and other Indians from the South added an explosive ingredient. Tension increased instantaneously. Natives were more than ever inclined to look upon both white men and Indians of other tribes as common enemies. Even the local Métis became sulky. Walsh was convinced that all newcomers had to be instructed about conduct on the Canadian side. But merely telling them was not enough; he knew from experience that they had to witness the administration of law, to see policemen acting with firmness and justice. Canadian Indians had formed an elementary understanding of the ways of the force and had learned to respect it. But the United States refugees either did not know how Canadian law was enforced or did not want to know. Walsh recognized the importance of winning the respect of all Indians. He vowed that the rules of order would apply to redmen and whites, regardless of the risks in enforcing them. Even a single failure or defeat seen by the Indians could undermine police prestige and effectiveness. The bold and successful arrest of White Dog had impressed the Sioux at Wood Mountain. But the lesson would have to be repeated in the Cypress Hills.

An opportunity presented itself in May, only three weeks after Sitting Bull's entry into the Canadian territories. The complaint came from a Canadian Saulteaux, Chief Little Child, described by Walsh as a "good and reliable man". With a band of followers occupying thirty or forty lodges, he had been hunting about thirty miles northeast of Fort Walsh and minding his own business until robbed and threatened by American Assiniboines from the Bear Paw Mountain country. The strangers, with two hundred lodges, camped alongside the Canadian Indians and sought to intimidate the members of the smaller band. The Assiniboines, United States agency Indians, were a lawless group, recognizing no authority except their own. Their insolent leader, Chief Broken Arm, known to some as Crow's Dance, ordered the Canadian Indians to join his camp and cease hunting except as he permitted. Refusing to become part of the bigger camp and surrender their independence, Little Child's followers informed the aggressors that they had first claim to this hunting ground. Speaking for his people, Chief Little Child said, "I have only a few warriors but I am a British Indian standing on my own soil and I will not take orders from strangers. The only Chief that I will obey is the White Chief at the Cypress Mountains fort."

The Assiniboine Chief left, only to return minutes later with one hundred and fifty young warriors. "Now you'll obey me," he said to Little Child. "You will surrender or flee from this hunting ground. And when your Red-Coated friends visit this camp, you will see how I will receive them." The

Assiniboines attacked, tearing down lodges, shooting horses and dogs, threatening women and children, and striking Chief Little Child in the face. With only thirty warriors, Little Child knew the folly of exposing his people to the dangers of a pitched battle and allowed them to fall back to the safety of the hills while he set out at once to inform Major Walsh of the threat to peace.

It was late in the afternoon when Little Child arrived at Fort Walsh. In less than an hour Major Walsh, Sub-Inspector Edwin Allen, Surgeon Kittson, guides, and the Chief were part of a twenty-five man troop riding toward the place where trouble seemed to be smouldering. It was arranged before departure that a bigger force would ride out from Fort Walsh if Indian resistance made it necessary. At 11 P.M., after a march of forty miles, the tired riders and sweaty horses reached the site of the Saulteaux camp. A halt was called to allow the scouts to ascertain the exact location of the Assiniboines. The camp had been moved northward and members of the police troop returned to the saddle at the weary hour of midnight. The sun was breaking over the horizon when the Assiniboine encampment came into view. "A perfect picture," recorded Major Walsh.

200 lodges fringed by young cottonwood trees on a beautiful plateau, a little stream running along the base ... not a sound. The warriors had at a late hour finished their war dance and were silent and slumbering, perfectly fearless. From this point we located the war lodge, fixed in the centre of the circle of lodges. We decided to attempt the arrest of Broken Arm and his sub-chiefs. To be successful, the war lodge must be surrounded without our presence being discovered, the Indians seized quietly if possible and carried out of the camp.[2]

Walsh's men ate a hasty breakfast and resumed the march along a narrow valley that allowed them to pass unobserved to within four or five hundred yards of the west end of the camp. Studying the topography carefully, the officers fixed upon a small butte less than half a mile from the camp as the point to which the men could retreat if necessary. Dr. Kittson, the surgeon, and two constables and a scout would remain there with instructions to commence building a breastwork of stones at the moment the camp was aroused or the police party discovered. And if the police mission was seen to be about to fail, the scout was to ride with all possible speed to Fort Walsh to summon reinforcements. Dr. Kittson was to hold his ground at all cost, providing a rallying point for men obliged to retire. There was a last-minute inspection of arms, then the orders to load carbines and revolvers and advance were given. Ascending the hill, the Mounties came into full view of the camp, still wrapped in an early morning silence. Walsh noted with pride:

...22 scarlet coats brilliantly bright in the red morning sun, moving against a force twenty times our number. ... No 22 men from the beginning of the days of Greece and Rome ever showed more valour. A Britisher had pledged his word that all who placed themselves under the care of the country's law would have his country's protection. The law was violated and they – the police officers – were ready to die or bring the trespassers to justice. ... the good horses seemed to respond to their masters' feelings and moved gently along. ... One by one we pass the lines of lodges; dogs bark but the war lodge is reached and surrounded. Troopers dismount and disappear under the lodge from every side. The arms of the warriors were seized. Broken Arm and 25 braves were captured and carried out of the camp while the alarm is being sounded. The hill is reached and the prisoners [are] shackled in pairs as far as there are manacles to do so. Horses were unsaddled and tied close together in the centre of our little fort and every man went to work with all his strength building breastwork. ... Even our prisoners were made to carry stones and soon we were ready, Kittson with his medicine-chest already opened, lint and bandages lying on the cover, ammunition boxes opened, Allen encouraging his men and instructing them what to do in case of attack, and interpreters listening to try to catch the words of the chiefs haranguing the camp and threatening destruction of our little fort and the rescue of their warriors. The camp was now in a great commotion and looked very threatening. Indians in hundreds commenced to advance toward us, then a halt and three or four chiefs moved to the front and asked for an explanation of our conduct.

Our commander pushed forward to within 300 yards of

the Indians and communicated to them the reason for the arrest of Broken Arm and his braves and now the Indians got a lesson read to them that not only impressed them but the police also. They were informed that they were in British Territory where the rights of man, no matter what his color, are sacred. Tyrants could not live in the air that floats over British soil. Our law demanded that men should live as brothers, as one family.... The police are the representatives of British law in this country. Under that law every man is free and safe.

The prisoners, it was explained would be taken to Fort Walsh and tried for offences allegedly committed. Those guilty would be punished; those who were not guilty would be set free. No man would be punished without cause.

The Indian spokesmen begged for the immediate release of the prisoners, promising they would never again commit an offense. They would respect British law. But the police knew they had to be firm and explained again that there could be no release until after the trial. They advised the Indians to retire to their tipis peaceably because demonstrations on their part would only place the prisoners in a more difficult position. While one Indian leader argued for an immediate attack in order to release the prisoners, others were being told that violence would only mean loss of life and the British brand of law and justice would still prevail. This brought the discussions to an end and the Indians withdrew, still muttering angrily.

Now it was for the prisoners to make a decision; they were being taken to Fort Walsh and they could either walk the long distance or they could try to persuade their friends in the camp to provide them with horses. One of them named Blackfoot called for horses and presently three or four young men came with the needed mounts. Men in the police troop were tired, but had no desire to remain in this unfriendly community any longer than necessary. The return to the Fort began at once. The horses were fully as tired as the men and had to be urged. Covered by a rear-guard, the party pressed forward as briskly as possible and reached the Fort at 11 P.M. In due course, the trial of the prisoners was conducted and those found guilty sentenced – Broken Arm to six months detention, and three others to one, two and three months respectively.

The expedition, carried out with typical Walsh dispatch, won much praise and some criticism. The story was widely publicized. Those who knew Walsh and knew his sense of justice were assured that his actions were carried out in the light of principle. But the opportunity for despotism was present and critics were quite right in noting that arresting officers should not be magistrates as well. That Major Walsh should issue a warrant to be executed by Major Walsh, policeman, and that Major Walsh, policeman, should make the arrests and bring the accused before Major Walsh, magistrate, was certainly not an ideal arrangement. An impartial administration of justice would, of course, demand judges and magistrates who were independent of the police. Major Walsh would have been the first to agree. But the frontier circumstances at Cypress Hills lacked many facilities which would have been more ideal.

In carrying out his hazardous exercise, Walsh was concerned about Indians of other tribes as much as with Broken Arm's Assiniboines. "This lesson," he noted, "which was heralded over the plains from North to South, from East to West, taught the Indians and everybody else upon the plains that the country was governed by law. The action of the police established for them an influence, a prestige, that made them respected throughout the country, even at the camp of Sitting Bull."

Assistant Commissioner Irvine reported the affair to the Government of Canada, saying: "I cannot too highly write of Inspector Walsh's prompt conduct in this matter and it must be a matter of congratulations to feel that fifteen of our men can ride into a enormous camp of Indians and take out of it as prisoners thirteen of the head men. The action of this detachment will have great effect on all the Indians throughout the country." In reply, the Secretary of State, speaking for the Government, asked Colonel Irvine to convey to Insector Walsh his appreciation of the courage and determination as shown by him and the officers and men under this command in carrying out the arrests.

Although Walsh did not say so in his own account of the adventure, John Peter Turner states clearly that Walsh led the early morning advance upon the war lodge. "No words were wasted in overture or argument. With a few curt invectives, for which he was noted, the superintendent reappeared almost immediately with the startled Assiniboine chief in tow."[3] In defence of Custer, Walsh had one comment "Custer died with his men". Walsh was never one to ask his men to go where he was not prepared to accompany them as their leader.

Sitting Bull at Fort Walsh, 1878
The only known photo of Sitting Bull taken in Canada. The photographer was
T. George Anderton, a North West Mounted policeman stationed at Fort Walsh.
Anderton was discharged in 1882 and later established a photograph business
in Medicine Hat. This photo was snapped up by various American photographers
who claimed it as their own.

Above: Major James Morrow Walsh

Right: From the *Walsh Papers*, March 24, 1879, quoting Sitting Bull.

your hand, when I first entered her country I told you that my heart was pale at how my people had been persecuted by the Americans and that I came to the White Mother country to sleep sound and ask her to have pity on me. that I never would again shake the hand of an American. I went at your request to the White Mothers Fort to meet the Americans (The Terry Comn) but I will never meet them again. I have forbidden my people to use my name to the Americans, I have always said to my people in Council. if any of you want to go back tell me. none of them have done so yet. I am looking to the North for my life and hope the White Mother will never ask me to look to the Country I left although mine and not even the dust of it did I sell

but the Americans can have it - I never look at the white mothers children with a side face I told you before and I tell you now. that I am never going to leave the White Mothers Country I see many roads coming they are the White Mothers I will live with them. Those who wish to return to the Americans can go, and those who wish to remain here if the white mother wishes to give them a piece of land can farm. but I will remain what I am until I die a hunter and when there are no Buffalo or other game I will send my children to hunt and live on Prairie mice for when an Indian is shut up in one place his body becomes weak

Above: Chief Joseph of the Nez Percé,
"one of the most remarkable men of his race".

Right: Major General George A. Custer

Left: Colonel James F. Macleod, 1870

Above: Red Cloud, 1875, "grand old man of the Oglalas."

Above: General Alfred F. Terry

Sitting Bull and Buffalo Bill Cody, 1886

Left: Spotted Tail of the Brule Sioux

Above: Standing Buffalo, chief of the Minnesota Sioux

Little Crow, 1858

Jean-Louis Légaré, the French-Canadian trader
who escorted Sitting Bull back to Fort Buford.

Above: North West Mounted Police officers at Fort Walsh, 1879

Back row: left to right: Percy R. Neale,
F. J. Dickens, W.D. Antoluis, J.H. McIllrie,
E. Frechette, Cecil Denny
Middle row: A.G. Irvine, James F. Macleod,
Dr. John Kittson
Front row: E.D. Clark

Above right: Lieutenant Colonel Acheson G. Irvine

Right: Fort Walsh, 1878

N.P. CAMP

Above: Sioux camp on Frenchman's Creek, 1874

Below: Group of Sioux Indians at Turtle Mountain between 1872 and 1875

The Wood Mountain Scene

No community that had Major Walsh as its leader and Sitting Bull as a resident could possibly be dull. For the first years after its construction, Fort Walsh mirrored the spirit of the vibrant and colourful commanding officer. Authorities knew it would be a difficult area to administer and needed no better reason for establishing a post there and naming Walsh to command it. Indians of many tribes congregated in and about the Cypress Hills to hunt and fight, and white men with varied shades of conscience came to trade.

But notwithstanding the serious character of frontier life, the Fort people paused at times for fun. On October 23, 1875, soon after the new post was ready for occupation, when the place reverberated from an all-day and all-night celebration. For want of a better excuse, the event marked the birthday of the commanding officer's small daughter, Cora Walsh, who lived with her mother at Brockville, Ontario, and had never been seen by the revellers. Flags fluttered in the autumn breeze and the roar of cannon fire echoed through the hills; Walsh who could sing and dance and fight with the best of men, was at the centre of every activity. A few weeks after that celebration, the Fort Benton press reported a Fort Walsh wedding. And who was officiating? Major Walsh, of course.

At first, Fort Walsh gave every indication of becoming a great city. The new Canadian Pacific Railway was expected to touch Fort Walsh or at least come close enough to give it the best possible claim to preferment when the territorial capital was being located. It was a beautiful dream but that was all.

Fort Walsh, in 1878, became the headquarters of the North West Mounted Police but it was bypassed by the railroad and, rather suddenly, the Wood Mountain district sprang to prominence and displaced it as the focus of interest.

The refugee Sioux, during their first winter in Canada, had camped beside Frenchman's River (Whitemud Creek), about twenty miles southeast of the present site of Val Marie. The next winter, with Sitting Bull among them, the same tribesmen camped deeper in the hills, roughly twenty miles north of the International Boundary and close to an old cabin constructed by men of the International Boundary Commission. Colonel French saw the cabin when the force was making its initial trek westward in 1874 and decided to acquire it as an emergency shelter for men who patrolled in the area. After a short time the hut was abandoned by the police but now, with new concern about Wood Mountain Sioux residents, Major Walsh recommended that it be made ready for use again. After his first meeting with the Sioux in 1876, Walsh saw the need for at least two outposts on the Wood Mountain side of Cypress Hills, one close to the Sioux and one which would be a halfway camp at the eastern approach to the Hills, where the Town of Eastend was later built. According to J. P. Turner,[1] Walsh recommended that Constable A. R. Macdonell be placed in charge of the Wood Mountain post and Constable J. A. Martin at the Eastend location. With the Wood Mountain post assuming more and more importance, Major Walsh decided to have a house built there for his personal use. Watching Sitting Bull, he knew, would be a full-time task.

Actually, the Wood Mountain-Willow Bunch settlement was not new. It began with the Métis who left Red River to escape the aftermath of the 1870 insurrection and the distasteful prospect of increasing immigration to Manitoba. They cared not at all for the white man's ambitious plans for exploit, preferring to live the free life of hunters and trappers. Here they hoped to live in their own way, beyond the greedy embrace of civilization. Late in 1870, the first group – some thirty or forty families – moved from Pembina, St. Joseph and White Horse Plains, following the border to halt at Wood Mountain, about a hundred miles southwest of to-day's site of Moose Jaw. It was essentially Assiniboine Indian country but was visited at times by Crees, Saulteaux and even

Sioux. All around was good buffalo country and the deep Wood Mountain coulees offering shelter, water, logs for burning and building as well as isolation, left nothing to be desired.

The Métis lost no time in building cabins and Wood Mountain became home territory. There the people found all the makings for pemmican and there they made their fun. Dancing was a principal diversion and the time-honoured Red River jig – a test of endurance when continued through most of a night – was their favourite. Customs and dress remained much the same as at Red River. With hair cut long, moccasins on his feet, leather clothing decorated with beads and the traditional l'Assomption sash tied around his waist, this mixed-blood was attractive and distinctive.

The men did not look for regular employment and had an indifferent interest in agriculture althought they were well qualified as guides and interpreters. Some engaged in freighting and when the International Boundary Commission was active in the region, a few of the Wood Mountain people accepted employment. With the completion of the Canadian Pacific Railway and the resulting market for buffalo bones, many of the Métis took to gathering and hauling. The bone business suited them; they could work at speeds of their own choosing or refuse to work at all. They would gather the whitened bones and haul them by ox or horse-drawn carts – about a thousand pounds to the load – to the railroad and sell them for five or six dollars per ton.

The great and unfailing friend of the Wood Mountain Métis and later of the Sioux and Sitting Bull was Jean-Louis Legaré, born in Lower Canada in 1841, but quick to acquire the spirit of the frontier. He went to Wood Mountain in 1870. The next year he took fifteen cartloads of trade goods and set up a trading camp in the Hills where he was to make his home. The native people recognized his fair play and furs and buffalo hides came to him in abundance. He was in the Hills to stay and in due course won the confidence of the Sioux and Mounted Police as he had won that of the Métis. When Sitting Bull made the long-awaited decision to leave Canada and surrender to United States authorities, it was Jean-Louis who escorted him to Fort Buford. The tall and bearded French Canadian with gentle and courteous mien came to be recognized as the leader of the Wood Mountain community.

Understandably, the Wood Mountain Métis did not accept the Sioux in good grace. They believed that Wood Mountain belonged to them. They were the first to settle there and to build cabin homes. But it was difficult for a small body of Métis to teach a desperate band of nomads about proprietory rights and there was considerable friction. As reported by the *Saskatchewan Herald:*

Sitting Bull warned some half-breeds who were encamped near Wood Mountain to move away or they would force them. The Half-breeds declined to go as they wanted some buffalo for themselves, whereupon the Sioux rode through the camp shouting and firing their guns....[2]

Rapidly, Wood Mountain became a centre of international interest and anxiety. It is not much of a mountain. At 3,371 feet above sea level, it is not quite as high as Fort Calgary. But what those bumps on the prairie landscape lack in towering elegance they make up in history. The impact of the few thousand Sioux Indians turned the region the political hotspot of the continent.

Sitting Bull from the time of his arrival at Wood Mountain was under some pressure from both sides of the border to return. He listened politely to the Mounted Police but the United States emissaries bold enough to enter his camp received a cool reception. Members of the first deputation in June, 1877 were seized and held like common prisoners. The Chief sent word to Fort Walsh, telling what he had done and asking the police to come and take the three captives off his hands. Major Walsh had to assume some responsibility, since he had told Sitting Bull to detain any strangers who came to his camp. Now Walsh had to go and Assistant Commissioner A. G. Irvine decided to go as well. In the party were Adjutant Dalrymple Clark. Sub-Inspector Edwin Allen, a couple of constables and two scouts.

The Chief did not hide his annoyance at the intrusion of the three Americans. One of the prisoners was a Catholic priest, Father Martin Marty; one was John Howard who had been a scout and interpreter with General Miles, and the third was the priest's private guide. Sitting Bull had no patience with missionaries and the priest was just another of the hated Americans to him.

The Fort Walsh men pitched their tents in the Sioux encampment and listened to Sitting Bull's complaints. There was a strong hint that the three men were lucky in not losing their scalps as well as their freedom. The Assistant Commissioner delivered a brief lecture, commending the Chief for keeping the men without harm and adding the same sentiment the Indians had heard previously from Major Walsh: "As long as you remain in the land of the Great White Mother, you must obey her laws. As long as you behave yourselves you have nothing to fear ... you must not cross the line to fight the Americans and return to this country. We will allow you enough ammunition to hunt buffalo for food but not one round of that ammunition is to be used against White men or Indians."[3]

Later that afternoon, when the priest was present, Sitting Bull spoke long and prayerfully. Taking the Peace Pipe, he pointed reverently to the four quarters and asked the Great Spirit to have pity on the Indian children. He then handed the pipe to Irvine and began his oration: "O God, remember this is the land I was brought up on, me and a woman. This is the reason I came back. I was brought up here.... Why do Americans want to drive me? Because they want only Americans here.... I have only two friends – the English and Spaniards."

Turning to the priest, he said defiantly: "I don't believe the Americans ever saw God and that is the reason they don't listen to me.... You know, as the messenger of God, that they tried to kill me. Why did you wait until half of my people were killed before you came? ... Do you think it's the will of God to have some of His people under your arms, so you can laugh at them? You are waiting for my people to come to your land so that the Long Knives may rush at them and kill them.... Are you here to ask me if I am going to throw my land away? I never thought of giving my land to the American people.... If I go back to the Americans, are they going to take all my stock away? God raised me on horseback to make my living. Did God tell you to come and make me poor?"

The priest listened soberly and replied: "After hearing all this talk and what the British officers say, I think you are better on British soil. If you wish to come back, I pledge my life that your lives and liberties will be safe."

Sitting Bull spoke again: "What would I return for? To have my horses and arms taken away. Once I was rich, plenty of money, but the Americans stole it all in the Black Hills." The Chief's decision was obvious.[4]

The police took charge of the three prisoners and Irvine spent the June evening mingling with the Indians. He was impressed by the cleanliness of the tipis and the order of the camp. He stopped to inspect a grey horse being ridden by a young brave. This one, bigger and better than most Indian horses, showed good breeding and a United States Cavalry brand on its rump. The Indians made no secret of the fact that they had many prizes of war from the Custer battle: horses, mules, army carbines, ammunition belts, and military uniforms, taken from dead soldiers.

Hundreds of stories about the tragic battle had been told but they differed widely. Because all the eye-witnesses who rode with Custer were dead and the Indian spectators were generally silent, the correct account might never have been known. But Irvine, to his surprise, was to get an account from the individual best qualified to relate it. Irvine and Clark, sharing a tent, had just retired for the night when they became aware of somebody peering in. Sitting up on his buffalo robe bed, Irvine recognized the intruder as the Sioux Chief and invited him in. Sitting Bull squatted on the ground and appeared to be in the mood for conversation. Irvine encouraged him and sent at once for his interpreter.

"What can you tell me about your battle with Custer?" Irvine asked, hoping the Chief might not object to discussing the delicate subject. Sitting Bull smiled. He was not a boastful person but he had no compunctions about talking about the war. He admitted that he had known about Custer's movements for several days before the meeting and had guessed his intentions. Early on the day of the battle, two American cavalry horses stampeded and dashed right into the Sioux camp, as if to give notice of Custer's approach. He recalled Custer riding toward the Indians to the sound of trumpets and waving flags. The display was more like a victory celebration than the advance of an army contemplating battle. The Chief saw it as an indication of Custer's arrogance.

Sitting Bull admitted that he did not identify Custer in person because of the wild confusion that followed the first exchange of shots. Having marched directly into a position where his men were exposed to Indian fire from three sides, Custer's troops and horses fell at an inordinate rate. When the mounted Indians encircled the Americans at a wild gallop and crowded close to them, Custer's men, unable to reload their carbines fast enough, tried to beat off the Indian attackers with the butts of their guns. In the hand-to-hand fighting, the Indians were far too numerous for their enemies and many of the soldiers were killed by blows from Indian coup sticks.

*

The atmosphere at Wood Mountain was unpredictable, exciting. For almost five years, Wood Mountain was like the proverbial powder keg. Dire prophecies were heard. An American editor warned that these murderous people, the Sioux, would rampage and massacre as they had in Minnesota in 1862 and in Montana in 1876. Other prophets of gloom predicted a great intertribal battle with Sioux pitted against Blackfoot and their allies with blood flowing like freshets in the spring. Still others feared that an alliance of the Sioux and local tribesmen would annihilate the white population in Canada.

None of these predictions came to pass but Canadian authorities spent an uneasy time as the two leading actors, Sitting Bull and Major Walsh, faced each other at Wood Mountain. American authorities were equally uneasy. They could never feel safe while Sitting Bull was close enough to attack but far enough over the International Boundary to be safe from counterattack. They wanted him where they could deal with him. But the great Chief had no intention of returning. He maintained that he was a British Indian and argued that the Wood Mountain hills should be allocated to him and his followers. He promised that if the Sioux could remain there, they would live in peace and be good Canadians.

International Complexities

There they were, 5,000 American Sioux, camping on Canadian territory where they were not wanted and close enough to the boundary to be a constant threat to American military posts. Sitting Bull told Major Walsh that he would refrain from acts of war as long as he was north of the border but nobody believed he meant it. James W. Taylor, United States Consul in Winnipeg,[1] wrote to the Secretary of State in Washington, reporting that the Sioux made no secret of their intention to renew the campaign in the Yellowstone Valley and that they seemed determined to lay in a supply of guns and ammunition, even though they had to steal them. He related how a war party of twenty-seven Sioux robbed Canadian traders of three kegs of powder and one keg of bullets.

Uneasiness reached right to the Prime Minister's office in Ottawa and to the White House in Washington. Canadian officials hoped the Sioux would suddenly vanish beyond the border like a migrating buffalo herd. The United States officials, unhappy about losing control of the Indians, hoped either for an early return of the wanderers or for an official acceptance of the Sioux by Canada so they would never return. Canada had no desire to adopt them and had no wish to run the risk of war by forcing their expulsion. And the United States authorities knew that to send their armed forces across the border to drive the Sioux back would be a serious breach of international law and would certainly be interpreted by Britain as an act of war.

Both sides hoped Sitting Bull could be persuaded to return voluntarily and thereby relieve the international tension which had been growing for several years. It started with the Fenians, those Irish revolutionaries who were seeking independence for Ireland and doing all in their power to embarrass the British Government. They were active in the United States and their raiding in border areas led to strained relations between Canada and United States. Their lobbying at Washington was blamed for United States refusal to allow use of the canal around rapids on the Ste. Marie River when Colonel Garnet Wolseley was taking the expeditionary force to Red River in 1870. The Canadians were slow to forgive. Then there was the attempt of just two years earlier to obtain the extradition of the Montana men who allegedly participated in the Cypress Hills massacre. The feeling over this affair reached its bitter peak at the court hearing in Helena and Assistant Commissioner James Macleod, who represented the Canadian Government, considered himself fortunate to get back to Canada with his life. Unkind editorials appeared on both sides of the border and now, just when the Helena trials should have been forgotten, the Sitting Bull trouble revived old animosities. The geographical setting was roughly the same – enough to make eastern skeptics louder in their criticism that it was a mistake to spend good Canadian money in the purchase of the prairie country just seven years before.

There were misunderstandings on both sides. Canada was critical of United States Indian policies and Americans chose to believe that Canada was unduly soft toward the Indians. Some Americans suspected Major Walsh of encouraging Sitting Bull and even of making it easy for him to obtain guns and bullets. The suspicion was totally without foundation. To his credit, he was friendly with Sitting Bull but knowing the Canadian Government's fear of being drawn needlessly into United States domestic affairs, he took precautions to practically stop the sale of arms by local traders. Jean-Louis Legaré was one of those instructed that he might furnish enough powder and shot to allow the Sioux to hunt buffalo for food, but no more. When the Wood Mountain traders were found selling guns to the Sioux in 1877, Walsh sent his men to seize all the supplies capable of being used in warfare.

Commissioner James Macleod, writing to Prime Minister Alexander Mackenzie on May 30, 1877, described what he believed the Canadian position should be:

*I would respectfully suggest that communications be opened
with the United States Government to ascertain upon what
terms they would receive them [the Sioux] back, and I fancy
they would be only too glad to have them return, as their
presence – so near the boundary – cannot but be a source of
continual anxiety and trouble, and it would be impossible for
the police to keep them in check over such an extended frontier; that the Indians be then told of the terms of the United
States Government; that they cannot be recognized as British
Indians; that no reserves will be set apart for them, and no
provisions made for their maintenance by our Government;
that by remaining on our side they will forfeit any claim they
have on the United States, and that after a few years their only
source of support – the buffalo – will have failed and they
will find themselves in a much worse position than they are
at present.*[2]

Members of the Canadian Government accepted the Commissioner's suggestions and lost no time in making official
representation to the United States to explain the Canadian
position. Canada would try to persuade Sitting Bull and his
people to go back to the United States. Early in August,
Honourable David Mills, Canada's Minister of Interior, went
to Washington. There he conferred with the President and the
Secretary of the Interior. On his return he could report that
both governments recognized "the gravity of the complications
that may arise from the presence in our territory of foreign and
hostile Indians".

The *Toronto Globe* concurred:

*The Canadian Government has only one course to pursue: to
insist that its soil shall not be used as a base for operations
against its neighbour, nor that whenever it suits Sitting Bull
to retire for a time from active strife he shall be at liberty to
retreat to the northern side of the boundary line in order to
recuperate and resume the offensive at pleasure.*[3]

Canadian policy was actually more sympathetic than
American citizens seemed to realize. The principal reason for
fear was the chance of an intertribal war of major proportions.

The Blackfoot, Assiniboine and Cree Indians, fiercely jealous of the presence of enemy Sioux on their buffalo range, were not overlooking the possibility of driving the invaders out. Such a conflict would have involved the whole of the western frontier, American as well as Canadian. American opinion was divided. Some believed that if the Government of Canada was not prepared to use force to effect the return of the Sioux the United States forces should invade and drive the Indians back. Others suggested that the United States declare the Sioux to be a Canadian tribe, thus making Canada responsible for their actions.

A news item published in the *St. Paul Pioneer Press* which produced consternation in Ottawa carried a Washington dateline, April 21, 1879, and seemed to bear the imprint of officialdom:

It has been decided after repeated conferences between the Secretaries of State, War and Interior that the troublesome individual on the northern frontier known as Sitting Bull, is a British subject; that he with his followers voluntarily left this country of the United Stares, and placed themselves under the protection of Her Majesty, who will hereafter be held responsible for their good conduct.

The Secretary of War has written a letter to General Sherman to this effect and the Secretary of State will notify the British Government. This may become a serious International question if Sitting Bull makes a raid on the frontier during the coming summer. General Ruger who has gone north to Dakota, four miles south of where Sitting Bull's camp lies, with the Eighteenth Infantry, who will build a military post in that locality, has been notified of this decision, and will govern himself accordingly.

But the Canadian Government was not consulted and received the news with surpise and dismay. The matter came before the House of Commons at Ottawa on May 5[4] when the Honourable Member, Mr. Dubuc, enquired if the Government had any official information about the Washington dispatch printed in the *St. Paul Pioneer Press*. Sir John Macdonald replied that the Government had nothing official on the subject – meaning that the members knew only what they had read in the press – and expressed the opinion that the report would have to be discounted because nobody in the government at Washington could properly decide who was a British subject and who was not.

But the idea was popular with western American politicians and the editor of the *Fort Benton Record*, noting that the Sioux had crossed the border and were hunting on the Montana side, chose to refer to them as British subjects who should be prevented from leaving Canada. Then, when the same Indians stole some Montana horses and ran them back to Wood Mountain, the editor became most indignant that Canadian Indians could do such a thing and get away with it.[5]

The most frequent demand was for Canada to surrender Sitting Bull and his followers, although nobody was certain how to effect it. The use of force seemed implicit but even in the United States there were informed individuals who knew that the use of Canadian arms in handing over the refugees would have been an unfortunate breach of British tradition. Such a sentiment was expressed in a scholarly open letter from Wendell Phillips of Boston, to Canada's Governor General, Lord Dufferin, appearing in the *Montreal Witness*, August 29, 1877:

SIR;
　　You will, I know pardon the intrusion – if you deem it one – of my calling your attention to the grave bearing of the United States Government's claim or request that you surrender the Indian Chief, Sitting Bull. It has been England's pride for centuries that her borders were ever a shelter for the victims of political misrule; and while she surrendered ordinary criminals she never gave up the defeated parties in a civil war or any like struggle. I need not tell you the long story of our Government's cruel injustices towards the Indian and gross misrule in all pertaining to him. Were this man a citizen, one of thousands who had rebelled against such injustice and sought shelter in his defeat, England would never surrender him. But the Indian is not a citizen or a simple subject, since we make treaties with him, asking his surrender of his land, instead of taking it by any claim of eminent domain, and leave him under an irregular tribal government, independent of our civil laws; we make war on him and we conclude peace with

him. Such a party, whatsoever his offence, cannot be treated like an ordinary criminal and reckoned within the purview of international treaties on such subjects. To surrender him is to surrender one in arms not against his own acknowledged government, but one in arms against a government which in a large degree, shuts him out from the limits of its civil polity; a government which he disavows and repudiates, and which, you know, will do him no justice. All our history attests this. Canada's success with the Indians since the proclamation of George II in 1740, grows from the methods she then adopted of making the Indian a full citizen and melting him into the common mass. Our failure is because we always put force in the place of law, and shutting the Indian out from the shelter of law, have treated him like an alien and an outlaw. In such circumstances we have no right to ask England's help to subdue him. Her granting it would be disloyalty to all her traditions, and a confession that she had ceased to be what poet, orator and statesman have so long claimed for her – the refuge of the wronged. I am speaking only of an insignificant race and a quarter million of people. But the principle touches the most sacred and honorable of England's traditions. Could the case be brought to the attention of the English people and fully understood, as it would be in the blaze of a month's discussion by your journals, I am sure no power on earth would ever drag the Indian chief from the shelter of English law. Every reason which made England refuse to give up the fugitive slave exists in the Indian case, and there are some considerations which make his claim to protection even stronger than the Negro's was. I beseech you, sir, let not the first time that England's magnanimity in this way fails be the case of this friendless and hunted race, meted out and trodden down alike by the greed and the neglect of a powerful and grasping people.

Respectfully yours,
WENDELL PHILLIPS

BOSTON, U.S.A., August 23, 1877

Although the Americans were reaching for an excuse to saddle Canada with some responsibility for their problem, the Canadian Government, with the better reasons for complaint, was either slow or needlessly charitable in failing to place more blame for the international aspect of trouble on American Indian policy. A serious comparison of Canadian and American methods in handling the native people was bound to reflect well on Canada. Even the *Fort Benton Record*, not always friendly toward Canada or the Mounted Police, offered the praise:

In what disgraceful contrast appears the agency system of the United States when compared with the just, humane and economical policy adopted by the Canadian Government. By a simple code of laws administered by a handful of incorruptible men, the very self-same Indians that here on the American soil will not be controlled, are not only prevented from plundering and murdering defenceless whites, but made to respect the people whose laws they dare not disobey.[7]

Although the House of Commons heard no proposal to charge the United States Government for costs arising from Sitting Bull's presence, there was a serious suggestion on February 1878, that Canada might ask the British Government in London to defray "the expenses incurred in relation to the crossing of our frontier by Sitting Bull". The Prime Minister replied that "It is not the intention of the Government to make any representation on that subject to the Imperial Government at present.... He [Sitting Bull] has no doubt caused us some additional expense and may cause more, but we do not think that to be a matter of such serious importance as to justify us in making any application of that kind."

Sir John A. Macdonald, sitting in opposition at the time, interjected a light comment: "I do not see how a Sitting Bull can cross a frontier," and Prime Minister Mackenzie replied in similar vein: "Not unless he rises."[8]

But something more than humour was needed to solve the problem created by the Sioux. Officials decided to try something new, a direct approach by United States officials.

And Then The Nez Percé

Get 'em together to talk about it, was the advice heard in both Ottawa and Washington. By bringing a deputation of high-ranking Americans to face Sitting Bull on Canadian soil, the Chief might be made to understand United States willingness to forget the past and give the Indians a chance to start a new life. Major Walsh was sceptical, but nobody had a more promising plan and the politicians were ready to try it.

Canada's Secretary of State, the Honourable R. W. Scott, sent a telegram dated August 15, 1877, to Commissioner Macleod notifying him of the proposed deputation. "Co-operate with Commissioners," he advised, "but do not unduly press Indians. Our action should be persuasive, not compulsion. Commission will probably reach Benton about twenty-fifth instant. Arrange to meet them."[1]

This message was followed a few days later, August 24, 1877, by a letter from the Honourable David Mills, Minister of Interior, to Colonel Macleod, communicating details, including the names of the commissioners, one of whom was "General Terry who is in active service in the Federal Army". Continuing, the Minister said:

I informed the United States Government during my visit to Washington, that should they decide to send these Commissioners, you or some other officer of the Police Force in the North-West, would meet them at the boundary with a suitable escort, accompany them to the Sioux lodges, and afford them all possible protection while they remained on Canadian territory.

*The Government are most anxious that the United States
Commissioners should succeed in inducing the hostile Sioux
who have come to our territory to return to the United States.
It is feared that should they remain in Canada, they will be
drawn into hostile conflicts with our own Indians: that in
going upon the hunting grounds of the Blackfeet, Assiniboines
or Crees, they will excite the opposition and resentment of
these tribes; and that ultimately, from a failure of the means
of subsistence and from other causes, they will become a very
considerable expense to the Government of Canada. It is not
at all improbable they may also be disposed to make hostile
incursions into the United States, and in this way become a
source of international trouble. The Indians, while engaged
in hostilities with the United States, were reported to be guilty
of acts of such barbarous cruelty that, should they again return for the purpose of scalping women and children, their
conduct would not fail to excite the indignation of the Government and people of the United States against this country.
It is therefore important that you should use your influence
to promote, as far as you well can, the object of the United
States Commissioners in securing the return of those Indians
to their reservations. Should you, at the time of the Commissioners' visit to Canada be engaged in the negotiation of treaties
with the Blackfeet and other Indians of our own country, you
can appoint Major Walsh or Major Irvine to take command.*[2]

The American commissioners left St. Paul, Minnesota, on
September 11 for Fort Benton by Union Pacific Railway and
then proceeded north by stage coach to meet the Mounted
Police escort "at the point where the usually travelled road
from Fort Benton to Fort Walsh crosses the boundary".

Initially, the commissioners intended to hold the conference at Wood Mountain. After considering the added distance
they would be obliged to travel and perhaps the danger in a
meeting close to the Sioux encampment, General Terry suggested by letter to the Secretary of War in Washington that it
would save time and effort if Sitting Bull and his councillors
could be induced to meet at Fort Walsh. He concluded by
mentioning that if the Indians consented to return, Fort Walsh
would afford the best facilities for starting them on their way.
The proposal for a meeting at Fort Walsh instead of Wood

Mountain was accepted by officials at Ottawa and Washington although no one in either capital considered Sitting Bull's reaction. By September 13, Canada's Secretary of State instructed Commissioner Macleod by telegram to plan for the meeting at the boundary.

As the Canadian Minister of the Interior had suspected, Macleod was indeed busy with negotiations leading to the Blackfoot Treaty. Indians of five tribes – Blackfoot, Blood Piegan, Sarcee and Stoney – were gathered at Blackfoot Crossing or "Ridge Under the Water", on the Bow River, about sixty miles downstream from Fort Calgary and eight or ten miles southeast of present-day Gleichen. Five thousand Indians were encamped in the valley and an estimated 12,000 horses grazed nearby, making it the biggest assembly of native people seen since the coming of the white man. Moreover, it was as crucial a conference as it was big; the Indians were being asked to surrender rights to 50,000 square miles of country. Colonel Macleod knew it was his duty to remain to the conclusion. There were delays, including one of three days occasioned by the late arrival of Chief Red Crow of the Bloods. But success came when Crowfoot, "Chief of Chiefs", and man of surpassing influence agreed on September 22 to sign the treaty.

Colonel Macleod left immediately for Fort Walsh in order to arrive at the Boundary in time to meet the United States Commissioners, expected on October 4 or 5. At Fort Walsh, however, Macleod received a message from General Terry, reporting an unexpected delay because members of his escort were needed to carry urgent supplies to General Miles who was being hard pressed in his battles against the Nez Percé Indians. By an escort, if one were to judge from the *Fort Benton Record,* General Terry meant a small army; in referring to Terry and the Commission, the paper's editor noted how it would be extremely hazardous to approach Sitting Bull with a small escort. "It would not be safe to treat with that treacherous villain unless there were five hundred soldiers within shooting distance."[3]

Rather than wait in idleness at Fort Walsh, Colonel Macleod decided to ride eastward in the hope of meeting up with Major Walsh who, with luck, would be on his way from Wood Mountain with Sitting Bull. Sixty miles along the trail, Macleod met Walsh and the great Chief with twenty of his supporters, including one squaw. As the Commissioner soon sensed, this had been a trying experience for Walsh, first in persuading the Indian leaders to make the journey and then in preventing them from turning back. Sitting Bull was still indifferent about meeting the American officers. He and his fellow-chiefs were more interested in a proposal for a feast to mark this meeting with the Paleface Chief and one member of the party promptly rode out and shot a buffalo. Before the animal heat had time to leave the carcass, chunks of hump were cooking over a fire of buffalo chips and during the night most of it disappeared.

While Macleod and Lieutenant-Governor Laird were toiling to bring Treaty No. Seven to a successful conclusion, Major Walsh had been at Wood Mountain, employing all the diplomacy he could command to persuade Sitting Bull to accompany him to Fort Walsh to meet the American representatives. The chiefs had no objection to going to Fort Walsh, especially when they were assured of rations furnished by the police. But the very mention of General Alfred H. Terry made Sitting Bull bristle with anger. General Terry was an enemy, the Chief insisted, and he did not wish to see him. But Bull – as Walsh was now calling the Chief – had come to respect the Major and found it difficult to refuse his requests. The sly old Chief had a secret motive in delaying. He knew all about the Nez Percé wars, knew that Chief Joseph and his warriors were retreating toward the Canadian boundary and Wood Mountain. He wondered if this might be his last chance to strike a blow at the pursuing United States forces. He did not tell Walsh of his hope to lead his fighting men across the line. He did inform the police officer that he might see Nez Percé Indians crossing into Canada, just as he had seen the Sioux crossing to safety. Neither Sitting Bull nor Joseph overlooked the possibility of joining forces for a great defensive battle and both believed they could win. Nor did the United States authorities overlook the danger; they were most anxious to prevent the Nez Percé from reaching the Canadian border.

Walsh, too, wanted to know as much as possible of the Nez Percé movements but his immediate problem was in persuading Sitting Bull to accompany him. He assured the Chiefs that they would still have the right to decide for themselves about returning to the United States. He brought two influential Métis to add their advice. After days of discussion, the Chief said he would go, even though he hated the prospect of associating for even a few hours with Terry. Well aware that the Indian Chief might change his mind, Walsh was eager to be started. They would leave early the next day, he said, and named an exact time for departure. But just hours before they were to leave, Sitting Bull's scouts reported about a hundred Nez Percé, battered and bloody, approaching from the south. As Major Walsh reported: "several little boys and girls had legs and arms broken by bullets. One woman was shot through the breast, the bullet entering just below the nipple passed through and came out of her back. This woman rode over the line on a horse, carrying a child tied upon her back with a shawl."[4]

As Walsh had feared, Sitting Bull announced his refusal to see General Terry. The police officer must have been discouraged but he did not give up. He reminded Sitting Bull that he had promised not to raid the United States forces from the Canadian side. Finally, Walsh was able to convince the Chief that it was now more important than ever that he meet Terry. And so the little party started for Fort Walsh.

White Bird's Story

The presence of the Nez Percé on the Canadian side of the border presented an entirely new element for the Terry Commission deliberations. Sitting Bull and his Sioux leaders had the full story of the summer-long campaign which ended disastrously for the Idaho and Oregon Indians and saw it as an exact parallel of the wars which had forced their own cruel expulsion. The plight of the Nez Percé people could only make it more difficult than ever for the United States representatives to convince the Sioux of good faith in urging their return. The old anger in Sitting Bull's heart burned more fiercely than ever. Only the fact that Walsh remained with him constantly held him to his promise to refrain from attack and to remain at the Fort for talks with the Commissioners. In restraining the Bull, Walsh was performing his duty, but after talking to the Nez Percé and spending his last evening at Wood Mountain in the company of White Bird, his sympathy was on the side of the Indians.

From the early part of the summer, Colonel Macleod and his fellow officers were aware of United States pressure to eject the Nez Percé from their homes in the intermountain valleys. From the time of gold discovery in Idaho in 1860, the fortune seekers pushed into Indian Territory, demanding that Washington clear away the native occupants. That these were progressive Indians, living on land held by their tribesmen for generations was not considered. That they lived in permanent homes instead of tipis, cultivated fields and maintained herds of cattle and horses did not seem to matter. That they were the only North American natives to make a lasting contribution to animal development – the Appaloosa breed of light horses – was overlooked. They would have to settle elsewhere, on poorer soil, whether they liked it or not. And, of couse, they did not like it. The idea of being forced to abandon their own homes and lands and settle on small and poorly located reserves was totally unacceptable.

Nobody in government defended the Nez Percé and only in very few instances was the tribal character recognized at all. The United States general who served the final notice upon Chief Joseph to vacate the area seemed to sense it, and the *Fort Benton Record*, generally anti-Indian in its sentiment, declared in complimentary terms:

Who are these Nez Percé whose band of rebels under young Joseph the U.S. Government is fighting? Not savages as the word is usually understood. They are half-civilized Indians who have been deceived and defrauded until a revolt has resulted. They number about 3,000 people, 400 of whom are warriors. They are brave and intelligent. One or two hundred can read English and many can write. They till 3,000 acres of land, and own 14,000 horses, 70 mules, 9,000 cattle and 500 hogs. Last year they raised about 30,000 bushels of grain and many vegetables. They have a saw mill and a grist mill. Last year they sawed 50,000 feet of lumber for houses. Some of these are carpenters, masons, blacksmiths, tinsmiths.... And now they have broken into rebellion because the Government has cheated them, has lied to them, has diverted their securities, has stolen their goods.[1]

After the flight of Sitting Bull's Sioux, only the Nez Percé had not retired to reservations. Their only crime was in occupying lands coveted by the whites. They were peaceful people, these Indians from the intermountain regions, but capable of fighting ferociously when there was reason. They could not believe they would be forced from their homes in the beautiful Wallawa Valley of eastern Oregon and adjacent Idaho. But the orders of early 1877 called for Indian removal, and quickly. Young warriors went on the rampage, even killed a few settlers. United States troops were dispatched to administer punishment. Chief Joseph, peace-loving and superior in intellect, went to Washington to intercede for justice. But the authorities were determined to remove the Indians. General Oliver Howard conveyed the final order. The Indians had to be out in a matter of days.

Chief Joseph would have made terms with the authorities but War Chief White Bird could not bring himself to accept this kind of surrender. His will prevailed. With three or four hundred warriors and the great handicap of a thousand women and children, he fought a rear-guard action for the remainder of the summer, dodging superior numbers of United States soldiers when he could, facing them in battle when he had no choice, and nearly always outguessing them.

The summer struggles were marked by daring and danger – the attempt to get through the Big Hole Pass blocked by General Gibbon, the countermarch over the trail with General Howard in pursuit, the detour south to reach the headwaters of the Yellowstone River, the virtual encirclement by pursuing forces at one point lower on the river, the march across a settled part of Montana, the successful crossing of the Missouri River and arrival at the Bear Paw Mountains with a ragged but unbeaten remnant of his people, there to face the impossible odds which led to the surrender of part of the band and a miraculous breakthrough and flight to Canada for the remainder. When all seemed hopeless, Chief Joseph had raised his hands in despair, saying: "Lost, all lost! Oh my people, my children, what have we done that God should finish us thus?" But White Bird, strategist extraordinary, devised an escape, fought his way out of the snare, and continued to embarrass his pursuers.

White Bird's own story, as told to Walsh through an interpreter, was melancholy, tinged with "romance as beautiful in sentiment and picture as Rome and Greece could record":

Our home was in Oregon Territory, located in a beautiful valley; our herds, horses, cattle and sheep, covered every hill. We lived in houses, had churches and schools. We were becoming acquainted with agriculture, had given up the chase as a means of livelihood. Our children were being educated and our people Christianized and no period of our nation's life was more prosperous than the year that Howard came to move us from our homes. The hereditary Chief of our nation was Joseph. He succeeded his father, also named Joseph. Old Joseph, as he was called, like his son, was an exceedingly good man and very fond of the whites and anxious to have them settle around him. In this respect, he differed from most of his people. I remember the first white man who came to our country and asked to remain among us. Joseph was pleased with the idea and consented to give him horses, cattle and land. I was then a young man and loved Joseph. I had a sort of suspicion of white men and that their association would be of no advantage to us and expressed my feeling to Joseph. He said I was wrong, that we should encourage the white men to come to us. There was much we could learn from them in growing grain and vegetables and cultivating the soil. He wanted his people to improve and they must have instruction.

Only a short time elapsed when another white came and Joseph held out his hand as he did to the first. I again protested against whites joining us and told Joseph the day would come when we could regret the course he was now pursuing, that white men would deceive him and bring misery upon his people. He dismissed me saying I was blinded by prejudice and the inborn feeling of my race towards the whites. I could not quarrel with Joseph.... Year after year, white men came to locate in our country. Poor old Joseph was happy and always their friend. Joseph knew the presence of white men did not suit me.... Joseph died and his son became Chief and continued the policies of his father. Our people were at this time rich in herds, horses and cattle. We were happy and prosperous. More white men came but could find no room. Our hills and valleys were all occupied with herds of the Indians and their white friends. But the white men saw our good grass, our thousands of animals and their hearts grew hungry. They asked the Great Chief at Washington to give them Joseph's country and remove the Nez Percé to some other locality. It is a beautiful country and should be opened to white settlement, let the Indians be moved over the other side of the gravel range. The country there is good enough for them.

The white Chiefs in Washington said 'Yes, move Joseph.' Our people were notified of this decision. Consternation *filled every heart. Were we to be driven from the homes our fathers gave us and, if so, why? Joseph's head was bowed. Upon him the blow fell the hardest. 'Oh my Father,' he asked, 'what have we done that this misfortune comes upon us?'*

Joseph called a council of all the head men of his tribe. The question was placed before them and discussed. Joseph was crushed in spirit. I objected to the decision from Washington and advised a protest immediately. He made it but a reply came that it was settled; the Nez Percé must move. Another Council was called. Joseph, always peaceable and obedient, recommended that the Government command be complied with. I could not agree with him and asked if he fully realized what such a move meant. Were the hills not covered with our stock? Was not our fortune in these herds? Were we, after years of toil by our fathers and by ourselves, going to throw this property away? Who were richer than Joseph and his people?... We shall not give away our country, handed down from our fathers whose graves mark a period of possession of 200 years. We will not surrender. ... If I have to leave this home, I shall never accept another south of the British line.

Joseph considered and begged that we, on account of our families, should accept the change and move across the mountain to the new territory selected by the Government for us.

... Joseph meets Howard and places the matter before him. Howard's ears are dumb and he replied you must move and your departure must not be delayed longer than one week.... Joseph was so oppressed he knew not what to do. To go to the new reservation meant paralyzing of his people; to resist the order meant war and killing of his people. At this juncture I felt I should speak and act and I said: 'Joseph, I shall never submit to this.'

Which direction do you go, my friend?' Joseph said. 'North,' I replied, 'to the red coats' country....' Looking Glass said: 'You shall not go alone. I will accompany you.' 'And I and I,' was resounded from a hundred voices and Joseph, the last to speak, said: 'And I'.

The following day, with women's hearts breaking, children weeping and men silent, we moved over the divide that closed our eyes upon our once happy homes, forever, and made us wanderers on the prairie and for what? White man's avarice. He wanted the wealth our nation had accumulated and he got it. We who yesterday were rich are today beggars, made so by the orders of Christian White Chief of Justice at Washington.[2]

White Bird's hope was to clear the Big Hole Pass and retreat to Canada, but General Howard, hearing of the Nez Percé flight, declared the Indians hostile and pursued. General Gibbon, too, took to the field to intercept them at Big Hole. The United States forces could keep White Bird moving but they were unable to catch him. For two and one-half months that war chief, notwithstanding the encumbrance of the women and children he refused to leave behind, was one day ahead of General Howard. The Nez Percé horses, with the spotted rumps, were too good for the more aristocratic cavalry stock. The fleeing Indians failed to reach the Crows or to find reinforcements along the way. After seventy-five days, more than 1,200 miles of travel. and the loss of more than one-third of their warriors, the Nez Percé came to the Bear Paw Mountains, hoping to be able to remain for the winter. But there was no rest and at the end of September, as trees were losing their foliage and weather was turning cool, General Nelson Miles moved up in the night and attacked. The white general's force was repulsed with heavy losses but reinforcements were on the way and the Indians had no chance. The embattled Nez Percé, cold, hungry and exhausted, hung on for three days and then, on October 5, 1877 with no assistance in sight, Chief Joseph issued his famous surrender message, deserving a place among the oratorical gems of all times:

I am tired of fighting. Our Chiefs are killed. Looking Glass is dead. Toohulhulsate is dead. The old men are all dead. It is the young men who say yes or no. He who led the young men is dead. It is cold and we have no blankets. The little children are freezing to death. My people, some of them have run away to the hills and have no blankets, no food. No one knows where they are, perhaps freezing to death. I want to have time to look for my children and see how many of them I can find. Maybe I shall find them among the dead. Hear me, my Chiefs: I am tired; my heart is sick and sad. From where the sun now stands, I will fight no more, forever.

But even the Bear Paw trap failed to hold the indomitable White Bird who broke through the Miles line "with 98 men, 50 women, about as many children and 300 horses", and made his way to the northern boundary, to place himself in the hands of a new and understanding friend, Major James Walsh. There the exhausted Nez Percé leader was received warmly by Sitting Bull and his thousand warriors, eagerly looking for an excuse to get back into the fight. Had it not been for the Walsh restraint, the Sioux would have crossed to Joseph's assistance. White Bird found peace on the Canadian side of the border but at an awful price. As Walsh recorded it: "The last words this great Hannibal of our mountains said to me was that he had no country, no people, no home – and did not desire longer to live and prayed morning and night that the Great Spirit might remove him."[3]

Walsh was an admirer of brave and resolute men, no matter what their race and colour. And having seen White Bird and Sitting Bull side by side at Wood Mountain, the officer could no fail to make comparisons. The Sioux Chief, he thought, was the more savage of the two, capable of making more trouble and furnishing more excitement; White Bird, on the other hand, appeared to be a more reliable friend. Said Walsh: "We found White Bird – while not much of a speaker – a very intelligent man of fine and good judgment, less diplomatic than Bull but more clear in perception and quicker in decision – a greater General than Bull."

Walsh did not have the opportunity to meet Chief Joseph. He was not an aggressive warrior like White Bird but even United States officers admitted respect for the Chief. He, too, had been in many battles but it was never his choice to fight. With fine intellect and high ideals, he was the great Indian gentleman. He won the right to be remembered as a man of peace at a time when the warpath was the surest road to fame. He was in many ways ahead of his time. He might well be remembered for his plea for freedom, delivered a couple of years after surrender: "Let me be a free man, free to travel, free to stop, free to work, free to trade when I choose, free to choose my own teachers, free to follow the religion of my fathers, free to think and talk and act for myself." In declaring for such freedoms, was Chief Joseph not speaking for all the Indian people?

True to his promise, Joseph did not fight again. He was told that he and his people would be allowed to return to Idaho. But they were taken to Fort Lincoln, then to Fort Leavenworth and Oklahoma. Seven long and unhappy years passed before they again saw their home. In the meantime, disease and privation made devastating inroads upon the once-proud band. Most of those who followed Joseph and White Bird in 1877 were now in their graves or in Canada.

Bull Faces The Commission

Snow blanketed the Cypress Hills when Commissioner James Macleod and thirty members of the Force, including Jerry Potts as guide, rode in from Blackfoot Crossing on the first day of October, 1877. But warm weather followed and by the time Major Walsh arrived with Sitting Bull and his party, Indian summer in all its glory had come to the Hills. There was a stir of excitement about the Fort as preparations were being made for the visit from the high-ranking United States officials. Nothing like it had happened before and there was enough uncertainty about the outcome to furnish an air of suspense.

Colonel Macleod paused to write a short letter to his wife whom he had not seen for weeks.

MY DEAREST MARY,

I have just got to this place [Fort Walsh] with Sitting Bull and a lot of his Chiefs. It was quite a job getting them this far, they are so very suspicious. However, here they are, safe within the fort, about 25 of them. I expect General Terry at the Boundary on Sunday and am going to meet him myself. I hope to get thro with them on Tuesday or Wednesday and then, if possible, I shall start for home. How I do look forward to getting there, day and night. Winder writes by Mr. Powers that you were not well. I sincerely hope it was only that cold you spoke about. Perhaps you will see me before you see this. The messenger is waiting for my dispatches so good-bye my own darling.

I am, as ever, your own, JIM[1]

The proposed meeting between the Sioux leaders and United States representatives had been a Canadian idea and it was now up to the Police to make it a success. Observers in Ottawa and Washington were confident. Major Walsh who had been assigned the task of bringing the Sioux chiefs to the Fort in the Hills and the only man who could have accomplished it was not optimistic. Sitting Bull was recalcitrant and while General Terry had the reputation, in non-Indian circles at least, of a gentleman, Walsh knew that his role in the recent Indian wars made him not the best choice to head a mission intended to convince the tribesmen of United States willingness to show compassion.

Members of the United States Commission left St. Paul, Minnesota, on September 14 and reached the International Boundary, south of Fort Walsh, a month and a day later. Commissioner Macleod, having received a letter from General Terry reporting his hope to be at the border by October 14, ordered a twenty-five man escort and rode south to meet him. But for those who left Fort Benton on October 10, there was further delay and the two groups finally met late on October 15. As though rehearsed for the stage, the two leaders on horseback came face to face, saluted, dismounted, took one step forward and greeted each other with a handclasp.

General Terry, a big and affable fellow, six feet six inches tall, and dignified by a sharply trimmed Vandyke beard, introduced the members of his group: Commissioner A.G. Lawrence; Commission Secretary Captain H.C. Corbin; Aide to the General, Captain E.W. Smith, and newspaper correspondents, Jerome B. Stillson of the *New York Herald*, and Charles Dehill of the *Chicago Times*. The American escort consisted, according to J.P. Turner, of an infantry company and "three companies of the 2nd Cavalry that participated in the battle against Chief Joseph at the Bear Paw Mountains".[2] The General did not hide his surprise at the small size of the Police escort. But he was impressed by the smart appearance of the twenty-five mounted men in red coats and pillbox caps carrying long lances.

It was late in the day and General Terry did not expect to march toward Fort Walsh at once. In making the suggestion, Colonel Macleod was thinking of the extreme difficulty Major Walsh had experienced in bringing the Sioux Chiefs to the

Fort and in holding them there. It would have been humiliating to the Police if, after escorting the visiting Commissioners to Fort Walsh, it was discovered that the Sioux contingent had disappeared. General Terry, although tired from long hours in the saddle, indicated willingness to proceed without further delay but there remained a point concerning the escort to be settled. He understood enough about international protocol to know that armed forces are not permitted upon foreign soil except by permission or under circumstances of extreme provocation and he issued instructions for the cavalry units to make camp on the south side and to employ themselves enjoying the prairie landscape and the view of the Sweet Grass Hills until his return a few days hence. Because of the small size of the Police escort and his personal unpopularity with certain Indian tribes, he felt he would be more comfortable if his infantrymen were to accompany him. Commissioner Macleod may have had some misgivings, but he would have found it difficult to refuse the General's request. He permitted the United States infantrymen to ride in wagons as personal attendants.

The little cavalcade was on its way with General Terry and Commissioner Macleod chatting as they jogged stirrup to stirrup. When a halt was called at sundown still forty miles from the Fort, the Police looked with envy upon the American soldiers preparing their night camp with the luxury of stoves to warm their tents. By making full use of daylight hours, the travellers reached their destination the following evening. Officers moved inside the stockade while the infantrymen set up their tents within view of the Sioux tipis.

Major Walsh, relieved that the Sioux Chief and United States Commissioners were within speaking distance or at least shouting distance of each other, paid a visit to Sitting Bull's tipi. Sitting Bull repeated in emphatic terms that he had no intention of being talked into returning to the United States. The Commissioners could make fine promises and offer gifts but he would not yield in his determination. The Treaty of 1868 was broken; promises were not honoured; he did not trust these people and would not give them another chance. His Indians might experience hardships in finding sufficient food in this country where buffalo herds were shrinking but for the first time in years they were sleeping at night and living without fear of bloodshed. Walsh reiterated that Sitting Bull's people would be better off if they accepted the Commission's proposals and returned to the United States but, as long as they behaved themselves, they would not be forced to leave Canada.

The Fort Walsh mess hall, the biggest room at the post, was chosen for the meeting which got under way in the mid-afternoon of October 17. The American Commissioners and reporters were the first to enter. Sitting Bull, with a wolfskin hat on his head, an old shawl draped about his shoulders, a pair of beautifully beaded moccasins on his feet and an angry scowl on his face, swept into the hall. If he saw the American Commissioners, he ignored them completely, but recognizing Colonel Macleod, shuffled directly toward him and shook his hand amiably. Then, passing the visitors with disdain, he squatted on a buffalo robe spread on the floor. Shifting so that his back was unmistakably toward the visitors, he prepared his pipe for a relaxed smoke.

Spotted Eagle, a younger man than Sitting Bull, taller, handsome, and naked to the waist, sat down close to him. Other chiefs followed; Bear's Cap, Flying Bird, Whirlwind Bear, Medicine Twinround, Iron Dog, Bear-That-Scatters, The Crow, Little Knife, Yellow Dog, and about a dozen minor chiefs, all took squatting positions on the robe. Finally a lone squaw, wife of Bear-That-Scatters, entered and sat on the bare floor. That a squaw should attend a tribal council meeting was unthinkable and the lady's presence was intended as nothing less than a premeditated insult to the Americans.

In the cramped and somewhat polluted atmosphere of the mess hall, casual spectators could not be accommodated and only a few people were to enjoy this notable scene in western history. And regrettably, representatives of the press at that period were not equipped with cameras. No photographic record was made.

The main dialogue was between General Terry and the Indians. Colonel Macleod made his own summary of the discussions and later shared his notes with the American Commissioners. General Terry was the first to speak. The General's interpreter, Constant Provost – better known as Old Provo – stood in readiness between the Indians and Commissioners. Rising to his full height and standing with an exaggerated straightness, the General read the official message, pausing after each sentence to allow the interpreter all the time he needed. The statement, as recorded by the Mounted Police, was in clear and simple terms:

We are sent to you as a Commission by the President of the United States, at the request of the Government of the Dominion of Canada, to meet you here today. The President has instructed us to say to you that he desires to make a lasting peace with you and your people. He desires that all hostilities shall cease, and that all shall live together in harmony. He wishes this not only for the sake of the Whites alone but for your sakes too. He has instructed us to say that if you return to your country and refrain from further hostilities, a full pardon will be granted to you and your people for all acts committed in the past, and that, no matter what these acts have been, no attempt will be made to punish you or any of your people; what is past shall be forgotten and you will be received in as friendly terms as other Indians have been received. We will explain to you what the President intends to say when he says you will be treated the same as other Indians who have surrendered. Of all the bands who were hostile to the United States your band is the only one not surrendered, every other Band has come into their Agencies. Of these Bands that have come in not a single man has been punished, every man, woman and child has been received as a friend, and all have received the food and clothing supplied for their use. Every one of you will be treated in the same manner. It is true that these Indians have been required to give up their horses and arms, but part of these have been sold and whatever money has been received from them will be expended for their benefit. Already 650 cows have been purchased for the use of the Indians on the Missouri River. If you abandon your present mode of life the same terms are offered to you.

The President cannot nor will not consent to your returning to your country prepared for war. He cannot consent to your returning prepared to inflict the injuries you have done in the past. He invites you to come to the boundary of this country and give up your arms and ammunition and go to the Agencies assigned for you, and give up your horses except those required for peaceful purposes.[3]

The Indians sat in silence as the message was read. Old Provo tried to transmit it accurately. The General was most anxious to convey the impression of sincerity without adding to the already long list of promises that could not be carried out. But the Indians were not receptive. Their angry frowns showed their determination to place no reliance on further promises from these people. Sitting Bull waved his contempt as he would wave a tomahawk, refusing to look directly at the Commissioners.

Sitting Bull knew he was expected to reply. He exchanged words with Spotted Eagle and took time to tie his moccasin and brush some dirt from the robe on which he was sitting. Then he rose slowly to his feet and inclined slightly toward the Commissioners but did not face them. Suddenly, the man who had been languishing in indifference became a showman. He paused as if waiting for inspiration from the Great Spirit and then waved his arms and began. His voice rose and fell; he gesticulated with his hands; his face beamed; he was aroused. The Mounted Police records are not quite the same as those reproduced in the eastern papers but there could be no question about the intent:

For 64 years, you have kept and treated my people bad; what have we done that caused us to depart from our country? We could go nowhere, so we have taken refuge here. On this side of the line I first learned to shoot; for that reason I come again; I kept going round and was compelled to leave and come here. I was raised with the Red River Half-breeds, and for that reason I shake hands with these people [Colonel Macleod and Major Walsh]. In this way I was raised. We did not give you our country; you took it from us; see how I live with these people [the Police]; look at these eyes and ears; you think me a fool; but you are a greater fool than I am; this is a Medicine House; you come to tell us stories, and we do not want to hear them; I will not say any more. I shake hands with these people; that part of the country we came from belonged to us, now we live here.[4]

Other Chiefs spoke briefly. Runs-The-Roe repeated some of Sitting Bull's expressions: "For 64 years you treated us bad; don't like you at all; you came here to tell us lies; I shake hands with the police in peace. . . . We did not give our country to you; you stole it away from us; you come here to tell us lies; when you go home take them with you."

Then the squaw made a statement. She complained that the United States forces kept her people on the run to such an extent that she did not find time to raise children. The General failed at first to catch the significance of her remarks and asked the interpreter to explain further. Bringing a new inflection to the woman's comment, the interpreter replied: "She say you never gave her time to breed." Whatever she said, her meaning was fairly clear, that she would stay on the Canadian side and raise children in peace.

General Terry sensed the futility of his endeavors. Although deeply disappointed, he tried to smile as he asked a concluding question: "Are we to say to the President that you all refuse the offers made to you?"

Sitting Bull answered: "I have told you all I have to tell. This part of the country does not belong to you; all on this side belongs to these people." The Chief shook the hands of Colonel Macleod and Major Walsh and by-passed the Americans. Then the other Sioux, including The Crow, embraced the Police officers and similarly displayed their disdain for the visitors from the south.

General Terry thanked Colonel Macleod and Major Walsh for making the meeting possible. Perhaps it was a failure, the General conceded, but the effort was one which had to be made.

Colonel Macleod and Inspector Walsh, who took no part in the proceedings, followed the Chiefs back to their lodges. Accompanying them were the interpreter and Sub-Inspector Dalrymple Clark, the latter carrying pencil and paper for notes.

The Police officers had several reasons for seeking out the Indian company so soon. Walsh knew that Sitting Bull's refusal was final but the American Commissioner and Colonel Macleod wondered if the relaxed atmosphere of the tipis might produce some hint of a compromise. If anything of value were to be accomplished, it had to be at once because Terry and Lawrence were planning to leave Fort Walsh on the following morning. And if Sitting Bull's announced determination to remain in Canada was the last word on the subject, the Police Commissioner could take this opportunity to offer some further instruction about the conduct Canadian law would demand from the Sioux.

With the chiefs squatting around him, Macleod told them bluntly that they would always be recognized as American Indians. "The answer you have given the United States Commissioners today prevents your ever going back to the United States with arms and ammunition in your possession. It is our duty to prevent you from doing this. I wish to tell you that if any of you or your young men cross the line with arms in your hands that then we become your enemies as well as the Americans. . . . As long as you behave yourselves the Queen's Government will not drive you out. You must remember that you will have to live by the buffalo on this side of the line, and that the buffalo will not last forever. In a very few years they will all be killed. I hope you have thought well on the decision you have given today, not only for yourselves but for your women and children."

The Chiefs listened but showed no indication of changing their decision. Sitting Bull admitted that it was only his respect for the Police and the desire to abide by Police wishes that he and his fellow chiefs had condescended to listen to the Americans. "Today, said The Bull, "you heard the sweet talk of the Americans; they would give me flour and cattle and when they got me across the line, they would fight me. I hope they will not come here a second time . . . the Americans robbed, cheated and laughed at us. . . . I would never live over there again."

Colonel Macleod reported to the Americans that the Indians were unyielding. At the same time, he delivered a letter which was a summary of the instructions he had given.

North-West Mounted Police,
Fort Walsh, Oct. 17, 1877

Gentlemen:
In answer to your note, I beg to inform you that after the interview of the Commissioners with the Indians, I had a 'talk' with the latter.
I endeavoured to press upon them the importance of the answer they had just made; that although some of the speakers to the Commissioners had claimed to be British Indians,

we denied the claim, and that the Queen's Government looked upon them all as American Indians who had taken refuge in our country from their enemies.

I pointed out to them that their only hope was the buffalo, that it would not be many years before that source of supply would cease, and that they could expect nothing whatever from the Queen's Government except protection as long as they behaved themselves.

I warned them that their decision affected not only themselves but their children, and that they should think well before it was too late. I told them they must not cross the line with a hostile intent, that if they did they would not only have the Americans for their enemies, but also the Police and the British Government, and urged upon them to carry my words to their camps and tell all the young men what I had said and warn them of the consequence of disobedience, pointing out to them that a few indiscreet young warriors might involve all in the most serious trouble.

They unanimously adhered to the answer they had given to the Commission, and promised to obey what I had told them.

I do not think there need be the least anxiety about any of these Indians crossing the line, at any rate not for some time to come.

In haste, Most respectfully yours,
JAMES F. MACLEOD,
Commissioner[5]

General A.F. Terry,
General A.G. Lawrence,
Sitting Bull Commission,
Fort Walsh

The Commissioners had their answer, and the American people were waiting for news of the outcome. It was a challenge for the journalists at Fort Walsh to find ways of reaching telegraphic facilities. When the *New York Herald* carried the story three days later, many people wondered how it had been accomplished. The explanation lay in a remarkable ride by Johnny Healy of Fort Benton, who, according to the story, came to the meeting place with the avowed intention of shooting Sitting Bull if the Chief refused to accept the proposed terms for his return. When warned that hanging could be the punishment, he was supposed to have replied: "Give me ten minutes start and all the Mounted Police in Canada won't catch me". He was diverted from his plan by the challenge to carry the dispatch for the *New York Herald* to the nearest telegraph office at Helena, about three hundred and forty miles from Fort Walsh. He boasted that he would deliver the papers in forty-eight hours. General Terry laughed, saying it couldn't be done. "I'll do it and maybe carry the news about Sitting Bull's death too," Healy replied. According to the Saskatchewan historian, George Shepherd,[6] he rode all night, covering the first hundred miles before changing horses at Milk River. The second stage of the relay brought him to Fort Benton twenty-four hours after leaving Fort Walsh. Changing horses there and twice more en route, he reached Helena forty-three hours after he set out.

Early on the morning of October 18, the day after the meeting, the American officials said their farewells to Colonel Macleod, thanked him again for his co-operation and conceded that the Police had done all possible to facilitate the Commission's purpose. Then, with Major Walsh heading the Police escort and General Terry riding close to him, the mule teams carrying United States infantrymen fell in line and marched away toward the Boundary. Two days later, Walsh was back at the Fort to keep his promise to Sitting Bull that he would accompany the chiefs when they returned to Wood Mountain.

The outcome was not a surprise to Walsh who had come to understand the Sioux temperament. "These Indians," he said, "are going to be guided by their own good judgement and their own good conscience. They are generally very sound. Don't under-rate them."

New Risks and New Dangers

The winds of change were blowing briskly across the West in 1878. Settlers were coming in larger numbers to Manitoba. Among them was Pat Burns from Kirkfield, Ontario, who walked from Winnipeg to Minnedosa to file a claim on a homestead quarter-section. And still further westward in the foothills, the first herds of range cattle were being winter-tested on grassland which had long supported buffalo herds. The outlook for immigration and settlement was bright except for one serious deterrent, the growing anxiety about Indian hostility.

The decision to move the North West Mounted Police headquarters from Fort Macleod to Fort Walsh in May, 1878 was the result of mounting fears for the Cypress Hills and Wood Mountain areas. It was the second time the Police headquarters had been changed. The first had been the transfer from Swan River to Fort Macleod in 1876. Southern journalists did not hide their astonishment when they wrote about Walsh and twenty-two noncommissioned officers and constables at Wood Mountain and another little force of fifty or sixty at Cypress Hills standing against Sitting Bull's hordes and thousands more Indians in the vicinity.

The *Fort Benton Record* termed the situation critical:

On the northwest side of the Hills are camped 350 lodges of Bloods and Blackfeet under Big Crow Foot, Red Crow and Hind Bull. South of this, on the west side of the Hills, are camped 150 lodges of Crees and North Assiniboines led by Little Chief, Medicine Bull, Big Bear and Bear's Head. On

*the east side of the Hills the famous Sitting Bull is camped
with 400 lodges of Uncpapas and Tetons. South of the camp
on a stream called Swift Current, are 150 lodges of Yanktons,
commanded by Chief Nine who was present at the Terry-Bull
commission. Close to the latter are 50 lodges of Sauntees,
under White Cap. On White Mud River, a tributary of Frenchman's Creek, and 25 miles east of Cypress Mountains, are 275
lodges of Sioux under Crazy Horse. This camp crossed the
line from Milk River country on the 18th of last month.
On the other tributaries of Frenchman's Creek are camped
about 200 lodges of Ogalalas, Brules, Sans Arcs and Blackfeet
Sioux, deserters from Agencies. They are divided up into small
camps.... On Frenchman's Creek are camped 250 lodges of
Yanktonais under Black Catfish. Near Wild Horse Lake there
are 30 lodges of Assiniboines under White Dog, and on Milk
River, near Sweet Grass, are camped about 50 lodges of Gros
Ventres and Assiniboines under Little Chief and White Eagle.
The main camp of the Bloods, Piegans and Blackfeet, includ-
ing 30 lodges of Kootenais and 50 lodges of Sarcees, is between
Fort Hamilton and the Cypress and is travelling towards the
Sand Hills.*

*Sitting Bull is apparently sparing no effort to form a league
among these congregated tribes. At a council held by the
Sauntees he appeared with 30 of his best warriors, dressed in
the clothing of soldiers killed in the Custer Massacre, and
called upon the assembled Indians to witness how he had
treated the soldiers and how easy to clean out all the whites
and have the country among ourselves. The Sauntees are a
small tribe who took part in the Minnesota Massacre.... Mr.
Thomas O'Harlon, in charge of Fort Belknap, considers the
situation critical.*[1]

Members of the Mounted Police were not surprised at the
rumours of an Indian alliance. There had been a warning
about tribal unions two years previously, as recorded in the
Police report for 1876. Sub-Inspector C.E. Denny told of the
unsettled state he had learned of from communications received by tribes of the Blackfoot confederacy from the Sioux
in Montana.

About a month ago, the Sioux sent a message to the Black-

foot camp with a piece of tobacco which the Blackfoot Chief showed me. The messenger told the Blackfeet...that the tobacco was sent them to smoke if they were willing to come across the line and join the Sioux in fighting the Crow Indians and other tribes with whom they were at war, and also the Americans whom they were fighting at the same time. The Sioux promised to give the Blackfeet, if they would join them, plenty of horses and mules they had captured from the Americans; they also told the Blackfeet that they had plenty of white women whom they had taken prisoners, and they promised to give them to the Blackfeet if they would join them. They also told the Blackfeet that if they would come to help them against the Americans, that after they had killed all the Whites they would come over and join the Blackfeet to exterminate the Whites on this side.[2]

According to Denny, the Blackfoot leaders replied that they were on good terms with the whites and would not smoke the tobacco. Offended, the Sioux messengers came again, this time to notify the Blackfoot people that if they would not be allies, they, the Sioux, would fight the wars alone and in due course come to the Canadian side, kill all the soldiers and then take on the Blackfoot warriors.

All this took place during the year of the Custer massacre; now, two years later, Sitting Bull repeated the offer. If the Blackfoot tribesmen "would join him in the conflict with the hated American Government, he would help them with any conflict they might have with the Canadian Government."[3] Would the reaction be any different this time? Indian sentiment could change and nobody was sure how the most recent proposals about alliance would be received. One thing, to be sure, was unchanged: Sitting Bull's dream of America for the Indians. It was the same as that of the great Pontiac who, more than a century earlier, led the Ottawa-Ojibway confederacy and tried to unite all the tribes between Lake Superior and the Gulf of Mexico in a revolt against British posts. The Pontiac plan failed but there was no guarantee that Sitting Bull's scheme would fail.

When the Terry Commission seemed doomed to failure, writers warned repeatedly of a "devastating Indian war". "Sitting Bull Preparing For Spring Campaign," the *Fort*

Benton Record announced in headlines and went on to explain how other tribes would join him. The Assiniboines, Gros Ventres and River Crows appeared certain to unite and the Piegans had been presented with an ultimatum to join the Sioux in their new war against the white race or refrain from hunting north of the Milk River. Said the editor: "That there is mischief brewing there can be no possible doubt."[4]

Readers were being reminded to keep their eyes on Wood Mountain, Northwest Territories, which "could erupt at any time". A dispatch from Helena, Montana, made it appear certain that Sitting Bull was about to lead all the northern tribes against the United States forces. Such a story carried by the Toronto *Globe* worried eastern Canadians by informing them that "Nearly all the northern tribes are ready for revolt and all can cross the Canadian line in three days." Moreover, it would be a formidable army – 5,000 ferocious warriors – the like of which had never been seen before. And "Sitting Bull is amply supplied with ammunition" the report added.[5]

The statement about ammunition was probably inaccurate, but rumours of impending trouble continued throughout the season. From Battleford on the North Saskatchewan came a story which was printed in Montana. Battleford, the reader discovered, "was greatly excited yesterday" as a result of a report from Red Deer that Sitting Bull had formed a confederation of Sioux, Blackfoot and Stoney tribes and made overtures to the Crees. Leaders intended to call the Indians of these various tribes together at the confluence of Red Deer and Bow Rivers as soon as the trees were in leaf and from there they proposed to embark upon a widespread programme of raiding. And before the Battleford correspondent finished writing his story, a man arrived from Cypress Hills, reporting a camp of seven hundred lodges of Sioux at the Sand Hills, sixty-five miles from Fort Walsh, and growing with new arrivals hourly. He added that

four wagon loads of cartridges arrived at the camp the day he passed; that the half-breeds are all leaving Cypress Hills and moving toward Carlton; that the Nez Perces, Little Blanket, Little Dog and Blackfeet have all formed a treaty with Sitting Bull; that the Blackfeet are on Belly River in force; that it is not known what these movements portend but it is supposed that an attack is to be made on the Cypress Hills and Fort Macleod.[6]

Nor was Sitting Bull alone in plotting for a grand alliance of prairie Indians to win back the buffalo country. No less eager for a test of battlefield strength was the fox of the dissident Crees, Chief Big Bear. This leader who had refused to take Treaty at Fort Pitt in 1876 was a source of consternation to authorities on both sides of the International Boundary. He was frequently in the Cypress Hills, inviting other tribesmen to follow him in his resistance to the white man's order. His fighting methods were direct and savage. He did not possess the cunning and leadership of a Sitting Bull and he was not a co-operator. He invited other tribesmen to follow him but he was not so ready to follow another leader. P. G. Laurie, founder and editor of the *Saskatchewan Herald* at Battleford, had a particularly good chance to know Big Bear and was well aware of the Chief's hope to form a confederation. But the effort, as Laurie saw it, was a failure. "He was willing enough to be made a Chief over all the bands on the plains but the Blackfeet, the Sarcees and some others whose adhesion he sought, declined to give him their allegiance."[7]

Walsh did not discount the dangers of an Indian alliance but there was speculation about another alliance which bothered him almost as much. He had heard proposals for a unification of the United States military forces and the North West Mounted Police for the purpose of combating the Indian menace. It was not for a police officer to criticize public policy but he had strong convictions and condemned this proposal. The Canadian force, he said emphatically, should never be part of an operation in which extermination is even remotely considered. The Police had tried to cultivate understanding and to win respect more than fear. To depart from these methods would completely undermine the confidence the Police had succeeded in gaining and destroy a relationship which had enabled a comparatively small force to supervise thousands of natives. "They," said Walsh, speaking of his American friends, "would be greatly pleased if they could manage to embroil us in a war against the Indians and by so doing make us take common ground with them. . . . The Indian looks upon the Mounted Police as his friend. Anything which would tend to make the Indian believe or even imagine that we are forming an alliance with the Americans would quickly injure us and completely destroy our influence with him."[8]

It is unlikely that an alliance of soldiers and police then in the country could have stood against a massed army of the native warriors. Had the design to unite the Indians under a single commander possessing the skills of a Sitting Bull or Crazy Horse been carried through, the force would have had both the numbers and strength to drive the whites from the frontier. Fortunately for the newcomers, ancient tribal jealousies and animosities prevented it from happening and the year 1878 passed without the much-feared bloodbath.

More Trouble On The Way

Sitting Bull's scouts kept him aware of the movements of his friends and enemies, near and far. Consequently, he was one of the best informed in the country and even though he did not tell all he knew, he communicated enough pertinent information to his friend, Major Walsh, to make the Police officer the first white man to anticipate many new problems.

He did not, however, relate all he knew concerning Louis Riel's activities and Walsh had to hear through other channels that the outlawed former resident of Manitoba had actually visited the Wood Mountain Métis in 1879. Sitting Bull knew about the successes and reverses of General Miles' army, sometimes before the official reports reached Washington. It happened again and again that Mounted Police scouts returning with what they believed to be important information were only confirming what Sitting Bull already knew. Late in 1877, he told Walsh about the Nez Percé and the probability of their ultimate flight across the boundary. And a year later, he warned Walsh to prepare for the Cheyennes, who were trying to stay beyond gunshot of their American pursuers. The Cheyenne ordeal seemed like the brutal implementation of the idea expressed by an American editor: "The fact is becoming very evident that starvation is the greatest and only successful Indian civilizer, except bullets and hemp rope."[1]

Those who supposed the Sioux and Nez Percé refugees would soon go home were very much mistaken. Instead of disappearing, the boundary problems grew in complexity. The official United States attitude remained noticeably antagonistic. Again the Secretaries of War and of the Interior were declaring publicly that Sitting Bull, having voluntarily placed himself under the British flag, became a British subject and that the Canadian or British Government had to assume full responsibility for his conduct.

"All right," said Patrick Gammie Laurie, whose *Saskatchewan Herald* was the first newspaper to be published between Winnipeg and the Rocky Mountains, "by the same reasoning, the Fenians are American citizens for whose behaviour and acts the United States Government is responsible."[2] But for the responsible people at Wood Mountain and Fort Walsh, local problems seemed more important than international debates. At the precise time that the Battleford editor was printing his observations, Sioux and Blackfoot Indians, with Sitting Bull and Crowfoot present, were hunting and camping side by side near the mouth of the Red Deer River. And the future direction of Cheyenne resistance was uncertain.

Those doughty Cheyennes who had shared battlefield fortunes and misfortunes with the Sioux on many occasions – including the 1876 battle of the Rosebud and the later and bloodier struggle beside the Little Big Horn – never reached the Canadian border. Many were shot by the troops sent to destroy them and those who survived were only a remnant. Members of the Algonquin linguistic family, they had roamed the Minnesota country in earlier times, then migrated westward to live and hunt in the Black Hills area and along the Cheyenne River. In the course of time the tribe divided to form the southern and northern bands and only after suffering the aggressions of intruders and the violation of treaties did they become hostile.

Their quarrels were similar to those of the Sioux, a fact which accounted in part for warriors of the two tribes fighting so often as allies. They did not forget the outrage of Sand Creek, Colorado, in 1864, when United States guns killed many men, women and children. With Colonel J. M. Chivington and Major Scott Anthony were some five hundred armed men; their objective was a camp of about one hundred lodges at a bend in Sand Creek, a tributary of the Arkansas River. The occupants of the camp were Cheyennes and a few Arapahoes. The attack was in early morning when the camp was just beginning to stir.

At the sight of soldiers, Chief Black Kettle seized a United States flag and a white flag and held both aloft to indicate friendliness but the soldiers took no notice and began firing. Outnumbered and unprepared, the Indians began firing back and the unequal battle continued for much of the day. The exact number of dead Indians was never established, probably five hundred, more than half of them women and children. In the initial public reaction, the soldiers were hailed as heroes but when the circumstances of the attack were disclosed, elation gave place to shame. The surviving Cheyennes could not forget and could not forgive. For the next few years they were periodically at war with the new authority and frequently indulged in plunder and killing.

Custer, in 1868, administered them another beating at the Washita River, in Indian territory, to settle the Cheyenne problem for a short time. The military, hearing of Custer's night march through the snow and cold of late November to surprise the occupants of the native village and kill one hundred and three warriors, said it was a great triumph for the forces of civilization. Among the dead was the Chief, Black Kettle. The operation was undertaken, ostensibly, for the protection of settlers but it was a cruel affair which concluded in the burning of the lodges, the shooting of many Indian ponies, and the capture of women and children. With only six of Custer's men killed and a few wounded, it was a one-sided engagement and must be remembered as a massacre. It was a severe setback for the Cheyennes but the determined people returned to the warpath as soon as they were able and constituted a formidable force when they fought side by side with their Sioux allies on that fateful day in June, 1876, killing Custer and all who followed him.

After the Custer defeat, the United States drive to subdue the Indians was doubled. Sensing futility in further fighting, a substantial body of Cheyenne under Chiefs Dull Knife and Little Wolf camping with Sioux Chief Crazy Horse on the Powder River accepted an army promise of good treatment in return for surrender of their guns. But instead they were marched as prisoners to a reservation in Indian territory far to the south where food proved to be inadequate and living conditions were foreign to them. Hungry and homesick and decimated from fever after almost a year in the south, three hundred unhappy survivors – less than one-third of the number making the southward trip – resolved upon a bold break to trek back home. They were pursued and ordered to return but they fought and continued on. Again they were deceived by promises and gave up their guns. Again they were told they must return to the south. Again they refused, making a desperate dash from Fort Robinson, fighting and struggling to reach Pine Ridge Agency. That final break for freedom was one of the most determined and courageous operations in the history of warfare, certainly not one in which the white race could take any pride.

The long journey of 1878 – roughly five hundred miles to the Yellowstone – coupled with terrible hardship and suffering, made a story even more pathetic than the 1877 flight of the Nez Percé tribesmen under Chiefs Joseph and White Bird.[3] But the Cheyenne fortitude and sacrifice won nothing more than starvation, bullets and imprisonment. The desperate, ragged, and helpless creatures were ready to die rather than surrender – and many did die. They did not succeed in reaching Sitting Bull and White Bird on the Canadian side as they had hoped.

Canadian authorities wanted no more refugees of any tribe and were ready to co-operate in trying to influence both Sioux and Nez Percé to leave. Father Genin came for a second time to advise Sitting Bull to return. But when, about the same time, Sioux hunters crossed the border southward in pursuit of buffalo, army guns were turned on them. It was enough to strengthen Sitting Bull's determination to stay where his people could hunt without being molested and where reservation fences would not be forced upon them.

The Indians could not determine if the United States authorities wanted to feed them or fight them. And the Canadian Government, aware of American accusations of pampering the refugees, wanted to avoid criticism either of starving these people or encouraging them unduly with food. Leaders on both sides wished the controversial natives would vanish.

"Be patient," Major Walsh advised. "Don't hurry them. Their judgment is sound and they'll know when the time is favourable for their return."

And just as Sitting Bull had received more emissaries from the south inviting him to return, so White Bird and his Nez Percé followers were being pressed to join the others of their tribe, then at Fort Leavenworth in Kansas. They admitted their desire to be reunited with their beloved Chief Joseph from whom they were separated at the Battle of Bear Paw, but Sitting Bull's scouts brought reports about the continued suffering felt by the Cheyenne and their hope to flee from their pursuers and take up residence on the Canadian prairies alongside the Sioux and Nez Percé. With dwindling buffalo resources, it should have been evident that the Canadian prairies could not support the Indians already there, let alone more outsiders. The Blackfoot Chief was already complaining: "They are eating our buffalo."

In seeking the return of the Nez Percé people, the American authorities now elected a subtle technique, sending three tribesmen captured at the Battle of the Bear Paw. These were to testify to the good treatment received at the hands of the American officials and make the refugees want to join their kin. The spokesmen were authorized to promise safety and rations as soon as White Bird's followers surrendered.

Lieutenant George Baird of the United States Infantry was delegated to meet the Nez Percé leaders at Fort Walsh and render all possible assistance. Commissioner Macleod and Assistant-Commissioner Irvine of the Mounted Police were present and the meeting resembled the earlier one at Fort Walsh when General Terry and Sitting Bull confronted each other. On this occasion, however, the exchanges were less bitter and White Bird found it possible to smile. But the Nez Percé Chief was making no snap decisions. He wanted to know more about Joseph. Was he well? Was he getting enough to eat? Did he have any liberties to roam and hunt? Why was he still at Leavenworth when he was promised return to his west country? When would he be allowed to return to the traditional homeland?

Baird answered the questions as well as possible and pressed White Bird for a decision, promising to escort him and his people personally to the meeting with Joseph. White Bird could not hide his yearning to be united with old friends and see them all back in the beautiful Wallawa Valley, but wanted time to consider and confer with those who shared his camp. He agreed to give his answer on the following day.

He and his friends laboured with the question throughout the night, weighing the apparent advantages of regular meals and an end to strife with the less apparent disadvantages. Had there been the promise of an early return to the old surroundings in the West, the decision might have been different. He wished he could send one of his men to talk with Joseph, but Baird looked upon this with disfavour. He wanted White Bird's answer right away. Finally, it was what White Bird knew about the experiences of the Cheyenne that made him conclude that there was really no official change of heart on the part of the Americans and that he would stay on the Canadian side.

And then there was Riel. Walsh had received hints about the proposed return to Canada of the controversial Louis Riel who had been outlawed following the insurrection at Red River almost ten years before. To the Métis he was still a hero and, having failed to obtain a satisfactory solution to their complaints, the people of mixed blood needed leadership as much as ever. Most of those making up the Métis population around Wood Mountain had come from Red River in 1870.

Born at St. Boniface beside Red River, in 1844, Louis Riel grew up to know all about hunting, boating and freighting. He tried farming on one of the long river-lot farms and even studied for the priesthood. But with his gifts of oratory and leadership, there was no chance of escaping a political role. After two hundred years of overlordship, the Hudson's Bay Company was surrendering territorial claim to Rupert's Land and the Canadian Government was taking over. These aggrieved people saw government employees coming from the East to lay out a strange new survey on land the Métis felt was theirs. They were angry and young Louis Riel emerged as their spokesman.

Hudson's Bay Company rule ended before the Government of Canada was prepared to take over the administration and before the Province of Manitoba was created. Hence the area was without constituted government for a time and it was into this political vacuum that Riel and his friends entered. Technically, it was not rebellion because there was no recognized authority against which to rebel. It was insurrection and on October 30, 1869, Riel's men of the New Nation halted William McDougall who was en route to Fort Garry to become Lieutenant-Governor of the new province. A few days later, November 6, they seized Fort Garry, seized the local newspaper, the Nor'-Wester, and formed a provisional government.

Members of the federal government were worried and sent

Donald A. Smith to mediate. The New Nation issued a bill of rights, a list of quite reasonable demands, and Riel was gaining local support. His great mistake was in condemning one of his prisoners, Thomas Scott, to death and in carrying out the sentence. The action infuriated the East and almost immediately a military force under Colonel Garnet Wolseley was marching west. At the approach of the army, Riel abandoned Fort Garry. He lost his place as head of a provisional government but he did not lose his convictions or his friends. He was elected to represent a Manitoba constituency in the House of Commons but eastern parliamentarians voted for his expulsion and, later, a warrant of outlawry was issued against him by the Court of Queen's Bench of Manitoba. Riel moved to the United States. He married; he taught school in Montana and became a citizen of the United States.

But Riel's heart was still north of the border. He was considering an Indian-Métis pact with enough muscle to ensure winning if there were a test of strength. He communicated his ambition to gain Indian support for justice in settling native grievances to Crowfoot and Sitting Bull.[4] The Sioux Chief had failed to achieve a federation of prairie Indians to stand against the whites but perhaps Riel could be more successful.

Having learned that Riel had actually visited the Wood Mountain Métis community, Walsh instructed his scouts to watch Riel's movements and determine his purpose. It was discovered that Riel was spreading stories intended to discredit the Police, among them that Walsh was planning to co-operate with General Miles in increasing military pressure on both Indians and Métis in norther Montana. Riel, it appeared, had the promise of support from the South Assiniboines and was trying to reach other branches of the Sioux and then the Blackfoot. Had he succeeded, he would have an alliance of the strongest warriors in the country. The news of the proposed scheme created new fears in the East and West, fears of an uprising of Indians and Métis co-operating as they never had before.

Acting quickly, Walsh persuaded the South Assiniboines to withdraw their promise of support to Riel and then expressed himself optimistically about the Sioux remaining loyal to him. As Turner told it,[5] Walsh reacted to the Riel threat by saying that if the Sioux remained loyal to him, he would want no other help.

Short Tempers, 1879

Manitoba people remembered 1879 as the year that the railway from the East reached Winnipeg. Residents at Wood Mountain might have remembered it as the year of almost continuous crisis. Major James Morrow Walsh and Chief Sitting Bull now lived almost side by side as neighbours. Walsh was in residence at his new log house a mere hundred yards from the Wood Mountain Post and Sitting Bull was at home wherever his tipi happened to be in nearby coulees.

Walsh and Bull remained on good terms, enjoying each other, except now and then when annoyed. That they managed to understand each other so well was a matter of the greatest fortune for Canada, but when they did disagree people who witnessed it had reason to tremble. Neither was apt to compromise. Any of several incidents involving Sioux and Police in that summer of 1879 could have exploded into a war. Walsh gave the impression that he thrived on crisis. He had a cool and courageous way of approaching dangerous tasks and there was never any hesitation. In the face of danger, his personality was unchanged and no one would know from the expression on his immobile face how he assessed the situation. Ottawa and Washington were kept informed although it is doubtful if they fully understood the seriousness of what was happening. Only those who were present at Wood Mountain realized how close the Major came to the brink of more serious trouble on several occasions.

Walsh believed that, even at great risk, it was essential for him to win every contest in which he was in the right. If it were otherwise, the Police would lose the hard-earned respect and Walsh would lose the authority so essential to his tasks. Fortunately, he was the winner in the serious confrontations of that year, so much so that the United States press described him as "Sitting Bull's Boss".

The chain of disorders in that summer began when fifty or sixty horses belonging to Pierre Poitras vanished mysteriously. Horse stealing was the most popular of all outdoor pastimes, one in which men of all races could participate, and it was taking much of the police time. It was not clear how Poitras happened to have so many horses in the first place but in the loss of his stock the evidence pointed to theft by a group of young Sioux. Poitras accused the Indian suspects and tried to recover the animals. The young men, without denying guilt, laughed at him and tried to exact a ransom for their return. Poitras took his complaint to Major Walsh who at once rode out with a small escort consisting of Constable Jack Mount and an interpreter. Unsuccessful in locating the animals, he altered his course to find Sitting Bull and demand the Chief's assistance in returning the animals to Poitras.

The Major was growing tired of repetitious horse stealing and was showing impatience. The police, he believed, would have to be tougher in dealing with such offences. His language – not overly genteel at the best of times – was more vitriolic than usual. For Sitting Bull, too, it was not one of his more amiable days and he reacted by becoming stubborn. "Look here, Bull," Walsh ordered impatiently, "you know where those horses are and you know where they belong. Now, by gad, if I don't get them damned fast, I'll lock you up until I do get them."

The Chief bristled angrily at a threat, any threat. Walsh may not have actually threatened to invite the United States army forces across the border to round up and take the Sioux back where they belonged but it seems to have been implied. The Chief, shocked as well as angry, soon produced the horses and turned them over to Poitras.[1]

But Sitting Bull did not forget the indignity and days later when he and several fellow-chiefs – Black Moon, Four Horns and Little Feather – were at the Wood Mountain post and feeling the pangs of hunger, they went boldly to the Major's quarters and demanded rations of meat and tea and tobacco.

They were in a mean mood and making no attempt to hide it. Walsh was not impressed and after listening briefly to the sulky complaints and poorly disguised taunts, he replied brusquely, "Who do you think you are that you can come to me with your gripes, looking for handouts every time you want something? Remember, you're not even Canadian Indians and you've got your nerve. Don't try your luck too far. We have trouble enough feeding our Canadian Indians. Now quit making a nuisance of yourselves. Go to Jean Louis Legaré's store if you want tea and tobacco and get these things the way other people get them, by trading something for them."

Sitting Bull stood close to Walsh and more erect than usual. "Nobody speaks to a Sioux Chief that way," he said. Then, imitating one of Walsh's remarks, he added: "Who do you think you're talking to?"

The Major knew there could be trouble but he would not be intimidated. "I know who I'm talking to all right and if you become troublesome, you'll be in irons, same as any other Indian or white man who takes the law into his own hands."

The Chief's fists were clenched and he was crouching as if to leap but Walsh, muttering some profanities, leaped first and seized the Chief by one arm and the loose of his jacket and swung him through the doorway to the ground outside. Then, before the Chief could regain his feet, Walsh was over him, delivering a humiliating kick to his buttocks. Filled with rage, the Indian reached for his gun but his friends removed the weapon and grabbed the Chief to restrain him. The enraged Bull strained to get at the man who insulted him and had shamed him with his hands and the toe of his boot.

Walsh suspected further trouble. Returning to the barracks he ordered his men to prepare for an attack. "Place a poplar log across the path a few rods away from the building," he instructed, "and then stand ready with your carbines. We'll warn them not to come this side of the log and if they disobey by advancing nearer, it will be just too bad for them. We don't want to shoot anybody but they have to know that we mean what we say." As Walsh expected, the Indian mob formed quickly and moved toward the barracks where they heard the Major's warning. "As long as you stay beyond that log, no police gun will be fired. But don't make the mistake of defying a police order to stay on your own side." The Indians were angry but knew they could not afford to forfeit the privileges and shelter they had enjoyed and even Bull had time to see the situation in a fairer light. The mob hesitated and gradually the anger subsided. Sullenly, the men drifted away, realizing that here was a white man who was about as unbending as the steel barrel of a buffalo gun.

Peace seemed to return to the community, only to be threatened again when some of Sitting Bull's people became infuriated at Manager Allen of the Kendell and Smith trading store at Wood Mountain. The big Indian population had attracted various traders: C.A. Broadwater, Powers, Cadd, Kendell and Smith, and of course, the pioneer Jean Louis Legaré. Too often the natives were treated with less than justice, sometimes obliged to pay one buffalo robe for a pound of sugar or two buffalo robes for a pound of tea. The Allen operations had come in for the loudest complaints and increasing hunger stiffened the Indian resolve to settle some old accounts. A mob moved upon the store for a showdown and Daniel "Peaches" Davis who had retired from the Mounted Police and was working for Allen at the time, was able to leave an eyewitness account.[2]

The store was built into the stockade which surrounded various other buildings, including the manager's home. Allen was a rough-and-ready sort who had never tried to cultivate Indian good will. Now, as the natives demanded admittance to the store and pounded on the barricaded door, he was satisfied to let them scream while he sat inside with a loaded Winchester resting on his knee. Nor did he seem concerned for his wife, alone in their house with her small baby. She sent for Davis to plead with her husband to come to the house at once, but Allen ignored the plea.

As night fell the Indian mob dwindled but when Allen opened the store in the morning, the natives reappeared and rushed inside. One of them marched straight to the Allen house where he forced his way inside, seized the baby from its mother's arms and brought it to the store for what was obviously a preconceived demonstration. He would murder the child before the father's eyes if the Indian demands for flour and bacon and tobacco were not met promptly.

As Father Rondeau recorded the story, the Indian holding

the baby addressed Allen, saying: "You refuse to give us food even if our children are dying of starvation. To show you what it is to watch your child die, we shall kill yours right before you."

Entering breathlessly at that moment, Mrs. Allen rushed frantically to grab her baby. But her strength was not adequate and she could do nothing more than cling to the little one's clothing and scream her pleas. Davis was ready to intervene and as he raised his rifle to aim at the man holding the baby in one hand and a raised tomahawk in the other, Allen called out telling him not to shoot because he had another weapon for use if necessary. The trader was sitting with the muzzle of his gun in the open top of a keg of gunpowder. If they harmed the child, he was ready to fire and blow the post and all its contents, including humans, sky high.

Davis had another idea, a better one. "Hold everything, he whispered to Allen. "I'm going to the fort for help. I'll be back in a few minutes."

"But you'll never get there with these savages watching you," Allen replied.

Davis charged and succeeded in getting through the door. After dashing to the Police post, he learned to his dismay that Major Walsh was confined to bed. But the Major received the report and ordered Sergeant Henry Hamilton and three constables and an interpreter to accompany Davis back to the store for the express purpose of bringing Mrs. Allen and her baby to the post. And Walsh had a message for the Indians: leave the store at once or he would come in person to deal with them.

At the trader's quarters, the Police found the Indian still with the baby under his upheld tomahawk and the father still sitting with the muzzle of his gun pointing at the gunpowder. A big constable led the way, pushing Indians right and left until he reached the one holding the Allen baby. Grabbing the offender the constable forced him to release his grip, thereby allowing the distraught mother to regain her baby. The officer's inclination was to administer punishment then and there but he was prevented by the sergeant from so doing.

With Mrs. Allen and the baby in their care, the Police returned to the post where Major Walsh sat with blankets over his shoulders awaiting an account. He approved the Police action and had some further advice to be communicated to the Indians; they were very lucky that no harm had befallen the baby or the consequences would have been serious for them. Also, he had a message for Allen, one he wished to deliver in person. It was to inform him that he was getting what he deserved because of his dishonest and greedy trading practices and if the Indians had seen fit to lay a charge against him for cheating, he might have ended up in jail. Finally, Walsh advised Allen to leave Wood Mountain to try for a better reputation elsewhere. If he decided to move away, Walsh promised him Police protection from the Sioux, who might feel constrained to pursue him until he was a safe distance away. As it turned out, Allen took the hint and departed.[3]

Famine in Buffalo Country

Robins, ducks and wild flowers came in their own good time in 1879 but the buffalo herds did not come. Police were puzzled, traders were disappointed, and the Indians who stood to suffer most were worried. The great brutes, whose numbers had run to many millions and whose migrations had been as unfailing and regular as the rising and setting of the sun, seemed to have vanished.

The prairie Indians and their half-brothers, the Métis, were practically carnivorous and a meat failure was famine – worse than crop failure for the wheat growers who come later. For the growers there was always next year's crop but in the case of the buffalo, there was no guarantee that there would be more. Here, indeed, was the most serious crisis to strike the Indian society at a period which seemed to be marked by recurring crises.

The gradual decline in buffalo numbers for several years was common knowledge. The fewer hides being marketed through prairie trading posts reflected the diminishing population; at Fort Macleod, for example, the 5,764 hides traded in 1879 was less than one-fifth of the 30,000 handled in 1877.[1] The average price to the hunter of two dollars per skin was still profitable as long as animals were numerous. But while the decline was one thing, this sharp drop to almost nothing was quite another.

Was the Great Spirit angry at the native people, Indians asked, or was this another manifestation of the white man's wicked schemes? Had the buffalo herds been destroyed or were they simply off their traditional course? Whatever the answer, it offered unlimited opportunity for speculation and accusation. The Blackfoot Indians blamed the Sioux for killing too many of the wild beasts. The Sioux blamed the Blackfoot for setting fires in the dry grass of the buffalo country. Louis Riel's Montana friends did not escape suspicion in connection with the burning; their motive, it was surmised, was to embarrass the Canadian authorities and force the Wood Mountain Métis into Montana where they would be more likely to rally if and when Riel called for a militant stand. Even the United States army was accused of arresting the northern migrations and turning the buffalo herds back from the Canadian boundary. It was easy to make accusations; proof was more difficult.

Probably the food crisis facing thousands of native people resulted from a combination of circumstances. An overpopulation of natives on the Canadian side was certainly a contributing factor. The addition of Sioux and Nez Percé tribesmen from across the border and an increase in the number of Métis relying upon the herds were simply taxing the land beyond its capacity to produce wild meat: too many consumers for the resources of the prairie area. Chief Crowfoot of the Blackfoot Nation, seeing his old enemies taking a big share of the buffalo in the previous couple of years, had warned of the coming famine.

The hide-hunters, with no conscience for preservation of the wild herds, had increased greatly on both sides of the boundary and killed lavishly. "Buffalo Bill" Cody was supposed to have shot 4,280 of the animals in his best year. J. A. "Dad" Gaff, who ranched on the south slope of the Cypress Hills, related his buffalo hunting experiences in Kansas and boasted of bettering Buffalo Bill's record by killing 5,200 in one season. It was wholesale slaughter and the legislation passed by the first Council of the Northwest Territories, sitting at Livingstone beside Swan River in March, 1877, "to protect the buffalo from wanton destruction" had the best of intentions but was too late.

Nobody was sure who started the prairie fires that autumn but there was evidence of deliberate mischief. Flames blackened the countryside as far west as Fort Macleod and the foothills. Those who made an inspection after the conflagration saw where the original fires had been started at several places along its course.

Commissioner E. Dewdney wrote in his report for 1880:
*When I left the Territories in the month of November, 1879,
large numbers of our Indians were starting for the buffalo,
which they expected to meet near the boundary line. . . . Prairie
fires, however, were started at different points almost simultaneously, as if by some preconstructed arrangement, and the
country north of the boundary line was burnt from Wood
Mountain on the east to the Rocky Mountains on the west,
and nearly as far north as the latitude of Qu'Appelle.*

*This alone would have been sufficient to keep the buffalo
south, if nothing else had stood in the way, but the continued
residence of the Sioux on our side of the line and the large
number of Indians who, after our payments, went south and
met the buffalo in the front, prevented any reaching those
Indians who had settled on their reserves in the north.*[2]

Those who blamed the Blackfoot Indians for starting the
fire suspected a plot to starve the Sioux and force them to
abandon the Canadian range. Of course, the Blackfoot stood to
suffer as much as other tribes and did. Their plight was so
bad that almost the entire tribe, including Chief Crowfoot,
went south in October and remained in Montana for most of
the next year.

All the prairie tribes relying on the buffalo were in trouble,
except the Treaty Indians remaining on their reserves who received some food assistance. But the limited amount of beef
rationed to them was not enough to keep the aggressive ones
on the reserves and hostility mounted as hunger became more
intense. In their determination, nothing was going to stop
them from going to the buffalo if it was possible to find them.
Indian feeling on this point was expressed later when Chief
One Spot was about to lead five hundred Blood and Piegan
braves from Fort Macleod.

"We are going to the buffalo," members of the band said
defiantly. "The Whites must be stronger than we are to turn
us back, and if that happens, then we will camp along the
boundary line and steal every horse and drive off every head
of stock that crosses until the Whites [Americans] allow us
in the country that belongs to us."[3]

The Sioux, heeding warnings to avoid travelling to the
inhospitable south, spread northward and eastward in search

of game of any kind. Many wandered as far as Battleford where the editor of the *Saskatchewan Herald* found some doing menial work like cutting firewood and fence posts. The Sioux were versatile and they could be adaptable. One group reached Prince Albert late in 1878 and a year later, according to Indian Agent W. Palmer Clarke, there were seven hundred and fifty of them trying to find enough to eat.[4] Settlers in those more northerly districts regarded them with dire suspicion and were ready to blame them for every unexplained misdeed. But they conducted themselves very well and many of the cattle they were blamed for killing and consuming were found later in good health.

The Wood Mountain Métis – five hundred families of them according to Father Rondeau[5] – could not escape this privations following the buffalo failure any more than the Sioux and when the hunger became serious, they followed the Blackfoot example and wandered southward into the United States. Crossing the border was not a new experience; many times they crossed to hunt, generally ignoring the line as though it did not exist. Certainly they could see no reason why they should not go again, especially when the buffalo happened to be on that side.

But the sudden increase in the population of native people worried the American authorities and General Miles, eager to prevent a dangerous concentration of hostiles, took to the field to keep them moving. One of his early encounters was with the big party of Wood Mountain Métis searching quite innocently for the buffalo herds. He had long ago blamed these people for supplying his Sioux adversaries with guns and ammunition. He impounded them all and delivered some sharp reprimands. The constant running back and forth across the boundary would have to stop, he told his prisoners. And now they would only be granted release if they were ready to settle down at Turtle Mountain or Judith Basin on the American side.

What could the Métis prisoners do? They sent a message to Major Walsh, the man who had never failed them when their need was deserving. At once, he rode south to locate General Miles for whom he held much respect. The two distinguished officers met beside the Missouri River and there Walsh won Miles' consent to allow the prisoners their freedom. They would be granted a choice between settling on the United States side or returning to Canada. As Father Rondeau found, one group settled near Lewiston; a second band located at Turtle Mountain, and the balance of the people elected their home territory and accompanied Major Walsh when he rode back to Wood Mountain.

It was a bad year for the buffalo-eaters; it was no better for the buffalo. If the army had, as alleged, turned back the migrating herd to prevent its return to Canada, there had to be a reason. Was it to deprive the Sioux of food in order to force their return or was it to hold the big animals where they could be more effectively destroyed? The theory was that the Indians would never fully accept reservation living as long as buffalo remained.

The editor of the *Fort Benton Record*[6] conceded that a herd of buffalo should be kept in a national park but otherwise, he would be satisfied to announce "today, that there was not a buffalo within a thousand miles of this Territory. For as long as buffalo roam over any part of it ... cattle killing and horse stealing Indians will continue to plague our settlers. The buffalo is the dirty vagabond of his genus." Continuing, the editor explained that he had "very little faith in the civilization of Indians as long as there remains a buffalo within fifty miles."

The disappearance of buffalo was soon to be complete. The Indian Commissioner, in his report for the year, hoped for a few buffalo "to help us in feeding the destitute Indians" in the next winter but felt it his

duty to say that in the future the same source of relief ... cannot be depended upon. For the last four or five years the buffalo have gradually been creeping south, making it difficult for the Indians on the Saskatchewan to reach them. Those that did had not only to encounter hostile American Indians ... but also whiskey traders who robbed them of their horses and the robes they had made by the hunt ... I feel that no dependence can be placed in buffalo in the future.

For prairie Indians who clung to the hope of escaping the horrible fate of life on a reservation, the hungry winter of 1879-1880 was both revealing and sobering. As long as the buffalo remained, they had a chance; without the buffalo, there was no means by which they could keep their independence. When the buffalo vanished from the plains, so too, would vanish the old way of life the native people were struggling to preserve.

And for no one was the grim fact more depressing than for Sitting Bull. He was a still a fighter and ready to go again on the warpath; but what was there to fight for? As the buffalo receded, so did the hope of his people living like Indians. It was awful to contemplate but if he and his people were to eat in a land devoid of buffalo – the traditional staff of life – it would have to be through integration with the white man's economic order or by the white man's charity. What horrible thoughts! But what alternatives?

You Can't Continue This Way

I will remain what I am until I die, a hunter, Sitting Bull told Superintendent Walsh in March, 1879. "And when there is no buffalo or other game, I will send my children to hunt prairie mice, for when an Indian is shut up in one place his body becomes weak."[1]

The bigger question was one he preferred to ignore: what would his children hunt when the mice were gone? Although he was showing marks of age, the spirit was still strong and he was quite sure that on a favourable battleground and with roughly equal numbers of men, he and his thousand mounted warriors could send the best American army to flight. His opinion of the United States soldiers was not high. "They could neither ride nor shoot," he told Walsh. "The Sioux with their stone coup-sticks would fight and defeat Americans with their guns." Bull promised Walsh that if the Americans should come north of the Medicine Line to create problems for the Mounted Police, "just send me word and every young man in the camp will mount his best horse and come to your assistance".

"I told him I would not need any assistance," Walsh replied to the Chief's obvious disappointment, "but if I did, I would send for him." Walsh knew how the old warrior hoped he would be needed for what might be his last chance to engage his enemies.

There was no question about where he stood on issues. It was most disturbing to him, therefore, to learn of one disloyal Sioux, Black Wolf, who, accompanied by twelve dissidents, travelled to the Lower Yankton Agency in the United States and gave the totally false impression of being sent by Sitting Bull to request admittance to an agency. The Chief was furious and longed to lay his hands on the scoundrel. In his anger, he chose to talk to his friend, the Major. In detailing the Chief's visit, Walsh recounted how Sitting Bull, Sitting Bull's wife, one child, two sisters, Little Assiniboine, One Bull and Bad Soup arrived on the afternoon of March 20 and camped "at my house". The Chief's first concern was about provisions, inasmuch as he and his friends had not eaten for a full day. Walsh provided the sustenance, with the result that next day all the head men of the tribe arrived, all bringing huge appetites.

"I want to tell you why I came to see you," Sitting Bull began with a flourish. "It is to contradict a report carried by one of our men, the Black Wolf, to the Americans." The Bull's anger burned as he related the mischief this man was trying to do. The very idea of anybody insinuating that the Sioux Chief would surrender to the Americans was both preposterous and insulting. "I request you to let the Americans know that the man – a rascal – was not sent by this Council to make such a statement.... What I wish to say to the White Mother is that I have but one heart and it is the same today as when I first shook your hand.... I went at your request to the White Mother's Fort to meet the Americans [the Terry Commission] but I will never meet them again. I have forbidden my people to use my name to the Americans. I have always said to my people in Council: 'if any of you want to go back, tell me.' None has done so yet. I am looking to the North for my life and I hope the White Mother will never ask me to look to the country I left although it is mine and not even the dust of it did I sell, but the Americans can have it.... I am never going to leave the White Mother's country."

Walsh never missed an opportunity to advise Bull to accept the terms offered by General Terry on behalf of the Government of the United States. It might be an exercise in futility but, now, he did it again.

"Bull, you know damned well you can't continue to live by the buffalo and you can't live on mice. Now, what's left? Don't you realize that the sooner you and your people begin to plow and cultivate some ground and grow your own crops and livestock, the better it will be for you? The American Agency Indians don't have all the freedom they would like but they are treated well. Just think of being assured of food and clothing for yourself and children, of getting household utensils and all the necessities of life. You might find you could enjoy it."

The Chief repeated: "I will die a hunter," but hoped those of his people who wished to become farmers would find opportunity right here on Canadian soil. "For many months," he added, "you have been advising us to think of getting our living from the ground. Will you tell me where we will get the ground?" Again he was asking Walsh if he would make request for an area of land to be set aside for his people. Walsh reiterated that in keeping with Government policy which recognized the Sioux as American Indians, there would be no reservation for them in this country. Those who considered farming should certainly return to the United States.

It was then that the Chief, with sadness in his voice and his eyes fixed upon the northern horizon, declared, "Those who wish to return to the Americans can go, and those who wish to remain here if the White Mother will give them a piece of land, can farm. But I will remain what I am until I die, a hunter."[3]

Some, like Sitting Bull's nephew, the clever Watogala, urged yet another appeal for land in Canada. Taking the matter in his own hands, he wrote a letter in May, to Prime Minister Macdonald, pleading in the name of starving children for a reservation on the Canadian side. He asked for an official reply "so its answer will be final to the Indians". The answer, forwarded in due course, held no encouragement. The Government was committed to a policy and would not yield. It seemed to be the last word as far as the Prime Minister was concerned.

Watogala received his reply but, obstinate like his uncle, he refused to accept it as final. He tried again, using a different approach. This time he wrote the letter to Major Walsh. Carefully worded – perhaps by a non-Indian friend – its purpose was clear and not in the least unreasonable:

OGALLALLA VILLAGE, N.W.T.

Maj. Walsh
DEAR SIR,
I ask your advice concerning a subject that really interests me.

In our conversation before I told you I would do all in my power to try and get Sitting Bull to cross the line and return to his former reserve. This I find impossible; he will never go back and if he does not, neither will I. Now this kind of life does not suit me and having given my promise to remain always with my uncle, I would rather that I could get a small piece of land from the Canadian Government, some farming implements, seeds and help to build a house, fences, etc., a cow, pig and few chickens, and commence farming, and thereby show the Indians a good example so that they would relinquish their ideas of a roving life and settle down on their former reserves and commence farming. I believe that is the only way that they can be induced to return to their former reserves. I ask all this of you to ask the Canadian Government to give it to me. I do not want it gratuitously. I will pay the Government for it in year instalments. I believe if you try you can get this for me. Do it and you will not be sorry. I should like a piece of land close to your post so that I could furnish the Post with vegetables, the payments from which would enable me to pay you part of the principal. I have resolved to remain in this country and become a farmer. It is the only independent life I know of. I can always be assured of enough to eat and a house to live when winter comes.

Your friend,
ECHARGHAHA WAKA
WATOGALA[4]

Less than four weeks after Sitting Bull's discussions with Superintendent Walsh, a party of his hunters wandered fifty miles inside the United States. The main camp remained a few miles north of the boundary with Sitting Bull. But driven by hunger, the hunters were hoping to locate a buffalo herd. As on most hunting expeditions, the squaws accompanied them to perform the chores like skinning, gutting, drying the meat and making pemmican. Nevertheless, the hunters were unable to hide their identity and a rumour spread that the Sioux were invading.

For two years the American newspapers had carried false reports about Sitting Bull being back and threatening war. Now, the Sioux presence in northern Montana was confirmed and American editors called for military action to capture or annihilate the offenders. William Evarts, United States Secretary of State, was not letting the British representative in Washington, Sir Edward Thornton, forget that because Canada failed to intern the Sioux refugees, Britain would have to answer for any of their misdeeds.

General Terry was under pressure from Washington and from the Agency Indians who resented the idea of sharing the few remaining buffalo. Deciding to clear the northern plains of all uninvited native visitors, both Indian and Métis, General Nelson Miles set out from Fort Keogh at the beginning of July with a force of five hundred. Crossing the Missouri River, he marched upstream along Milk River, expecting to encounter a hunting party of Wood Mountain Métis. Instead, his scouts came upon the camp of the Sioux hunters, altogether about four hundred men and women. Sitting Bull had not been in the camp but when his scouts brought word that Miles was in the area, the Chief left his camp on the Canadian side to be with his people who might come under attack. The Sioux were not ready for war.

Miles attacked. He was too strong for the Indians whose first concern was to get their women and children out of danger. They retreated toward the Boundary, fighting a rearguard battle as they moved. But unprepared as they were, Sitting Bull believed that by the time they reached the Boundary, his Indians could mount a strong counterattack which would drive Miles back. He would have attempted it had it not been for his promise to Walsh that he would not carry a fight to the Americans and then recross into Canada. In any case, this clash, in the Major's own words, "put an end for the present to the Indians having any desire to return to the United States".

Back on the north side of the line, Sitting Bull faced the problem of explaining to Major Walsh that his excursion into the United States and his encounter with General Miles were not a breach of trust. Walsh was satisfied that Bull was telling the truth and while he urged the Indians to avoid hunting on the other side as far as possible, he resolved to come to an understanding with Miles. Happily, Walsh and Miles had become friends and Walsh had no hesitation in travelling to visit the General. He defended Sitting Bull's presence on the

Montana buffalo range. As far as he could discover, said Walsh, the Sioux who accompanied Sitting Bull on that particular hunting expedition had refrained from all hostile acts. Any fighting that occured after Miles overtook them was strictly for self-defence. Miles did not argue. He was carrying out his duties and his main purpose in these discussions was to make plain his intention to drive all Canadian Indians indulging in crime and plunder back to the Canadian side and all American hostiles to cover. "Fair enough," Walsh said; "and if you have proof of Canadian Indians committing crimes on your side, let me know and I'll co-operate in making the arrests."

It was only a few days after returning to Wood Mountain that Major Walsh received the message from the Canadian Métis in Montana, telling him of their capture and internment by General Miles. Resolutely he set out again to find Miles, this time to intercede for the Wood Mountain half-breeds. Although Miles had moved, Walsh located him and obtained agreement for some concessions which would probably be satisfactory to the Métis.

On his return, Walsh had an unexpected companion, John Finerty, correspondent for the *Chicago Tribune*, who was to make an appraisal of the Sioux situation in Canada. Walsh saw the advantage in honest reporting which would place the Sioux in a fair light. Journalists liked Walsh at any time, admired his forthright manner and appreciated his willingness to speak boldly. He was glad to take the reporter to the Sioux camp and give him a chance to meet with and talk to Sitting Bull. Under other circumstances, an American newspaperman would not gain entrance to a Sioux camp. In the company of Walsh, he was safe.

By this time the Sioux camp was located just five or six miles west of Wood Mountain post and as the Major and the correspondent rode in on that early August morning, they were surprised to find the Sioux in an uproar. Young men wearing fresh warpaint were gathering their horses and women and children in preparation of war. Finerty wondered if his decision to make this visit was a colossal mistake.

Strangely enough, the Indian reaction to Walsh's appearance was no less surprising. They gazed at him in disbelief. Then their astonishment changed to obvious relief and Indians, young and old, gathered around, muttering excitedly as if witnessing a miracle. Not until Sitting Bull on his favourite palomino horse rode up to Walsh and shook his hand as though welcoming an old friend back from the dead, did the officer learn the reason for the demonstration. Just an hour earlier, a Métis on a sweating horse galloped in from the south bearing the awful news that Walsh and Long Dog and others accompanying them to the camp of General Miles had been murdered. The report spread among the Sioux like fire in dry grass and everybody from Sitting Bull to the lowliest Indian was filled with shock and anger. The thought of revenge was in every Sioux mind. Surely the atrocity would release the Sioux from all promises to refrain from attacking across the border. The warriors were making ready to ride out against the Long Knives to avenge the death of their friend – and, incidentally, to settle some long-standing accounts. Sitting Bull, by this time, could mount 1,200 or 1,500 warriors, every one on a good horse.

Finerty watched in amazement. Walsh called for an interpreter, even though, by this time, he could speak the Sioux language moderately well and used the occasional Sioux word. Now, moved by the demonstration of feeling for him, he had to speak seriously to these people. He told them about his visit to the Miles camp and assured them that he had been well received. But he had to warn again about crossing the boundary, even to hunt, unless they were prepared to go to stay.

But the Sioux were not permitted to forget about going back. Father Martin Marty came again from Dakota to advise the Chief and members of his council of the advantages of seeking a new life on an American reserve. Ottawa officials communicated similar messages and Major Walsh took every opportunity to reason with the Indian leaders in a friendly way. The response was slow. Only in Walsh did the Sioux have confidence. As the weeks passed, however, more of the tribesmen showed interest in an American agency and even the Chief, without admitting any change in his thinking, was slightly more willing to listen. He resolved to seek direction from the Great Spirit.

He has been called a pagan and savage, but on the contrary, he was a man of strong faith. He believed the Great Spirit brought the Sioux to Canada and would not abandon them now. Father Rondeau wrote that the Chief was "very opposed to Christianity."[5] It is doubtful if he was opposed to the religion of others as much as he was devoted to his own. Sitting Bull ordered preparation for that great tribal exercise in prayer, a sun dance. The ceremony was held in the White Mud Badlands, about twenty miles west of the Wood Mountain post. There the sun dance lodge was erected with all due ceremony, with the usual forked log of poplar for a central support, poplar branches for the roof and a spacious interior. There the Sioux danced, fasted, prayed, made braves and, near the conclusion, called upon the Great Spirit to give His children a message. They waited for the medicine men to announce the message. It came but was not what the Sioux hoped to hear. It was almost as if Major Walsh had written it: "You can't continue to live this way."

Dissension

Men who watched Major James Morrow Walsh at Wood Mountain said that if he had been born a Sioux, he would be another Sitting Bull. It was intended as a compliment but not all who knew Walsh were complimentary. Such a forceful fellow could not escape criticism. Citizens conscious of the dangers to human life in the area were grateful; some with whom he worked were jealous; and wrong-doers hurt by his unbending discipline were bitter. He was not one to compromise and criminals brought before him for sentence knew they were more likely to receive the maximum than the minimum penalty. As the records show, when three whiskey traders arrested in 1876 were brought before Magistrate Walsh and convicted, the penalty for each of the two principals in the case was a five hundred dollar fine and three months imprisonment.[1] The Secretary of State at Ottawa took note and offered commendation but Commissioner Macleod warned that such sentences were very severe and might not be justified unless the convicted men were selling the liquor to Indians.

Policemen could expect resistance from outside their working circles but Walsh, unhappily, encountered it from within. He was not totally blameless. He was a strong and able fellow but he was an indivialist more than a co-operator. It suited senior officers to have Walsh move from Fort Macleod to take command of the new post in the Cypress Hills in 1875 and even at a distance of one hundred and fifty miles there was no guarantee against discord.

When decided about what should be done, Walsh demanded action with a minimum of waste time. Mounted Police correspondence for 1876 shows Walsh communcating directly with the Secretary of State in Ottawa about his conviction that the new and high-powered guns should not be sold to Indians. He should have conferred with the Commissioner and Assistant Commissioner. A letter from the Minister brought the matter to the attention of Commissioner Macleod and the latter, angered, replied:

When at his post he informed me that he had stopped the sale [of improved firearms] except upon his permit and I approved of his course ... but he never mentioned to me and I am informed by the Asst. Commissioner that he never mentioned to him any apprehension he had on account of the improved arms. I respectfully submit that the officer in command of his district should at any rate have been made aware of the danger, at the same time that Insp. Walsh wrote his letter to you. ... I am quite satisfied that Inspector Walsh is mistaken. ... There is not the slightest foundation for the [idea that] Indians are storing up arms and ammunition for any disloyal purpose. ... I think, therefore, that the less we interfere with the sale of breech loading arms and ammunition to our Indians the better.[2]

But within days, Commissioner Macleod seems to have changed his mind, saying: "The hostile Sioux in the United States must be prevented by every means in our power from procuring either carbines or ammunition in our Territory".[3]

Again, late in 1879, Walsh took matters into his own hands. This time it was on account of the hungry Métis and Sioux who were crossing the border in the hope of finding wild meat. The Indian Agent at Buford complained to Washington and, quite innocently, referred to a letter he had received from Walsh. The Major, still struggling on behalf of the Canadian Métis whose hunting on the Montana side had been abruptly ended by General Miles, submitted that most of those who were then camping on the United States section of Milk River were Canadians in origin and should be eligible to take land in Canada. These people, he argued, should be encouraged to end their dependence upon hunting and settle on land in their own country. It was logical enough but when the Walsh letter was quoted to Washington and then comm-nicated to Ottawa, it took on the appearance of officiality. Min-isters were concerned and wrote the Commissioner to enquire what a police superintendent was doing writing letters to serv-ants of a foreign government concerning matters of policy. Ottawa called for a reprimand.

Macleod transmitted the censure but Walsh, fully aware of the urgency of the Métis and Indian situation, found it diffi-cult to understand why any Canadian should not invite Cana-dian Métis to return to their own ground, especially when their presence on the American side was largely responsible for preventing the few remaining buffalo from migrating north-ward to give Canadian-based Indians the chance of a shot at them. Moreover, Walsh was aware that Louis Riel was active in attempting to weld the Métis people into one big commu-nity on the United States section of Milk River and he was sure there would be fewer dangers of upheaval if the Canadian Métis were settled on Canadian land pursuing a peaceful way of life. Walsh may have been too hasty, but Indians could starve while a message was being transmitted to Fort Walsh and then to Ottawa and back to Wood Mountain. The man who had done so much to save human lives by forthright and deliberate action found official censure difficult to accept.

Naturally, the whiskey traders hated Walsh. And when those who felt the sting of his forthright administration of justice were from south of the boundary, American editors spoke up. The *Fort Benton Record*, the newspaper most wide-ly read at Fort Macleod and Fort Walsh, carried the Walsh name often, but not always cordially. One day the Benton paper would have a warm testimonial: "The thanks of the re-sidents of this community and of every white settler in North-ern Montana are due to Major Walsh."[4] A short time later the writer was proclaiming Walsh as "the right man in the right place and deserving great credit for his energy and pluck".[5] But writers can be fickle and another time the sentiment was very different: "Sitting Bull is only a second rate Chief and Walsh a third rate policeman."[6] On still another occasion, it read: "This excellent officer deserves a public reception from the people of Benton and vicinity for his efforts to stop the trade in arms and amunition in this section, and also for his kindness in sending scouts to inform the unprotected posts on

Milk River of the threatened danger from hostile Indians".[7]

There was no reason to suppose that the opinions expressed by Montana newspapers made the slightest impression upon Walsh as he carried out his duties. But he was disturbed at the thought that the editorial attention directed at him might have a damaging effect on his relationship with fellow officers in the Force. He was receiving more newspaper coverage than any other officer.

Unfortunately, an officer visiting the East allowed himself to be interviewed by a reporter from the *Chicago Times* and the resulting story was more flattering to Walsh than to the Commissioners. It was bad enough that such opinions appeared in the press, but, quite unjustly, Walsh was blamed for them and a friend of Assistant Commissioner Irvine, living at Fort Walsh, wrote to the Benton editor alleging that:

Major Walsh has used every dishonorable means to oust his present commanders and obtain supreme control of the police stationed here, but failing in this he has endeavored to obtain a separate command at Wood Mountain where neither Col. Macleod nor Col. Irvine could interfere with his management of the Indians or the police.

The correspondent, using only the pen name, Veritas, resorted to slander to discredit the officer:

The Major's record is hardly calculated to enhance his claim to military skill, although it speaks volumes for his ability as a propagator of the half-breed race. If there is a personal feeling on the part of Col. Macleod, it is probably owing to the licentious life that Walsh is leading here, which is a burning disgrace to the Force, and deserves immediate investigation from the Canadian authorities.[8]

The writer alleged that Walsh, instead of counselling the Sioux to return to the United States, had used every means at his command to induce them to stay and had visited Indian encampments near Fort Belknap, Montana, to invite more Indians to come. The object, according to Veritas, was to so increase the Indian population at Wood Mountain that a huge army of police would be required and Walsh would be in command.

The allegation appears irresponsible and not at all in keeping with the evidence. Walsh had urged Sitting Bull to go back to the United States and the Chief admitted it. Moreover, the accusation of empire building seems ridiculous when at the time of the criticism, Fort Walsh had about one hundred and forty policemen and Wood Mountain, with a bigger Indian population nearby, had fewer than twenty-five men in uniform. Having regard to the surrounding population of disgruntled natives and the potential for rebellion, the Wood Mountain police strength was small, as Walsh pointed out in his last report after leaving the area: "With so small a force it was hard to keep proper discipline but the conduct of the detachment was extremely good, as can be seen by the few entries against the men composing it, in the annual defaulters' sheet for the force."[9]

Rumour breeds rumour. There was one about Walsh trying to prevail upon Sitting Bull to accept a promoter's proposal which would have placed the Chief on public exhibition in various Canadian cities. One of the papers carrying the story was the *Saskatchewan Herald*[10] which linked the names of Major Walsh and Captain Allen in overtures to Sitting Bull, seeking his agreement to a circuit of engagements at which he would be on display. According to the *Herald*, the Chief agreed to the plan but after eating well for a time at the expense of the promoter, changed his mind. A few years later, after his return to the United States, he was indeed on tour with Buffalo Bill Cody's Wild West Show but as the Major took pains to point out emphatically in his annual report for 1880:

Idle and absurd as such reports may seem, yet I feel it my duty to emphatically contradict them, and to say, though I have been asked to assist in securing engagement of Sitting Bull, I have always declined to do so. Another report, as I am informed, has also gained currency, that Sitting Bull would have surrendered during the last summer, and it not been for the encouragement which I held out to him, of possibly being able to return to his camp with better terms of surrender than the United States had accorded to other Indians. As to this, I beg to say that the report is likewise false, for I have never given Sitting Bull any such encouragement. As I have already stated, after most urgent requests made by Sitting Bull, I told him if the Canadian Government would permit me, I would see the President or Secretary of the Interior for him. I never heard Bull demur very much to the conditions of surrender offered him by the United States Government. His only objection appeared to be the doubt that the conditions would be carried out, and particularly with regard to himself.[11]

The situation became serious when a letter appeared in the Toronto *Globe,* sharply criticizing the Assistant Commissioner at Forth Walsh. Colonel Irvine's friends were incensed and blamed somebody close to Walsh. Whoever was responsible, it showed that unfounded aspersions were being made on both sides and the Commissioner, hoping to end the animosities decided upon a general reallocation of post commands.

During June and July of 1880, Superintendent W.D. Jarvis left Fort Saskatchewan and took over the command at Fort Macleod. Superintendent W.M. Herchmer gave up Shoal Lake in favour of Battleford. Inspector James Walker was moved from Battleford to Fort Walsh. Superintendet L.N.F. Crozier took over the difficult Wood Mountain assignment and Superintendent James Morrow Walsh was assigned command of the Eastern Division at Qu'Appelle. The Qu'Appelle assignment looked important, but for Walsh it did not hold the interest or the challenge of Wood Mountain. The man who had manoeuvred so skillfully from the moment of the Sioux arrival was leaving. He was not well and he was not happy.

An Old Hat and an Old Horse

Sitting Bull's manner was grave. He did not want Walsh to leave Wood Mountain and told him so. He spent more time alone, squatting and brooding in his tipi. Everything seemed to be going against him. He was making no headway in his aim to be recognized as a Canadian Indian and was still the object of hate in the eyes of most Americans. The position of his people was more pitiful than ever. They were reduced to eating the decaying flesh from horses which died the previous winter. Now, in addition to all else, he would shortly lose his paleface friend, "Meejoor", as he called Walsh.

Walsh could only tell the Chief that he preferred to stay at Wood Mountain where he would expect to fight with Sitting Bull's people periodically, as he had done for three and a half years, and to help them at other times with understanding and guidance. The two men found the bonds of attachment growing stronger although neither had allowed cordiality to stand in the way of an argument. Both could set aside all feeling of personal friendship as quickly as two combatants could shed their coats, just as they did one day when the Chief was bemoaning Walsh's impending departure.

On this occasion, the natives made an ill-advised attempt to rescue a young Sioux arrested for creating a disturbance at Jean Louis Legaré's trading post. Young bucks responded to the prisoner's shrieks for help and Sitting Bull joined them. Walsh hurried to the scene and it required twenty policemen to repel the agitated mob and take the prisoner to the post. With feeling running high, it was rumoured that the Sioux were not giving up and would attack the post to recover their man. Walsh did not place much reliance in the report but thought it prudent to barricade the approaches to the post anyway. The barricade was maintained for several days until "Bull came and apologized for his conduct and asked forgiveness which I granted him".

Sitting Bull would have put up a fight for the Major as he would for his own followers. During the same week in which the Sioux were contemplating attack for recovery of a prisoner, Walsh had the Chief's co-operation in recovering and returning nine stolen horses, some of them the property of the United States government, to the American Indian Agent at Poplar Creek.

Bull's visit to apologize was one of the last they would have. Both welcomed the opportunity. After the varied experiences of three and one-half years, Walsh could communicate moderately well in Sioux. The Chief made no claims to progress with English, except to know when Walsh's language was predominantly profanity. In the clear light of that June morning, Walsh saw Sitting Bull as a man whose dreams had turned out to be empty. His leather smock hung loosely like drapes, hiding heavy muscles shrunken by hunger. But his eyes still sparkled like black diamonds and in spite of lameness, he walked proudly, planting his heels down hard with every step. But there was sadness in his expression and dejection in his voice. And for no apparent reason, he was wearing his ancient war bonnet, adorned with eagle feathers and rich in battlefield associations. It was the headpiece the Chief wore on the day of Little Big Horn.

Walsh raised the old question of return to the United States, saying that he hoped for the Chief's own sake as well as that of his followers that he would soon decide to accept the American offer of a permanent home on a reserve. It was now apparent that the buffalo would not come back, ever. Too many shared the views of an American editor that: "Our Territorial Legislature ought to set a bounty on the head of each one killed instead of trying to prevent their disappearance".[1]

Sitting Bull reiterated that he would be the last to go back to the United States. He recalled his promise to his people, that those who wanted to return to American agencies could do so. Many of his people were already on their way or pre-

174

paring to go. Walsh knew of the movement which began in March when thirty families departed carrying letters from him to the United States Army officers and Indian agents along the way, requesting protection and assistance while en route to specified agencies.[2] Chiefs Broadtail and Little Knife came to Walsh to report the arrival of Poplar Creek, Montana, of one hundred more lodges of Sioux, all drawing rations at once. Throughout April groups following Chiefs Iron Dog, Waterspout, Hairy Chin and The-Man-Who-Killed-The-White-Man were setting out for Spotted Tail and Red Cloud and other agencies south of the border. Before Walsh left Wood Mountain to go to Qu'Appelle, by his own count, "10 Chiefs with 250 families moved out of Canadian territory and reported to the United States officials on the Missouri River of their intention to return to their reservations and this migration continued until the great camp of one hundred lodges in 1879 was reduced to about 50 lodges of Bull's own relations."[3]

Even with the smaller population, the general state of nutrition was at a low point and the number of fresh graves betrayed the necessity of eating decaying horse meat and other dangerously damaged foods. But even in their impoverished state, as Walsh took pains to note in his report, "the conduct of these starving and destitute people, their patient endurance, their sympathy, and the extent to which they assisted each other, their observance of law and order, would reflect credit upon the most civilized community."[4]

Sitting Bull, for the first time, admitted that he "might be willing to shake hands with them," meaning the Americans. But he knew he was not just another Indian. He was blamed personally for the deaths of Custer and his cavalrymen, and would be a marked man wherever he appeared. And in Walsh's view, there was justification for the Chief's fear that he would be made to suffer for all the sins of his people. In addition to all else, he was blamed for the killing many years earlier of several government scouts and mail carriers and knew on his return to the United States he would be tried for murder and perhaps hanged. That accusation concerning the murder of scouts and mail carriers was not new to him but he denied vigorously having any part in the killings. He could name the guilty person if necessary. And as for the celebrated Custer affair, he was afraid the American people would continue to think of it as a massacre rather than just a battle in which one side won overwhelmingly.

The Chief made a final plea: "If the White Mother is determined to drive me out of her country and force me into the hands of people I know are waiting like hungry wolves to take my life," would Walsh not see the President of the United States and ascertain from him the best conditions on which the Chief, personally, would be permitted to return and "if the conditions would be faithfully carried out."[5] Could he, the Chief, be assured by the President that the same treatment accorded other returning Sioux would be extended to him or would he be singled out and held responsible for every depredation committed on the prairies in the past twenty years?

To this Walsh replied: "If the Canadian Government permits me to do it, I will comply with your request and see the President."

Tough as Walsh and his Sioux friend could be, both disliked the prospect of parting. "I won't forget you, Bull," Walsh promised, "and I hope I'll see you again. And by the way," he added, "when I ride away from here in a few days, it'll be on your old grey gelding, the one your boys rustled from the battlefield."

The Chief's eyes brightened with pleasure. Of course he remembered the horse and hoped it would remain permanently in the possession of his friend. Now known as "Custer", the horse was a war veteran with a distinguished record. Nobody was sure where the good grey was foaled but his teeth showed him to be twelve or thirteen years old and his quality of bone and body could be seen as a mark of good breeding. Possessing the approved conformation and refinement, he was acquired by military purchasing agents and assigned to the Seventh Cavalry. After seeing action in various skirmishes with Indians on the northwestern frontier, the grey gelding was one of the horses ridden into battle beside the Little Big Horn on that fateful 25th of June, 1876. Like others who followed Custer that day, the horse's rider did not return. Most of the horses died by gunfire, but a few, including the grey, escaped to be taken as prizes of war by the victorious Sioux.

Only one of the horses being ridden by Custer's men that day returned to the Cavalry. That one was severely wounded and Indians searching for loot left him to die. But men of the

United States forces found him later and thought enough of him to make a litter and carry him back to the base where he was cared for until he recovered. The horse then called Comanche was retired to ease and all the good treatment the army could furnish for the remainder of a very long life. Comanche was reported to have lived to the age of forty-five years.

The Indians were skillful horsemen and knew a good horse when they saw one. They recognized the grey as a good one and its captor was happy to be its owner, just as other warriors were happy to have various new possessions like United States Army rifles and clothing and watches taken from dead soldiers. The grey gelding was still a war horse and with a proud young Sioux on his back, he saw more action in the engagements which followed the Battle of the Little Big Horn. When Sitting Bull's people fled across the International Boundary, the equine veteran was taken with them.

The horse was an excellent buffalo runner. Because of his reputation for versatility and his conspicuous colour, the animal naturally inspired would-be horse thieves to whisk him away. He was stolen on at least one occasion and recovered. Then, it seems, he was traded to a Wood Mountain Métis. At this point, the animal caught the attention of Superintendent Walsh who noticed the United States Army brand and immediately surmised what had happened to bring the horse to Wood Mountain. "Is the horse for sale?" he enquired at once. The answer should have been obvious because anything owned by these poor people could be bought, especially if real Canadian or United States money would be used in settlement. A price was named and Walsh agreed to pay it, and the horse was taken to the North West Mounted Police stable.

The officer admitted a great fondness for the horse but did not wish to be accused of being in possession of stolen property and wrote at once to General Terry at United States Army Headquarters to report the transaction that brought the grey and aging animal with a United States Cavalry brand on his hip to him. If the United States authorities wanted the horse returned, their prior claim would be recognized and the animal would be sent back promptly. But, Walsh admitted, he had formed a strong admiration for the old grey mount and if permitted to keep him, it would be a matter of very great satisfaction. If it should be his good fortune to retain the animal, Walsh promised, it would always have a good home.

Walsh received a reply to his letter and as recorded by John Peter Turner, it was exactly as he had hoped:

I have the honour to inform you that the Secretary of War authorizes Major Walsh to keep the horse.

E.D. TOWNSEND
Adjutant-General[6]

Sitting Bull was no less pleased than Walsh.

"Before you go away," Sitting Bull said to the Major, "I have something I want to give you, something else that came through the war." As Walsh stared in astonishment, the Chief removed his feathered war bonnet – the one he wore in the Custer battle and a score of other engagements – and passed it to Walsh. "I'm through fighting," he said with evident emotion. "I want you to have it."

Only now was the Chief's reason for wearing the famous headpiece on this day understood. The old bonnet was his most priceless possession and he wanted Walsh to have it. The old hat was destined to a place of honour among Canadian treasures. Some time after retiring from the Mounted Police, Major Walsh presented the hat to Sir William Van Horne, president of the Canadian Pacific Railway, who in turn, in 1913, presented it to the Royal Ontario Museum in Toronto.

Almost Persuaded

The gallant grey gelding, Custer, pranced like a three-year-old, demonstrating what oats and good care can do for a horse's spirits, as Walsh reined him away from Wood Mountain in July, 1880. B Division of the Mounted Police was starting for Qu'Appelle – a four-day ride – and as commanding officer, Walsh rode in front, presenting a picture which might have suggested Napoleon on his great grey charger, Marengo. The new posting in the beautiful Qu'Appelle Valley would offer a pleasant change for men who grew tired of the isolation of Wood Mountain. Henceforth they would see much of Cree and Assiniboine Indians and rarely any Sioux. Administrative problems would be very different and somewhat less dangerous.

For Walsh, the immediate future was uncertain. His health had deteriorated. There had been recurring spells of erysipelas and the difficult duties of the recent years seemed to aggravate the disorder. He was looking forward to a leave of absence. It took a few days after his arrival at Qu'Appelle to reorganize the administration and turn over the command temporarily to Inspector S.B. Steele. Then he left for Winnipeg and continued by way of St. Paul and Chicago to Ontario, hoping to confer with government officials at Ottawa and hoping to have a restful visit with his wife and small daughter at Brockville. Had he remained at Fort Walsh instead of going to Wood Mountain, he would have brought his wife and daughter to live in the Cypress Hills, but when the Wood Mountain assignment demanded his residence where he would be close to the Sioux, he concluded that his family would be safer and more comfortable at the Ontario home.

Wood Mountain, of course, would never be the same without him. Inspector L.N.F. Crozier was a highly regarded policeman with an excellent sense of duty, but try as he might, he could not captivate the Sioux as Walsh had done. He tried particularly to cultivate Sitting Bull's confidence. The Chief was not one to be easily won. As with water dripping on flint, it would take a long time to make an impression. Crozier had a long talk with Sitting Bull, hoping to convince him to make a complete surrender to the United States authorities and to do so at once. He misjudged the man. He was using almost exactly the same words as Walsh had used but the Indian was completely unresponsive. Crozier became impatient. He was not Walsh. Thinking the Chief was in one of his contrary moods, Crozier walked away.

To Walsh, Sitting Bull had hinted a willingness to go back to the south but he was not going to be rushed into it, certainly not by an impatient officer whose appearance and manner he did not yet understand. Furthermore, Sitting Bull hoped the Major would intercede on his behalf at Ottawa and Washington. The Chief was not going to move before hearing from his friend.

Crozier adopted a different tactic; he appealed directly to other Sioux chiefs and ignored Sitting Bull. In other words, he attempted to win the Indians away from their Chief and thus strip him of his influence. If enough of the Sioux left for Montana, the Chief, finding himself with little or no following, would be obliged to go as well. The plan worked well for a while and Spotted Eagle, an influential Sioux leader, left with a substantial group of the Sans Arc band, going to Fort Keogh. But while the technique had some success and lessened Sitting Bull's prestige and support, it only toughened his resistance and made it more difficult than ever for Crozier to talk to him. The Chief was left with a small group of loyal followers and their families, living almost without communication with the police.

Meanwhile, Walsh was making his way to Brockville and Ottawa. In Ottawa he was able to obtain an appointment with Prime Minister Sir John A. Macdonald. The Prime Minister was well aware of the service Walsh had rendered at Fort Walsh and Wood Mountain and he listened attentively as the officer described the Indian situation and pointed out the reasons why Sitting Bull hesitated to return to the United States. The Chief's fears were justified, Walsh contended, and the officer hoped something could be done to remove the danger of a direct vengeful attack if he returned. He asked permission to visit Washington and interview the President, from whom he had, through a secretary, an invitation to call at any time he happened to be in the American capital.

Sitting Bull's requests were entirely reasonable and it seemed likely the President would give assurances of the same treatment the Indians returning earlier had received. That would be enough to persuade the last of the Sioux to leave Canadian soil. After all, the conditions were almost exactly those offered by the Terry Commission and there was no apparent reason why they should not be repeated to make them apply to the Chief.

But the Prime Minister was not convinced that a Mounted Police officer should be taking matters of international concern to Washington; he did not have much sympathy for Sitting Bull anyway. Since so many of the Sioux had already gone back, Macdonald believed it was only a matter of time until Sitting Bull would be ready to join them. In the meantime, he inferred, it would be better for Walsh to attend to police duties and stay away from Washington. Macdonald was aware of the rivalry existing in Mounted Police ranks. He knew Walsh was a man of unusual courage but too forthright to be a diplomat, and under the circumstances, should be restrained. It was with that purpose, therefore, that Walsh was detained in the East.[1]

Sitting Bull could not understand why he had not heard from his old friend. Crozier was in constant communication with Major David Brotherton, officer in command at Fort Buford, and between them it was arranged that one of the Buford scouts and interpreters, Edwin Allison, would go to Wood Mountain in the hope of convincing Sitting Bull of the good treatment being accorded to all returning Sioux. Allison found the Indians on Frenchman's River (Whitemud Creek) and introduced himself by distributing presents. He was warmly received and invited to sleep in Sitting Bull's tipi along with members of the Chief's family – his two wives, sisters, three sons and two daughters. A seventeen-year-old daughter was the oldest of the children and twin boys of four were the youngest. Sitting Bull was congenial but his hospitality was not to be taken as an indication that he would be easily convinced. Allison's influence, however, was sufficient to convince the once-great Chief Gall to turn southward. It meant, also a rupture in the relationship between the two old warrior chiefs, Bull and Gall, but the latter's popularity was still strong enough to convince half the remaining Sioux to follow him. Sitting Bull said again he would not budge before receiving a message from Walsh. He knew it would come, even though Crozier told him Walsh had gone away to the East and might never be back.

On first of November of that year – 1880 – Colonel Macleod terminated his services with the Mounted Police to devote himself to the new duties as a stipendiary magistrate. Lieutenant-Colonel A.G. Irvine became Commissioner and, before the end of his first month in office, he journed to Wood Mountain to deliver the Prime Minister's message. As might have been expected, it advised acceptance of the American offer because there would be no reservation for the Sioux in Canada and there was nothing on the Canadian side to which the Sioux people could look forward. Irvine, in whom the Chief had some confidence, added his own counsel to wait no longer for Walsh to return.

A few days later, Scout Allison from Fort Buford, came to reopen discussions with Sitting Bull. Winter was fixing its icy grip upon the Canadian prairies, and Chief Low Dog, considered a dangerous Indian, said he would return to the States. Sitting Bull agreed to go part way and to consider as he travelled. Police officers breathed sighs of relief and communicated the good news to Ottawa. Mid-December found the Chief with a pathetically shrunken band – only about sixty lodges – trudging southward toward the International Boundary.

Some of the young bucks with Low Dog could not resist temptation and picked up forty-five horses along the way, expecting that once across the border they would not be challenged. The Métis owner pursued them but had no success. Not only did the Indians keep his horses but they took his gun from him. He returned to Wood Mountain and reported his troubles to the Mounted Police who at once invited him to ride back in the company of a constable and identify the stolen horses. The Métis had no desire to see more of the Sioux and refused. A Police constable and guide went southward anyway and, in the best tradition of the force, overtook the Indians and returned with the stolen horses.

But it was too soon for official rejoicing. A short distance south of the border, the Chief's followers saw an American troop attacking Chief Gall's camp and concluded that United States policy had not changed. There was a time when Bull would have been keen to engage such a force of Long Knives but now, with only a few warriors, he knew it would be folly to fight. The able old warrior, Gall, was slow in completing his trip to Fort Buford and while camping at Poplar Creek, was ordered to report at the Fort by the second day of January. When he showed no willingness to obey such an order, General Terry sent a force to hurry him along. It was poor planning on the part of the military command to stage such a demonstration when other bands might be on the way to complete the long-awaited surrender. Sitting Bull concluded that he could expect no less in the way of reception. Low Dog and his band were some distance ahead and continued toward Buford but Sitting Bull's followers, cold, hungry and depressed, saw themselves walking into the jaws of a trap and decided to turn back to Canada. As soon as news of Bull's change of course reached the American military authorities, a troop was sent from Fort Assiniboine to intercept him. But the soldiers were not clever enough, and on January 24 he and his little band crossed the Boundary again, resolving that they would never leave.

Eastern papers carried the story that Sitting Bull was at last back in the United States, never to return. Officials in both Ottawa and Washington were overjoyed but their relief was cut short when it was learned that the Sioux were back at Wood Mountain. Inspector Crozier knew he must again urge the Sioux to return.

By April, Sitting Bull agreed to let two of his young men accompany a Mounted Policeman to Fort Buford to observe how the Sioux who returned earlier were being treated. Major Brotherton made sure the visitors obtained a favourable impression and even provided a feast for the visitors. Sitting Bull was still unwilling to trust the Americans. If only he could consult Walsh or know what new information his friend had from Ottawa and Washington, he would be ready to make the great decision. He decided he would go to Qu'Appelle and then, if he found Walsh, he would know exactly what to do.

Qu'Appelle

The Canadian census for 1881 showed 56,446 people, excluding Indians, living in the Northwest Territories. Winnipeg had a population of almost 8,000. The Canadian Pacific Railway was completed as far west as Brandon. Senator H.M. Cochrane obtained one of the first 100,000-acre grassland leases under the terms of the Land Act and was driving the first big herd of cattle, 3,000 head, to graze on the Canadian buffalo range. And Sioux Indian residence at and about Wood Mountain was in its fifth year.

To the great relief of both the Mounted Police and the populace, Sioux numbers on the Canadian side had dropped greatly but the key figure, the man blamed for most of the Sioux crimes, was still there. To most people, Sitting Bull was the Sioux tribe as much as were the 4,000 Indians who had returned to reservations in the United States. Although his power within the tribe had declined with the departure of his tribesmen, he remained the Sioux phantom, capable, in the public mind at least, of all kinds of mischief.

Leaders in Ottawa, acting on advice from the Mounted Police, were trying to dispel this idea along with the fear that had discouraged settlement in the whole of the midwest. The Prime Minister welcomed every chance to make a statement on the subject. When Sir Richard J. Cartwright stood in the House of Commons on March 11, 1881, and asked: "What information can the First Minister furnish respecting Sitting Bull and his band?" Sir John A. Macdonald replied.

Said Sir John: "The main portion of the hostiles has surrendered to the United States. Sitting Bull with a much diminished body, numbering only 60 lodges out of the vast body of men, is in a starving condition, but is still obstinate more from apprehension, I think, than anything else, and refuses to surrender. The Americans promise the Sioux good treatment, and those who have surrendered have been well treated. Sitting Bull who is in a starving condition, receives no sustenance of any kind from the Canadian Government. They are told they will receive no food from the authorities, and that they must surrender to the American Government. Our offer of an escort for Sitting Bull to the frontier and also of protection till the American forces are ready to receive and protect them, has been made again and again. The Indians are afraid of being attacked by some of the western men who suffered from hostile incursions of the Indians during the Civil War. Every inducement has been offered to those Indians to surrender, and I believe they will surrender to the United States authorities ere long."

Sir Richard Cartwright, satisfied with the reply, added a brief comment: "I am extremely glad to hear that, because Sitting Bull's Indians have always been a serious source of danger to us."[1]

Poplars and willows were in full leaf and the blanket of green on the prairie was broken only by whitened buffalo bones when Sitting Bull and about half of his shrunken band started for Qu'Appelle. Seeing no buffalo on the way, the travellers relied upon roots and gophers for food. On the third night out they camped beside the creek at Pile of Bones where a townsite was soon to be laid out and called Regina. And then, after another day of riding, the Sioux arrived at Qu'Appelle and learned to their disappointment that the report was true; Major Walsh had not returned from the East.

The Chief was downcast. He talked with Inspector Steele who was in command of the police detachment. With none of the arrogance for which he had a reputation, the Indian recited an old request, a Canadian homesite for his remaining people. And, of course, he did not overlook his immediate need for food supplies. Steele must have been overawed by the Chief if one may judge from his estimate of the number of Indians present. There is every reason to believe that Sitting Bull was there with fewer than one hundred of his people, including women and children, but Steele believed he saw twelve hundred Sioux in the party.[2] Anyway, Steele told Sitting Bull that he did not know when Walsh would return, if ever, and that Canada would never make land grants to American Indians. Nevertheless, Steele suggested that land was a matter which could be discussed more appropriately with Indian Commissioner Edgar Dewdney, then at Shoal Lake, one hundred and sixty miles to the East. Steele sent a message to Dewdney and suggested that he come to Qu'Appelle to talk to the Sioux.

Sitting Bull agreed to wait. He was not in a hurry to go back to Wood Mountain. But in the meantime, there was the problem of finding food; Star Blanket's Crees had already taken most of the wild game in the valley. The trader at the Hudson's Bay Company post was low in supplies and Indian agent Allen Macdonald had no more than he needed for local Indians. But a friendly Métis came to the rescue with a quantity of fish caught in nearby lakes, enough to meet minimum needs for a few days. Then there was the mission where Father Hugonard, a young priest from Grenoble, France, was alone. Needless to say, he was startled when eighty Sioux on horses halted at his place and issued three shrill shrieks. The visitors dismounted, except for the Chief, and made their need for food very clear, even to someone who did not understand the Sioux tongue. The worried priest invited the leaders to come in and sent for an interpreter.

The priest admitted that four Red River carts which had just arrived from Fort Ellice carried flour, six bags to the cart. The flour was brought from Winnipeg to Fort Ellice by riverboat and cost close to twenty dollars per hundred pounds. The priest had a reason for hoarding the flour: it was to be used if necessary by friends of the mission and could not be given away. Hearing this, the Chief, with a rifle under his blanket, said nobody had a greater need than his people and they intended to have some.

The priest yielded slightly and enquired what the Sioux had to offer in exchange. The Chief removed the blanket from his shoulders – a Navajo blanket, according to Zachary and Marie Albina Hamilton.[3] The priest said he would allow three dollars for it. Other Indians offered horses, knives, and watches and the priest fared very well in the trading which followed. There was one serious defect in the watches which had been taken from Custer's dead soldiers; the wheels and working parts had been removed for use as earrings and ornaments and the timepieces would not run. To the natives, the brightly coloured ornaments were more attractive than the watches which could only tell them what they already knew. The Sioux left the mission with six or seven bags of flour and whatever vegetables the priest could spare from his garden. It was poor fare for people accustomed to buffalo meat but better than living on wild turnips. Father Hugonard tried to win Sitting Bull to the white man's religion but he would have none of it. John Hawkes recorded after his interview with the priest: "Father Hugonard was anxious to carry the gospel to the Sioux, but Sitting Bull would not hear of it, and such was his authority that not one convert was made while he lived."[4]

Several days later, Indian Commissioner Dewdney arrived at Qu'Appelle and met at once with Sitting Bull. But he knew what the Chief's questions would be and his answers were repititions of those the Sioux had heard many times: no reservations for American Indians. "You go back to Wood Mountain," he counselled, "and if you're wise you'll get your people together and head straight for Fort Buford." The only help the Commissioner could offer was the promise to furnish rations for the return journey to Wood Mountain provided the Indians departed at once. It was sufficient inducement and the Indians were on their way.

Walsh, still not in the best of health and still not free to return to full police duty, had not been idle. He had been prevented from visiting the President of the United States to personally request a guarantee for Sitting Bull's safety, but he hoped to accomplish something useful outside the official channels.

"It would be criminal," he wrote,[5] "if something was not done" to relieve Bull of the fear of American vengeance at his return. He decided to take the matter to some influential friends in New York and Chicago. In Chicago, Walsh met General Hammond whose acquaintance he formed through the United States Indian department some years earlier and who was familiar with the Sioux tribulations. The man agreed with Walsh that Sitting Bull, on his return, should not be singled out for punishment, and assured his Canadian friend that he could tell the Chief to come to Fort Buford without fear of reprisals. Moreover, Hammond would secure promises from "several gentlemen friends with strong political influence with the Washington Cabinet, that they would, if it became necessary, intercede on behalf of Bull."

On the strength of this promise, Walsh resolved to send a message to the Chief. He wanted to avoid official channels, and he turned to Louis Daniels who served for some years with the Mounted Police and was then in Manitoba, contemplating a farming venture near Qu'Appelle. Daniels could be trusted. Walsh wrote, asking him to proceed to Sitting Bull's camp at Wood Mountain with the message that "he could with safety return to the United States, that the same treatment would be extended to him as that given to Broadtail, Spotted Eagle, Gall and other Chiefs."[6]

Daniels carried out the instructions faithfully. Sitting Bull had heard similar assurances from other people but was not convinced. If Walsh said it, however, it was now all the Sioux leader needed. He would take his remaining followers to Fort Buford.

The Inglorious Return

It was the most difficult decision Sitting Bull had ever been obliged to make. No doubt he repeated the unhappy sentiment communicated to relations at Standing Rock sometime earlier: "Once I was strong and brave, and my people had hearts of iron, but now I am a coward and will fight no more forever. My people are cold and hungry. My women are sick and my children freezing. I will do as the Great Father wishes. I will give my guns and ponies into his hands. My arrows are broken and my war paint thrown to the wind."[1]

With no hope of obtaining a reserve in Canada, he attempted to negotiate for some much-needed supplies for his destitute followers. Inspector A.R. Macdonell, who took over the Mounted Police command at Wood Mountain from Inspector Crozier in June, showed an inherited parsimony and was no more helpful than his predecessor. Sitting Bull's own body was emaciated and even the horses and dogs were weakened from hunger. Called to the Police headquarters a few days after his return from Qu'Appelle, Bull was as stubborn as ever and Inspector Macdonell, not knowing what was in the Chief's mind, became impatient and ordered him to leave.

Jean Louis Legaré, the tall, friendly and courteous French-Canadian trader – "one of the finest men I have ever known", according to Marie Albina Hamilton[2] – had befriended the Sioux from the day the first band crossed the Boundary to pitch tipis in Canada, almost five years earlier. After Walsh, Legaré ranked as the white man in whom the Indians had the greatest confidence. Most traders placed profits far ahead of a

189

reputation for honest dealing and cared but little for Indian welfare. Earlier in the summer, Legaré had provisioned a group of local Sioux and had accompanied them to Fort Buford. He was ready to go again, this time with a bigger prize, Sitting Bull. But he knew the necessity of caution and diplomacy; the Americans had hinted at a reward for anyone who succeeded in bringing Sitting Bull to surrender and if the Chief was given reason to suspect that the trader was using him for personal gain, he would certainly have shown how obstinate he would be.

Sitting Bull gave Legaré the opportunity to repeat the oft-sounded advice about returning and then surprised the trader by saying he would consider going back if assured of sufficient provisions for his immediate needs as well as for the long trip. One writer contended that Sitting Bull demanded money – three hundred dollars – in addition to ten bags of flour and other supplies.[3] It seems doubtful, however, that cash with which the Chief was quite unfamiliar, would be one of his demands. Jean Louis agreed to supply the necessities. He promised to furnish the wagons, carts, horses and helpers needed and to escort the Indians personally to see that they were properly received at the American post.

Having received Bull's word, Jean Louis became the man of the hour and the Police recognized the magnitude of the task he was undertaking. Moving about two hundred men, women and children with their tipis and belongings would require considerable equipment and Jean Louis, understanding from Major Brotherton that the United States would reimburse him for expenses, was prepared to back the operation with all the resources he could command. Since the freetraders had no business dealings with the Hudson's Bay Company, it was necessary to cart supplies over the long trail from St. Paul in Minnesota and costs were high. Jean Louis took stock of his reserves and furnished ten bags of flour as an advance payment and agreed to have ten more for the journey. But as the day for departure drew near, the Chief protested that Legaré was loading nine bags, not ten. Sitting Bull could not read but he could count.

When Legaré's cavalcade of wagons and carts was ready, the Chief announced that he would require another ten days to reconsider. Legaré was exasperated but he did not dare offend the Chief and run the risk of inviting refusal to go through with the plan. He accepted, with the understanding of a definite deadline, July 11. In the meantime, Legaré was feeding the Indians and as a means of sustaining their confidence, even provided a feast with gifts of tobacco.

It was not a joyful departure. Minutes before Jean Louis gave the signal to start, several families withdrew, determined to remain in Canada, whatever it might hold for them. The cavalcade was the biggest seen in those parts since the Mounted Police trek of seven years ealier. Thirty-five wagons, three carts, and undetermined number of horse-drawn travois and sixty or more horses with riders moved away in disorderly array. Wagons were piled high with supplies and tipis. Women and children rode on top or walked behind and kept company with the numerous dogs. There were still Indians, particularly men, who refused to ride on the white man's wagon wheels – which they saw as symbols of evil. To guide the carts and wagons, Jean Louis employed his Métis friends, among them, Jean Chartrand who lived long and often related the experiences of the trip. He recalled Sitting Bull's insistence that his own mounted warriors act as advance and rear guards for the expedition. The man who showed no fear on the battlefield was now fearful that his enemies would take advantage of his weakened position and swoop down to kill.

The travellers were ten miles along the way when they pitched tipis for the first night. Legaré ordered one of his Métis helpers to make the first distribution of supplies, flour, bacon, tea and sugar. Even then there was argument about the rations being too small. One excited Indian drew his revolver and blasted a bag of the flour until the contents were lost. Legaré was most anxious to avoid trouble and submissively replaced the damaged bag. But at this point he realized that his total stock of one ton of flour would not be enough to feed the two hundred or two hundred and twenty-five people until they reached Buford and knew he must make other arrangements. After the Indians had settled down for the night, he instructed two of his most reliable Métis to ride through the darkness and advise Major Brotherton at Fort Buford that he was on the way with Sitting Bull but faced a serious food shortage which could wreck the entire plan. He requested a wagonload of meat and flour to be sent forward with all possible haste – but without a military escort which might alarm the Indians.

Major Brotherton was as anxious as Legaré to see this mission completed. On his instructions, Captain Walter Clifford and a small staff proceeded with two loaded wagons to meet Legaré. The Major understood Legaré's worry about creating needless alarm and he took a further precaution. There existed a danger that an American force in the area might confront Sitting Bull's Sioux and spoil the plan by trying to effect a capture in the field. To guard against this, Captain Clifford carried specific orders to take immediate command of any troops in the area to ensure against any action likely to alarm the Indians or interfere with their voluntary surrender. Clifford accompanied the wagons while the Métis made a wide detour, rejoining Sitting Bull's party from the rear, thereby avoiding any appearance of collusion.[4]

As Legaré expected, Sitting Bull was disturbed by the approach of the American officer and wagons but when informed that the loads were made up exclusively of food supplies – flour and pemmican – and were intended for his people, he acceded. The supplies had arrived none too soon. Legaré's stocks were becoming dangerously low and now, in the best Indian tradition, the arrival of fresh provisions called for a celebration before going on.

Captain Clifford had a pleasant personality and his smile alone was enough to set the Chief at ease. He was able to answer certain questions which seemed to be bothering the Chief; one concerned the Chief's daughter who eloped with a young buck from Wood Mountain and then surrendered at Fort Buford. A rumour had reached her father that she was held prisoner in chains at Fort Yates. Clifford was able to tell the old man that the girl was well and free. Pleased with the good news, the Chief seemed almost ready to forgive Clifford for wearing the uniform of the United States army.

Two days later, July 19, Legaré's wagons reached Fort Buford and the Indians were apprehensive. Lined up imposingly were the United States troops with their guns ready. In the background was the fort, the symbol of the new authority in their lives. Major Brotherton advanced to greet Legaré and smiled at Sitting Bull who continued to sit stoically on his old cream-coloured horse. His blanket was drawn to hide his face and he was in no hurry to dismount or to indulge in handshaking. A sign of a smile came only when he recognized Inspector A.R. Macdonell who had ridden in from Wood Mountain to be present for this occasion. Sitting Bull had not known Macdonell long. He knew this Inspector could be firm and tough but he bore a resemblence to Walsh and the Chief liked him much better than the efficient and rather overbearing Crozier.

Macdonell greeted the Chief and told him what Major Brotherton had planned. The Sioux would give up their guns and some of their horses and could then pitch tipis beside the fort and prepare to eat all they wanted of United States government food. "And when you're ready," Macdonell added, "we'll have a meeting in Major Brotherton's office – Brotherton and Legaré and you and I will talk about the plans they have for you."

The Indians dismounted, dutifully deposited their guns, and then gathered in small groups or strolled aimlessly beside the river. Bull alone sat motionless on his horse until Macdonell signalled to him to come to Major Brotherton's office. The Chief responded slowly, his reluctance showing in every step. He took with him one of his young sons, the one named Crowfoot because of his admiration for the Blackfoot Chief. The officer was wise enough to know that the presence of Macdonell and Legaré would make it easier for him to give the impression of good faith on the part of the Government. Brotherton explained that as soon as possible, Bull and his followers would be transported down river to Fort Yates and Standing Rock Reservation where most of the Sioux from Wood Mountain were already located. There, the Major was sure, Sitting Bull could live peacefully and comfortably. As long as he refrained from hostile acts, he would not be molested by soldiers.

Sitting Bull sat as motionless as a marble statue – and just as silent. He knew it would be his last chance to speak in the presence of the Canadians. Finally, he broke the silence. He was now convinced that surrender on his part was the proper decision, distasteful as it might be. He hoped that he and his people would still be allowed some liberties. He hoped he would be allowed to hunt and even tramp back to visit Wood Mountain. He wished those of his tribe who remained at Wood Mountain would now decide to join him here. Turning to Inspector Macdonell and his friend, the trader, he said: "Tell them to come. Tell them I said so. They'll be all right here."

Then he lifted his old rifle from under his blanket, handed it to his seven-year-old son and said: "You take your father's gun. I surrender it through you. You must learn the ways of the whites and how to live with them. I'm too old to learn much. And remember, your father was the last Sioux to surrender his gun."

With the least possible delay, river-boats were requisitioned and Sitting Bull and all the disarmed Sioux were on their way to the Indian agency at Standing Rock, downstream on the Missouri. Captain Clifford, the officer in charge, had twenty soldiers with him but said he did not feel the need for any. The Indians were perfectly orderly. The dispatch from Fort Buford, dated July 29, 1881, reporting Sitting Bull and one hundred and eighty seven of his band leaving by steamer for Standing Rock that day added only: "Bull was silent and reserved."[5]

Along the way, the Chief became the object of great interest. Crowds turned out at stopping places to gaze at this man whose name had for so long filled North Americans with terror. He returned their stares with fixed defiance. With him were five other chiefs: White Dog, Scarlet Thunder, High-As-The-Clouds, Four Horns and Bone Tomahawk. With him, also, were his two wives, children, sisters and his aged father.

As the boat splashed its way downstream, nobody in the Indian party was finding more entertainment from passing scenes than Sitting Bull's father. Having made very few contacts with the new race except in warfare, much that the old man saw was strange and new to him. For the first time in his life he saw the white man's villages and towns, and even more amazing, a railroad track with a train on it. He had seen wagons on the trails and steamboats on the rivers and felt quite reconciled to these but steam engines running on rails frightened him. The old man was not alone in his disdain for rails and the locomotives which thundered over them. The feeling seemed to be shared by most Indians and Métis that those "iron horses" and "singing wires" were frightening the wild game away and inviting settlers to enter the land. Surely, they were among the most disturbing features of the new civilization, generally "bad medicine".

Even Sitting Bull failed to hide his fear, as a news report from Bismark, dated August 1, 1881, noted:

Sitting Bull arrived here yesterday.... He arrives at Standing Rock today.... He has great fear of locomotives. The terror of the North, the hero of a hundred battles, the Indian brave who never quailed before the arrow, the tomahawk or the rifle, is afraid of a locomotive. It evinces a power quite beyond his comprehension, and for once he feels himself awed into realization of his utter inability to cope with the forces of civilization. Wherever the locomotive penetrates, the savage is subdued.[6]

Bull's arrival at Standing Rock, without arms, without horses, marked the end of one of the most important chapters in North American history. The United States military beheld it with the sense of relief. The Indian Wars which plagued the West for so many years appeared to have ended.

To Whom The Praise and Payment

Ever since the day of Custer's "last stand", North American papers welcomed every available scrap of news concerning Sitting Bull. Had a vote been taken, he would probably have been acclaimed the most newsworthy citizen of the period. Even during his stay on the Canadian side, newsmen wanted to know his movements, ever trying to guess his motives. It was not surprising that the same editors wanted to identify the hero or heroes in the great game of persuasion which led to his decision to surrender to United States authorities.

It would have been easier to name some of those public figures who failed to make an impression upon the Chief. It is doubtful, for example, if Major Crozier deserved any of the credit, even though Commissioner Irvine in his annual report complimented him in glowing terms for his work with the Sioux during Sitting Bull's last year in Canada. Some observers suspected that the Commissioner was bored by the prolonged praised directed at Major Walsh and was trying to cool the public ardor for that gallant officer by extolling the name of another. It was rather obvious that Crozier, although a dedicated officer, only antagonized Sitting Bull and his successor, Inspector A.R. Macdonell, was not with the Chief long enough to make much of an impression.

An American editor nominated Commissioner Irvine for the distinction, saying: "There is no doubt whatever that Sitting Bull's surrender is attributable to the great exertions shown by Col. Irvine."[1] But Irvine did not see much of Sitting Bull. Colonel James Macleod carried more influence with the

Chief but, in his case as in Irvine's, he was only occasionally among the Sioux. The same editor presented a contrary opinion four weeks later, noting:

Just at present there is considerable discussion as to who is entitled to the credit of inducing Sitting Bull to surrender. . . . It is important that the credit of bringing in Sitting Bull in person should be given to the right person. This person is Mr. Louis Legaré, a French Canadian who carries on a trading post on the Canadian side, near the line. The Indians would come starving to his door and he would never turn them away hungry. . . . Legaré has accomplished what armies have failed to do, and therefore deserves the credit and a liberal reward from the Government.[2]

Major Walsh had been absent for a year but he should not have been overlooked when credit for the final success was being apportioned. Walsh's influence on Sitting Bull was strong and lasting, and produced a loyal friendship without parallel in frontier history. When Walsh was prevented from returning to counsel his Sioux friends, he had succeeded in sending a message, and it was only then that the Chief made his decision. But the fact remains that Walsh was absent during the last months and in providing the final impetus which placed the Sioux on the trail to Buford the credit belongs with Jean Louis Legaré.

For the French-Canadian trader, the provisioning of Indians was a costly activity and Jean Louis, who brought all his personal resources to the task of taking Bull back to Buford, was never fully compensated for his expenses. It was not the prospect of mometary reward that motivated him in aiding the Sioux. It is doubtful if money ever entered his thoughts in the early stages of his plan. His reputation was for generosity and fair dealing, "one of the most modest and un-assuming men in the world,"[3] as Z.M. Hamilton wrote when Secretary of the Saskatchewan Historical Society. Probably the idea of seeking payment for expenses and services did not occur to him until late in April, 1881, when he escorted a party of sixteen Sioux from Wood Mountain to Fort Buford. Apparently, Major Brotherton informed him that the United States Government would gladly pay all costs. The offer was never confirmed in writing and it appears that neither Brotherton nor Legaré was thinking at that stage of anything more than the most modest of sums.

And so, Legaré escorted a second group of thirty-two returning Indians in May, and finally, the large contingent of two hundred, including Sitting Bull, in July. In 1882, he travelled to eastern Canada, mainly to see his aging parents after an absence of seventeen years. When in Ottawa, he visited certain members of the Government who were already familiar with his contribution to the repatriation of Sitting Bull through a petition presented previously on the trader's behalf. Consequently, the Government voted a payment of $2,000 which was made to Jean Louis through Sir Hector Langevin.[4] There was, at the same time, a proposal for a grant of one township of western land in lieu of Jean Louis' service but it was not carried out and Legaré did not receive the all-important title.

Some critics, including personnel of the United States Court of Claims, believed Legaré tried to collect too much – that he was trying to take advantage of the Government. He made various trips to Fort Buford, each time reminding Major Brotherton on his hope for reimbursement. The reply was always the same, that payment for such expenses could come only from Washington. Accordingly, itemized statements of expenses were submitted to the United States War Department, and then the United States Department of the Interior, but no settlement was made. There was no authorization, government officials replied, and nothing could be done until the passage of a Bill for Claimant's Relief, then before Congress.

Jean Louis' account was finally filed with the U.S. Court of Claims on July 15, 1887. As presented by Legaré's lawyer, R.A. Burton:

The claimant states that he is a citizen of Canada.... That he is an Indian trader and freighter. That during the years of 1881 and 1882, and after the escape of Sitting Bull and his band of Indians from the United States, the petitioner, by the direction of the commander of the post of the United States Army at Fort Buford, Dakota, undertook to secure the return and surrender to the United States of said Indians, which undertaking he accomplished; that for said work he claims

*from the United States for money expended, stores and sup-
plies furnished, and for services rendered on behalf of de-
fendant, the sum of thirteen thousand, four hundred and
twelve ($13,412) dollars. An itemized bill of this claim is as
follows:*

1. 1881, April 20, Provisions, tobacco, pipes furnished Sitting
Bull and followers .... $ 350.00
2. Transportation, board for Indians from Wood
Mountain, Canada to Fort Buford, Dakota
Territory, 150 miles @ $32 per Indian
  1881, April 26,   16 Indians 512.00
          May 22,   32 Indians 1024.00
          July 11, 200 Indians 6400.00
3. Transportation and board for Indians from Fort
Buford, Dakota, to Wood Mountain, Canada,
150 miles @ $32 per Indian
  1881, May 2, Four Indians 128.00
  1881, June 1, Three Indians 96.00
  1881, June 19, One Indian 32.00
4. Provisions furnished 12 lodges of Indians, about
50 or 60 persons, from April 26, to July 2, 1881   990.00
5. 1881, July 2, Provisions and tobacco furnished
Sitting Bull and followers, 300 Indians 225.00
6. 1881, July 3, Twelve sacks of flour furnished
Sitting Bull and three headman @ $12 .... 144.00
7. 1881, July 11, One revolver to Sitting Bull 15.00
8. 1881, July 11, One looking glass for Sitting Bull   25.00
9. 1881, July 11, To one lodge 12.00
10. 1882, April 12, Board and clothing for one Indian
9 months @ $40 .... 360.00
11. 1882, April 20, One year's services 3,000.00
12. 1882, April 22, One pony turned over to account   45.00
13. Use of pony from August 25,'81 to April 22,'82 ...... 54.00

Total Amount Claimed .... $ 13,412.00

Having heard the case of the claimant, the court listened to
argument by the Attorney General on behalf of the United
States. He denied many of Legaré's claims and asked "that the
petition be dismissed".

In due course, the court delivered its judgment. There was no denial that Legaré had rendered an invaluable service in having brought "235 Indians, including Sitting Bull" to Fort Buford. "The Indians," it was conceded, "had become very troublesome to the Claimant because of their condition of want and poverty." But as the Judge took pains to note, the claimant had already received payment amounting to $2,000 from the Government of Canada. It was mentioned, also, that some of Legaré's actions were motivated by his own interest; there was, for example, the matter of a feast provided for the Sioux. The court saw this as an action intended to prevent an attack upon his own trading post. But the main point in the judgment was that no contract existed. Bringing the Indians back to the United States was a useful act but it was voluntary on Legaré's part because there was no promise on behalf of the defendant to pay the claimant for services.

The post commander at Buford, Major Brotherton, did recommend an allowance of $2,000 – exactly the same amount which was paid by the Government of Canada – but had promised nothing. As the judge was informed, Brotherton told Legaré "he had no authority to contract on behalf of the United States to pay him for services rendered or supplies furnished the Indians during their return but he thought the Government would pay him a reasonable compensation for his services, provisions, and clothing furnished the Indians. The statement was received by claimant without dissent or objection." In the light of evidence, "the court determines as a conclusion of law that the petition is dismissed."

Jean Louis was disappointed but he had learned to take reverses as well as triumphs. And in public gratitude he fared well. Many honours came to him over the years, among them a beautiful stone cairn in the Jean Louis Legaré Park at Willow Bunch. The plaque on the monument carried this tribute:

Jean Louis Legaré (1841-1918) was a founder of Willow Bunch where he settled in 1880 after ten years as a fur-trader at Wood Mountain. He operated a store, a ranch, a cheese factory and post office. He conducted Sitting Bull and 200 Sioux Indians back to the United States in 1881.

What Might Have Been

Wwhat would have been the consequences if Sitting Bull and his brave people had been granted a reservation in Canada or if they were still on the Canadian side when Louis Riel was urging the Indians to join the Métis? The student of history can only conclude that events may have been disastrous. In the light of what did happen in 1885, the Sioux departure proved more fortunate than Canadians realized.

Of the small number of Sioux who did remain in Canada, most of them hastened to the side of Riel and Dumont. And if the Sioux in strength had joined in the war, it would have been extremely difficult for other chiefs such as Crowfoot and Red Crow and Piapot to remain on the sidelines.

The south Saskatchewan trouble, nurtured in Métis unrest, took a serious turn on March 26 when Gabriel Dumont's well-armed half-breed troop clashed with a party of Mounted Police and Prince Albert Volunteers under Major Crozier, a few miles from Duck Lake. The result was a decisive victory for Dumont, and Crozier, after serious casualties – twelve killed and another twelve wounded – was glad to withdraw to Fort Carlton. It was then too late to halt the larger conflict and Riel's people sent runners to invite active support from all the unhappy and sometimes hungry Indians on scattered reserves. Most of the young tribesmen favoured revolt and became difficult to control. Most chiefs, including Crowfoot and Piapot, succeeded in restraining Indian participation only with difficulty. Big Bear and Poundmaker found it impossible to control their braves. Other chiefs, including Beardy and One Arrow of the

Crees and White Cap did not try very hard.

There was massacre at Frog Lake and the threat of attack at Battleford, Fort Edmonton, Prince Albert, Calgary and Regina. But the news of hostilities brought instantaneous response in eastern Canada and Major-General Frederick D. Middleton, former Imperial Army officer, was named to take command of a military force to be rushed to the scene of the rebellion. But bringing an army from the East to places far beyond the reach of new railroads was not an easy matter. The partially completed Canadian Pacific Railway helped to facilitate the journey by taking troops to Qu'Appelle, Swift Current, and Calgary. With the main body of his army, Middleton marched from Qu'Appelle toward Duck Lake; Colonel Otter's force went north from Swift Current and then westward to engage Poundmaker's Crees; and the Alberta Field Force under the command of General Strange, went over the Calgary-Edmonton trail.

Middleton met the Métis in the Battle of Fish Creek and discovered the toughness of the enemy. His losses were heavy and there was immediate criticism that he was not the best man for the command in this conflict. He was an experienced army officer and had a fine reputation, but he did not understand prairie conditions or prairie Indians and was inclined to treat the operation as an all out war. Some, like the author of a *Montreal Witness* editorial, proclaimed Major James Morrow Walsh as the man who should have been appointed. "There is in Canada one man, Major Walsh, whose knowledge of the country, of the Indians and half-breeds and their rights and wrongs, is not excelled by any living man.... The services of a man like this are now sadly required in the Northwest, and in the interest of both the half-breeds and Canada, he should be there with power to act." Other voices proposed that Walsh, with his unequalled record in dealing with the Indians, should be empowered by the Government to form a regiment of sharpshooters of his own choosing. With his experience, it was argued, "he would crush the rebellion in short order."

Walsh who had resigned from the Mounted Police on September 1, 1883, was by this time engaged in the coal business in Manitoba. He had successfully formed the Dominion Coal, Coke and Transportation Company, but remained a keen observer of the prairie scene and his opinions were sought continually. When asked for his views about the Métis revolt, he did not hesitate to say that the man who should have been appointed was his former superior officer, Colonel James F. Macleod. He did not wish to be critical of General Middleton whom he regarded as the best soldier in Canada for conventional warfare. But when it came to dealing with Indians and half-breeds on the Canadian prairies, he had everything to learn. "Had Macleod been in command," Walsh said to the *Globe* correspondent, "he would have secured the loyalty of the Blackfeet by his own personal influence. The Sioux, Assiniboines and Crees would have been secured by the men he would have selected for his Lieutenants."[1] Walsh was thinking of the technique used by General Miles in hiring scouts from among the very Indians he was trying to subdue.

In his usual outspoken way, Walsh declared that the Métis had legitimate grievances. He believed the uprising could have been put down without the firing of a shot. But with fighting already in progress, he emphasized, special precautions should be taken to guard the American boundary against the influx of hostile Indians. He was thinking particularly of the Gros Ventre and Sioux tribesmen who would still welcome a chance to deal a blow at the Europeans, regardless of which side of the border they happened to be on. It was not until May 12 that Middleton defeated the Métis at Batoche. Three days later, Riel surrendered. The rebellion was over except that Middleton considered it necessary to pursue Poundmaker and Big Bear.

The remark was heard many times: "Thank God Sitting Bull is no longer here." Only a few of the Chief's former followers remained at Wood Mountain but, true to their tradition, every healthy young man among them seized his gun and made his way to Duck Lake to join Riel and Dumont. At the same time, the Sioux chief, White Cap, whose people were in Canada from the time of the massacres in Minnesota and had been allotted a reserve south of Saskatoon, led his warriors to Duck Lake, leaving no doubt about his sympathies.

Wounded Horse, a seventy-six-old Sioux living on the small tribal reserve at Wood Mountain in 1971, remembered his grandfather of the same name fighting for Sitting Bull at Little Big Horn, then coming to Canada with the Chief and fighting on the side of Louis Riel in 1885. Pete Lethbridge, seventy-one years of age and still living on the same reserve in 1971, knew that his grandfather, Red Bear, fought in the Custer battle; he later fought alongside Riel's men at Batoche where he was taken prisoner and held in jail at Regina where he died.

There could be no doubt concerning Sioux sympathy in that troubled year and, with a leader like Sitting Bull, the seasoned prairie fighters might have given General Middleton the most serious defeat in his career. It is difficult to escape the thought that Canada might have experienced something resembling the Custer massacre. It was small wonder that Walsh repeatedly urged a close watch on the border and on Sitting Bull. But the old Chief was by that time completely cut off from his own people in North Dakota. Strange as it seemed, he was touring United States and eastern Canada as a leading attraction in "Buffalo Bill" Cody's Wild West Show. He was in no position to make trouble and knew no more about the rebellion than what his white friends told him.

Circus owners had cast covetous glances at the Chief for several years. The idea was discussed while the Chief was in Canada and Major Walsh had been accused, falsely, of trying to persuade him to remain in Canada with the idea of making a circus tour. Just as the Northwest Rebellion campaign was being concluded, the "Buffalo Bill" Cody show was appearing in Ontario, reaching Toronto for a three-day stand on August 22. For several days in advance of the appearance, the Toronto *Globe* carried announcements about this sensational public attraction. "The greatest novelty of the Century, featuring the Renowned Sioux Chief, Sitting Bull, White Eagle and 52 braves," the announcement read. Admission was fifty cents for adults, twenty-five cents for children and "Carriages admitted free."[2]

A few days later, the Toronto paper[3] carried a glowing review of the show built around one hundred and fifty cowboys, eighty horses, a herd of nineteen buffalo, some wild cattle, a few elk and a band of Sioux Indians. Throughout the programme, Buffalo Bill was the hero; the Indians were the villains, repeatedly swooping down on innocent people and having to be driven away by cowboys. In one scene the Indians attacked the Deadwood stagecoach, shooting it up until it could scarcely be seen for gunsmoke. But when all seemed lost,

Buffalo Bill and his posse galloped in to engage the savages and drive them to cover. In another act, the terrible Redmen attacked a settler's cabin and were ready for massacre when, again, Buffalo Bill and his boys appeared and gave the Indians such a gunbattle that they were glad to flee.

During his stay in Toronto, Sitting Bull agreed to talk to a representative of the *Globe*. He spoke reluctantly about his war experiences. "Do you reflect with horror upon the loss of life you caused on the occasion of your fight with Custer?" the reporter asked. The Chief replied calmly: "I have answered to my people for the loss of life on our side; let Custer answer to his own people for the loss on his."

He preferred to talk about his return to Canada and recall his years near Wood Mountain and his desire to remain in "the Great Mother's country". As he talked about his friendship with Walsh, his eyes brightened. He had hoped to see the Major at some point in the Canadian tour but his old friend was in Winnipeg. He spoke admiringly about Chiefs Crowfoot and Poundmaker and Big Bear – good Indians, no matter what the white man's courts might rule concerning them.

And yes, Sitting Bull knew about Louis Riel's return to Canada to lead the Métis and admitted that on five different occasions he had been asked to join in the Métis plan to regain the country for the native people. Were they temptations? Of course they were, but they had come too late for him.

Bull's Last Battle

After several relatively uneventful years, troubled times came again for the Chief. Throughout his life, trouble was never far away, following him, it seemed, like a wolf stalking a lame deer. A government commission wanting the return of certain lands allotted to the Sioux came to renegotiate an earlier agreement. It was the same old story and nobody knew it better than Sitting Bull. Many of those Sioux leaders who experienced the white man's infuriating record of broken promises were now dead. Crazy Horse was dead; Spotted Tail had been murdered; Red Cloud was old; but Sitting Bull's memory was still good and he was still capable of rebellion. Incensed by these white-skinned marauders, his old vigour returned and he was ready to fight for Sioux rights. He persuaded his tribesmen to refuse to relinquish their land and, in so doing, he incurred the displeasure of the government.

It was about this time that an Indian in Nevada saw a vision of a new Messiah, giving rise to what became known as the Messiah Craze. As the Indian reported it, he saw the Messiah standing on a mountain top, clothed in white buffalo robes, coming to bring aid to the native people. Most Indians, whether they had accepted or rejected Christianity, had learned something of New Testament story – enough, at least, to fire their imaginations. A Messiah whose special mission was to save the Indians from the grip of the white man could not come at a better time. Indians who heard the story became greatly exercised and believed that the Great One's coming would mean the return of lands, freedom and buffalo herds.

Sitting Bull was no less moved than the others. Although he had rejected the advances of the European missionaries, he had been a succesful medicine man and a respected religious leader. Perhaps he saw in this new movement an opportunity to recover the leadership and prestige he had lost. Ever sensitive to the mystical, Bull thought deeply about this apparent revelation and decided to conduct his own search for the truth. Ostensibly on a hunting expedition in the direction of the Shoshone Mountains, he found himself one evening following a particularly bright star moving westward across the sky. After pursuing it most of the night, the Chief came face to face with the radiant figure in white buffalo garments. His expression was kindly and his hair and whiskers were long and lustrous. Here, indeed, was the vision seen by the Indian mystic in Nevada. Here, surely, was the Messiah, anxious to meet and confer with Sitting Bull. The Chief fell into a deep sleep, in the course of which he had dreams and saw visions. He saw dead relations and forebears restored to life and buffalo returning to cover the plains.

Awakening, Sitting Bull engaged the Messiah in conversation. The stranger displayed his hands and feet bearing the unmistakable marks made by nails when he was crucified long ago by white men. He came on the earlier occasion to rescue the white race but was not well received. Now he was back to save the Indians from the trouble into which they had fallen and to bring back the buffalo. At nightfall, the mysterious stranger with the halo instructed the Chief to return to his people and urge them to search for the new strength their Messiah could bring. Although some days of actual travel from home, Sitting Bull found a power that enabled him to return in what seemed like only a few minutes and a few paces.

Sitting Bull told his story. It was exactly what the dejected Sioux wanted to hear. They crowded in upon the Chief, chanting and dancing through the night, until many were on the verge of collapse. Sitting Bull was the undisputed leader of the Messiah Craze.

Fearing new outbursts of trouble, Indian Agent James McLaughlin, with whom the Chief had been feuding for years, visited Sitting Bull hoping to persuade him to abandon this Messiah nonsense and spare his followers needless worry and frustration. But the Chief did not see it as nonsense. His experience in the presence of the spiritual figure dressed in white buffalo skins was more convincing that the Indian Agent and he offered to go again to the distant hunting ground if the skeptical agent would accompany him to witness the proof. McLaughlin showed no interest in such a journey. Moreover, if Sitting Bull was determined to pursue this foolishness which had already whipped the Sioux into a frenzy, something would have to be done to restrain him. It was decided that the Chief would have to be arrested and removed, but a legal excuse for apprehension was needed. Perhaps his refusal to send his children to school at the Agency would be enough, or the suspicion that in applying for a pass to leave the Agency, he was planning to escape. Anyway, a warrant was issued and the Indian Police, with support from the infantry, were instructed to make the arrest.

It was six o'clock on the morning of December 15, 1890, when the police under Sergeant Henry Bullhead stole into the Indian village and entered Sitting Bull's house. Taken by surprise and completely overwhelmed in number, the prisoner had very little chance to resist. But while the Chief stalled as he dressed, his son, Crowfoot, notified the neighbours. A crowd of angry Indians gathered and demonstrated threateningly. When the police emerged with their prisoner, one of the officers tried to reason with the angry mob but the Indians were in no mood to compromise. Sitting Bull called upon his friends to rescue him. Needing no more encouragement, two young men ran forward, shooting as they came. One shot struck Sergeant Bullhead and another hit the policeman, Shave Head. And just as he was shot, Bullhead fired and hit Sitting Bull. All three men fell together and in the wild shooting that followed a second bullet hit Sitting Bull. The Indian Police group was forced to withdraw to the shelter of an old house but a signal to awaiting infantrymen under Colonel Drum brought them to the scene and the enraged Sioux were repulsed.

Sitting Bull was seriously wounded but the old warrior did not give up. Having gained possession of a Winchester, he dragged himself to a sheltered spot and fought relentlessly until police and soldiers attacked him, seized his rifle, and broke it over his head. He died almost immediately, fighting to the last.

Some writers suggested that Sitting Bull's death was planned. No doubt some people wanted him out of the way but there is no good reason for presuming premeditated murder. Falling with him were his own son, Crowfoot, Little Assiniboine, Catch-The-Bear and three others of his friends, as well as members of the Indian Police. The Sioux, their hopes again shattered, mourned noisily and cursed their oppressors. The old Chief was buried at the post cemetery at Fort Yates. Sixty-three years later his remains were exhumed and moved to Mobridge, South Dakota, where a monument was erected to his memory. At his passing, the normally undemonstrative tribesmen left no doubt about their great admiration and love for the Chief. They proclaimed the greatness of his courage, the invincibility of his spirit, and his unfailing devotion to his people.

He was the great enigma of his generation; although often described by the white man as a cruel and murderous savage, Sitting Bull had unbending principles and adhered to them. He was a devout family man; he opposed liquor for his Indians; he would make any sacrifice for the sake of freedom; he tried to answer to the Great Spirit and believed in a life hereafter; and contrary to the usual allegations, he was not cruel and vengeful. White men would make unkind aspersions, but in the memory of the Sioux he would live as a hero.

At least one white man agreed with the Indian assessment. Major Walsh who had the best chance to know Bull, payed him a fine tribute. Writing the day after the Chief's death, Walsh had this to say:

I am glad to hear that Bull is relieved of his miseries, even if it took the bullet to do it. A man who wielded such power as Bull once did, that of a King, and over a wild spirited people, cannot endure abject poverty ... without suffering great mental pain, and death is a relief. ... The Indians were not receiving sufficient food. ... women and children crying for assistance ... his suffering from day to day becoming worse ... stronger appeals to the Great Spirit ... appearing to the white people as a craze. ... I regret now that I had not gone to Standing Rock and seen him. ... Bull has been misrepresented. He was not the bloodthirsty man reports made him out to be. He asked for nothing but justice. ... He did not want to be a beggar. ... He was not a cruel man. He was kind of heart. He was not dis-

honest. He was truthful. He loved his people and was glad to give his hand in friendship to any man who was honest with him. . . . Bull experienced so much treachery that he did not know who to trust. . . .[1]

Only in death did Sitting Bull's struggles end. He won most of the battles he fought but lost the important one, the long war against the oncoming hordes from lands across the sea. Strange people, these newcomers, and crafty. He could not understand them, try as he might. Their way of thinking was so foreign to his ideals. What they wanted was to him morally wrong. He found he could not trust them. He said so in that speech by which he might well be remembered, a speech marked by bewilderment and beauty, a speech revealing the depth of his imagination and the anguish in his heart:[2]

Behold, my friends, the spring is come; the earth has gladly received the embrace of the sun, and we shall soon see the results of their love! Every seed is awakened, and all animal life. It is through this mysterious power that we too have our being and we therefore yield to our neighbors, even to our animal neighbors, the same rights as ourselves to inhabit this vast land.

Yet hear me friends! We have now to deal with another people, small and feeble when our forefathers first met with them, but now great and overbearing. Strangely enough, they have a mind to till the soil, and the love of possession is a disease in them. . . . They claim this mother of ours, the Earth, for their own use, and fence their neighbors away from her, and deface her with their buildings and their refuse. They compel her to produce out of season, and when sterile she is made to take medicine in order to produce again. All this is sacrilege.

This nation is like a spring freshet; it overruns its banks and destroys all who are in its path. We cannot dwell side by side. Only seven years ago we made a treaty by which we were assured that the buffalo country should be left to us forever. Now they threaten to take that from us also. My brothers, shall we submit? or shall we say to them: 'First kill me, before you take possession of my fatherland'.

Notes

Pages 16-21

[1] Alexander Henry, *New Light on the Early History of the Greater Northwest.*

[2] Robert B. Hill, *Manitoba; History of its Early Settlement, Development, and Resources,* 120.

Pages 22-27

[1] Hill, *Manitoba.*

[2] *New York Tribune,* August 27, 1862.

[3] *New York Tribune,* August 25, 1862.

[4] *New York Tribune,* September 5, 1862.

Pages 28-36

[1] *Nor'-Wester* (Fort Garry, January 18, 1864.

[2] *Nor'-Wester* (Fort Garry, January 18, 1864.

[3] Hill, *Manitoba,* 225.

[4] *Nor'-Wester* (Fort Garry), February 18, 1864.

[5] *Nor'-Wester* (Fort Garry), September 1, 1864.

[6] *Nor'-Wester* (Fort Garry), September 1, 1864.

Pages 37-44

[1] *Nor'-Wester* (Fort Garry), July 4, 1865.

[2] *Nor'-Wester* (Fort Garry), September 16, 1864.

[3] *Fort Benton Record,* June 26, 1875.

[4] *Manitoba Daily Free Press* (Winnipeg), July 11, 1874.

Pages 45-53

[1] John McDougall, *On Western Trails in the Early Seventies.*

Pages 54-64

[1] House of Commons. *Debates,* April 28, 1873.

[2] James Morrow Walsh, Journal of proceedings of a detachment of Mounted Police Under Major J. M. Walsh, 1873.

[3]*Manitoban* (Fort Garry), October 4, 1873.

[4]*Ibid*, April 18, 1874.

[5]*Manitoba Daily Free Press* (Winnipeg), August 11, 1874.

[6]*Ibid*, July 6, 1874.

[7]*Ibid*, July 10, 1874.

[8]*Ibid*, July 8, 1874.

[9]*Ibid*, July 10, 1874.

Pages 65-71

[1]*Manitoba Daily Free Press* (Winnipeg), March 7, 1876.

[2]E. S. Godfrey, "Custer's Last Stand," *Scarlet and Gold*, XV (1933-4), 85.

[3]Flora Warren Seymour, *The Story of the Red Man*, 320.

[4]Norman B. Wood, *Lives of Famous Indians*, 455.

[5]*Manitoba Daily Free Press* (Winnipeg), July 21, 1876.

Pages 72-83

[1]Irvine to Walsh, July 5, in North West Mounted Police Letterbook for 1876.

[2]U.S. Bureau of Indian Affairs, *Famous Indians*.

[3]*Manitoba Daily Free Press* (Winnipeg), October 27, 1876.

[4]Walsh Papers, May 22, 1890.

[5]Walsh Papers, May 22, 1890.

[6]Walsh Papers, May 22, 1890.

[7]Walsh Papers, May 22, 1890.

[8]Walsh Papers, May 22, 1890.

Pages 84-89

[1]Adrien Chabot, *History of Willow-Bunch*, II, 1920-1970, 228.

[2]Walsh Papers, May 22, 1890.

[3]Walsh Papers, May 22, 1890.

Pages 90-96

[1]Walsh Papers, May 22, 1890.

[2]Walsh Papers, May 22, 1890.

[3]John Peter Turner, *The North-West Mounted Police, 1873-1893*, I, 325.

Pages 97-103

[1]Turner, *The North-West Mounted Police, 1873-1893*, I, 308.

[2]*Saskatchewan Herald* (Battleford), July 14, 1877.

[3]E. Dalrymple Clark, in *Sessional Papers of Canada*, 1878, No. 4, 39.

[4]*Ibid.*, Appendix E, 40-41.

Pages 104-110

[1]Taylor, James W. Letter to U.S. Secretary of State, in the *Globe* (Toronto), August 9, 1877.

[2]Macleod to Hon. Alexander Mackenzie, May 30, 1877, in *Sessional Papers of Canada*, 1878, No. 4, Appendix E, 34-5.

[3]*Globe* (Toronto), October 22, 1877.

[4]House of Commons. *Debates*, 1879, 1756.

[5]*Fort Benton Record*, May 7, 1880.

[6]*Montreal Witness*, August 29, 1877.

[7]*Fort Benton Record*, June 29, 1877.

[8]House of Commons. *Debates*, 1878, 353.

Pages 111-115

[1]Scott, Hon. R. W. to Macleod in *Sessional Papers of Canada*, 1878, No. 4, Appendix E, 42.

[2]Mills, Hon. David to Macleod in *Sessional Papers of Canada*, 1878, No. 4, Appendix E, 42.

[3]*Fort Benton Record*, September 14, 1877.

[4]Walsh Papers, May 22, 1890.

Pages 116-123

[1]*Fort Benton Record*, August 31, 1877.

[2]Walsh Papers, May 22, 1890.

[3]Walsh Papers, May 22, 1890.

Pages 124-133

[1]Macleod, James Farquherson. Letter to his wife, Mary Isabella (Drever), October 12, 1877.

[2]Turner, *The North-West Mounted Police, 1873-1893*, I, 363.

[3]*Sessional Papers of Canada*, 1878, No. 4, Appendix E, 47.

[4]*Sessional Papers of Canada*, 1878, No. 4, Appendix E, 48.

[5]Macleod, James Farquherson. Letter to American Commissioner in *Sessional Papers of Canada*, 1878, No. 4, Appendix E, 49.

[6]George Shepherd, "Wood Mountain Post", *Canadian Cattleman*, December, 1945, 123.

Pages 134-139

[1]*Fort Benton Record*, April 5, 1878.

[2]North-West Mounted Police Report for 1876 in *Sessional Papers of Canada*, 1877, No. 9, Appendix D, 21.

[3]*Montreal Witness*, August 16, 1877.

[5]*Globe* (Toronto), September 25, 1877.

[6]*Fort Benton Record*, April 19, 1878.

[7]*Saskatchewan Herald*, May 5, 1879.

[8]*Walsh Papers*, April 24, 1878.

Pages 140-146

[1]*Fort Benton Record*, March 12, 1880.

[2]*Saskatchewan Herald*, June 2, 1879.

[3]George Bird Grinnell, *The Fighting Cheyennes.*

[4]Turner, *The North-West Mounted Police, 1873-1893*, I, 409.

[5]Turner, *The North-West Mounted Police, 1873-1893*, I, 443.

Pages 147-152

[1]Camp Crier, *Scarlet and Gold*, XII (1930), 99.

[2]Daniel "Peaches" Davis, "Trading with The Indians at Wood Mountain", *Scarlet and Gold*, XVI (1935), 59.

[3]Clovis Rondeau, *La Montagne de Bois — Willow Bunch, Saskatchewan*, 76.

Pages 153-158

[1]*Saskatchewan Herald*, September 8, 1879.

[2]Edgar Dewdney, Annual Report of the Department of Indian Affairs

for the Year Ended 31st December, 1880, in *Sessional Papers of Canada*, 1880-81, No. 14, 93.

[3] *Fort Benton* (Montana) *Weekly Record*, August 25, 1881.

[4] W. Palmer Clarke in Annual Report of the Department of Indian Affairs for the Year Ended 31st December, 1880, in *Sessional Papers of Canada*, 1880-81, No. 14, 101.

[5] Rondeau, *La Montagne de Bois*, 93.

[6] *Fort Benton Record*, December 29, 1881.

Pages 159-166

[1] Walsh Papers, March 24, 1879.

[2] *Ibid.*, Nov. 9, 1878.

[3] Walsh Papers, March 24, 1879.

[4] Watogala, in Walsh Papers, undated.

[5] Rondeau, *La Montagne de Bois*, 86.

Pages 167-172

[1] Irvine to Colonel Bernard, April 26, in North West Mounted Police Letter-book for 1876.

[2] Macleod to Secretary of State, November 17, in North West Mounted Police Letterbook for 1876.

[3] Macleod to Walsh, November 24, in North West Mounted Police Letter-book for 1876.

[4] *Fort Benton Record*, September 29, 1876.

[5] *Ibid.*, June 8, 1877.

[6] *Ibid.*, August 8, 1879.

[7] *Ibid.*, December 1, 1877.

[8] *Ibid.*, November 22, 1878.

[9] Walsh, in Annual Report of the North West Mounted Police for 1880, in *Sessional Papers of Canada*, 1880-81, No. 3, 29.

[10] *Saskatchewan Herald*, July 5, 1880.

[11] Walsh, Annual Report of the North-West Mounted Police for 1880, in *Sessional Papers of Canada*, 1880-81, No. 3, 29.

Pages 173-178

[1] *Fort Benton Record*, December 29, 1881.

[2] Walsh Papers.

[3] *Ibid.*,

[4] Walsh, Annual Report of the North-West Mounted Police for 1880, in *Sessional Papers of Canada*, 1880-81, No. 3, 27.

[5]*Ibid.*, 28.

[6]Turner, *The North-West Mounted Police, 1873-1893*, I, 449.

Pages 179-183

[1]Gary Pennanen, "Sitting Bull, Indian Without a Country," *Canadian Historical Review*, June, 1970, 123.

Pages 184-188

[1]House of Commons. Debates, March 11, 1881, 1353.

[2]Samuel Benfield Steele, *Forty Years in Canada*, 159.

[3]Zachary MacCaulay Hamilton, *These are the Prairies*.

[4]John Hawkes, *The Story of Saskatchewan*, 365.

[5]Walsh Papers.

[6]*Ibid.*

Pages 189-195

[1]*Saskatchewan Herald*, March 24, 1879.

[2]Hamilton, *These are the Prairies*, 26.

[3]Chabot, *La Montagne de Bois*, 98.

[4]Turner, *The North-West Mounted Police, 1873-1893*, I, 583.

[5]*Fort Benton (Montana) Weekly Record*, August 11, 1881.

[6]*Benton River Press*, August 24, 1881.

Pages 196-200

[1]*Fort Benton Record*, July 28, 1881.

[2]*Ibid.*, August 25, 1881.

[3]Hamilton to Deputy Minister of Public Archives, October 26, 1939.

[4]House of Commons. *Debates*, May 13, 1882, 1508-9.

[5]Records of United States Court of Claims, C.J. No. 15713, J. Legare Vs. the U.S. Filed July 15, 1887.

Pages 201-203

[1]*Globe* (Toronto) April 8, 1885.

[2]*Globe* (Toronto), August 22, 1885.

[3]*Globe* (Toronto), August 24, 1885.

Pages 204-208

[1]Walsh Papers, December 16, 1890.

[2]Charles A. Eastman, *Indian Heroes and Great Chieftains*, 119.

Bibliography

Unpublished Materials

Walsh, James Morrow. Correspondence, manuscripts and miscellaneous papers, 1874-1905; Journal of Proceedings of a Detachment of Mounted Police under Major J. M. Walsh, 1-22 October, 1873, Public Archives of Manitoba, Winnipeg Man.

Hamilton, Zachary MacCaulay. Letter to Deputy Minister of Public Archives in Sitting Bull File. Public Archives of Canada, Ottawa.

North West Mounted Police. Letterbook for 1876. Public Archives of Canada, Ottawa.

Macleod, James Farquharson. Letter to his wife, Mary Isabella (Drever), October 12, 1877. Glenbow – Alberta Institute Archives, Calgary, Alta.

United States. Court of Claims. C.J. No. 15713, *J. Legaré* vs. *the United States,* filed July 15, 1887. National Archives, Washington, D.C.

Newspapers

Benton (Montana) *River Press*
Calgary Herald (Alberta)
Chicago Times
Fort Benton Record (Benton, Montana)
Globe (Toronto)
Manitoba Daily Free Press (Winnipeg)
Manitoban (Fort Garry)
Montreal Witness (Quebec)
New York Herald
New York Tribune
Nor'-Wester (Fort Garry, Manitoba)
St. Paul Pioneer Press (Minnesota)
Saskatchewan Herald (Battleford)
Winnipeg Weekly Times

Books, Articles, and Published Documents

Annual Report for the Department of Indian Affairs for the year ended 31st December, 1880. Ottawa, 1881.

Annual Report of the North-West Mounted Police, 1876 – 1880. Ottawa, 1877 – 1881.

"Camp Crier", *Scarlet and Gold,* XII, 1930.

Canada. Parliament. House of Commons. *Debates,* 1873 – 1882.

Chabot, Adrien. *History of Willow-Bunch, 1920 – 1970.* Winnipeg, Canadian Publishers, 1970.

Davis, Daniel Peaches. "Trading with the Indians at Wood Mountain", *Scarlet and Gold*, XVI, 1935.

Eastman, Charles A. *Indian Heroes and Great Chieftains*. Boston, Little, Brown, 1924.

Grinnell, George Bird. *The Fighting Cheyennes*. New York, C. Scribner, 1915.

Hamilton, Zachary MacCaulay and Marie Albina Hamilton. *These are the Prairies*. Regina, School Aids and Textbook Pub. Co., 1948.

Hawkes, John. *The Story of Saskatchewan and its People*. Chicago, S.J. Clarke, 1924.

Henry, Alexander. *New Light on the Early History of the Greater Northwest; the Manuscript Journals of Alexander Henry and David Thomson*. Edited by Elliott Coues, 1897. Minneapolis, Ross and Haines, 1965.

Hill, Robert B. *Manitoba; History of its Early Settlement, Development, and Resources*. Toronto, W. Briggs, 1890.

McDougall, John. *On Western Trails in the Early Seventies; Frontier Pioneer Life in the Canadian North-West*. Toronto, W. Briggs, 1911.

Pennanen, Gary, "Sitting Bull; Indian without a Country", *Canadian Historical Review*, June, 1923.

Rondeau, Clovis. *La Montagne de Bois – Willow Bunch, Sask.* Quebec, Action sociale, 1923.

Shepherd, George. "Wood Mountain Post", *Canadian Cattleman*, December, 1945.

Steele, Samuel Benfield. *Forty Years in Canada*. London, H. Jenkins, 1915.

Seymour, Flora Warren. *The Story of the Red Man*. New York, Longmans, Green, 1929.

Turner, John Peter. *The North-West Mounted Police 1873 – 1893*. 2 vols. Ottawa, King's Printer, 1950.

United States. Bureau of Indian Affairs. *Famous Indians*, n.d.

Wood, Norman Barton. *Lives of Famous Indians*. Aurora, Ill., American Indian Historical Pub. Co., 1906.

Index

Allen, Manager: 150-52
Allen, Sub-Inspector Edwin: 92, 100, 171
Allison, Edwin: 181-82
Anderson, Major: 59
Anthony, Major Scott: 141

Baird, Lieutenant George: 144
Bell, George: 49, 52
Benteen, Captain Frederick: 68-69
Big Bear, Chief: 10, 21, 138, 201, 205
Black Horn: 81, 83
Black Kettle, Chief: 142
Black Moon: 76, 148
Black Wolf: 159-60
Breland, Pascal: 33
Broken Arm, Chief: 91, 93
Brotherton, Major David: 187, 191-93, 197-200
Brown, Kootenai: 47
Bullhead, Sergeant Henry: 208
Burns, Pat: 134
Burton, R. A.: 198
Butler, William Francis: 54

Carrington, Brigadier-General H. B.: 39
Cartwright, Sir Richard J.: 184-85
Chabot, Father Adrien: 85
Chartrand, Jean: 191
Clark, Adjutant E. Dalrymple: 100, 102
Clarke, W. Palmer: 156
Chivington, Colonel J. M.: 141
Clifford, Captain Walter: 192, 194
Cochrane, Senator H. M.: 184
Cody, "Buffalo Bill": 154, 171-72, 204-05
Corbin, Captain H. C.: 125
Crazy Horse: 41, 44, 66-70, 142, 206
Crook, General George: 44, 66-70
Crow King, Chief: 68, 208-09
Crowfoot (Sitting Bull's son): 208-09
Crowfoot, Chief: 113, 154, 155, 201, 205
Crozier, Major L. N. F.: 172, 180-81, 189, 196, 201

Cullen, Commissioner W. E.: 163
Curtis, Charles: 32
Custer, General George A.: 42-43, 61, 65-71, 142
Custer, Captain Thomas W.: 43, 70
Cypress Hills Massacre: 47-50

Dallas, Governor A. G.: 29, 30
Daniels, Louis: 77-79, 188
Davis, Daniel "Peaches": 150-51
De Corby, Father: 88
Dehill, Charles: 125
Denny, Sub-Inspector C. E.: 135-36
Devereaux, Jeff: 48-51
Dewdney, Edgar: 155, 186-87
Drum, Colonel: 208
Dubuc, Honourable: 107
Dufferin, Lord: 108
Dull Knife, Chief: 142
Dumont, Gabriel: 201, 203

Evans, John: 48-52

Farwell, Abel: 47-53
Fetterman, Captain William J.: 39-46, 65
Finerty, John: 164-65
Fort Dufferin: 62-63
Fort Phil Kearney: 39
Fort Whoop-Up: 45, 48
Four Horns, Chief: 78-83, 148, 194
Frechette, Sub-Inspector Edmund: 76
French, Lieutenant-Colonel George A.: 59, 61-62, 98

Gaff, J. A. "Dad": 154
Gall, Chief: 68-70, 73-75, 182-83, 188
Genin, Father: 143
Gibbon, General John: 66, 118, 121
Grace, Ed: 50
Grant, President Ulysses: 41, 42
Grizzly Bear, Chief: 62

Hale, Trevanion: 48-52
Hamilton, A. B.: 46
Hamilton, Sergeant Henry: 151
Hammond, General: 187-88
Hardwick, Thomas: 48-52

Harper, Charlie: 48-52
Hatch, Major E. A. C.: 33-34
Healy, Joe: 45-46
Healy, Johnny: 132-33
Herchmer, Superintendent W. M.:
    172
Hole-In-The-Day, Chief: 25
Howard, General Oliver: 118-121
Hugonard, Father: 186-87

Iron Horn: 75
Irvine, Colonel A. G.: 72, 95, 100,
    102, 144, 170, 182, 196

Jarvis, Superintendent W. D.: 59,
    63, 172
Joseph, Chief: 114, 117-23, 125,
    143
Jumping Buffalo: 11

Kellog, Mark: 70
Kittson, Dr. John: 92-93

Laird, Lieutenant-Governor: 114
Langevin, Sir Hector: 198
Laurie, Patrick Gamie: 138, 141
Lavallie, Louis: 75-76, 77-78, 84-85
Lawrence, General A. G.: 125, 130
Lebombarde, Alexis: 53
Legaré, Jean-Louis: 99, 105, 150,
    173, 189-92, 197-200
Lethbridge, Pete: 203
Little Child, Chief: 91-92
Little Crow, Chief: 23, 26, 29, 31
Little Feather: 148
Little Salteaux: 79-82
Little Six: 31-32
Little Wolf, Chief: 142
Long Dog: 76
Low Dog, Chief: 182-83

Macdonald, Sir John Alexander:
    51, 54-55, 61, 107, 110, 180-82,
    184-85
Macdonell, Constable A. R.: 98,
    189, 193-94, 196
Mackenzie, Prime Minister
    Alexander: 61, 105, 110
Macleod, Assistant Commissioner
    James: 47, 51, 58, 63, 105-06,
    111, 113, 116, 124-33, 144, 168,
    182, 196-203
Martin, Constable J. A.: 98
Marty, Father Martin: 100-02, 165

McCutcheon, Sergeant Robert: 88
McDougall, Captain: 68-69
McDougall, Reverend John: 45
McDougall, William: 145
McFarland, John: 49
McLaughlin, James: 207-08
McLean, John: 31
Medicine Bear: 38, 82-83
Messiah Craze: 206-07
Middleton, Major-General
    Frederick D.: 202-04
Miles, General Nelson: 74, 113,
    121, 156, 163-68
Mills, Honourable David: 106, 111
Morin: 77
Morris, Lieutenant-Governor
    Alexander: 51, 60
Mount, Constable Jack: 148

New Nation: 146

Otter, Colonel William: 202

Page, M. C.: 51
Phillips, Wendell: 108-09
Piapot, Chief: 21, 201
Poitras, Pierre: 148
Potts, Jerry: 21, 63, 124
Poundmaker: 201, 205
Provost, Constant: 127, 129

Rain-In-The-Face, Chief: 43, 70, 75
Red Cloud: 37, 39-41, 206
Reno, Major Marcus: 67-71, 73
Riel, Louis: 140, 145-46, 154, 169,
    201, 203
Ross, Colonel Robertson: 54
Runs-The-Roe: 129-30

Schultz, Dr. John C.: 24
Scott, Honourable R. W.: 111
Scott, Thomas: 146
Selkirk Settlers: 18-19
Sheridan, General Philip Henry: 45
Sherman, General: 42, 107
Silbey, Colonel H. H.: 25, 29
Smith, Donald A.: 146
Smith, Captain E. W.: 125
Smith, Lieutenant-Colonel
    Osborne: 55, 59
Soloman, Gabriel: 84, 87
Solomon, Moses: 49
Spotted Eagle: 76, 85, 127, 129,
    180, 188

Spotted Tail: 206
Standing Buffalo: 31, 34
Stanley, General: 42
Steele, Inspector S. B.: 179-86
Stillson, Jerome B.: 125

Taché, Bishop: 29
Taylor, James W.: 104
Terry, General Alfred H.: 42, 66,
    70, 111-13, 125-33, 163-77, 183
Terry Commission: 125-130
Thornton, Sir Edward: 163

Vincent, Sam: 48, 57

Walsh, Major James Morrow:
    55-57, 64, 77-83, 85-89, 93-95,
    118-122, 148-150, 169-170, 172,
    174-179, 209-210

Walsh, Mary Elizabeth (Mowat): 57
Walsh, William: 58
Watogala: 161-62
White Bird, Chief: 116-23, 143-44
White Cap: 202, 203
White Dog: 87-9, 91, 194
White Eagle, Chief: 76, 204
Wolseley, Colonel Garnet: 105, 146
Wolverine: 32
Wood, Commissioner S. T.: 48
Wounded Horse: 203

Young Chief: 62

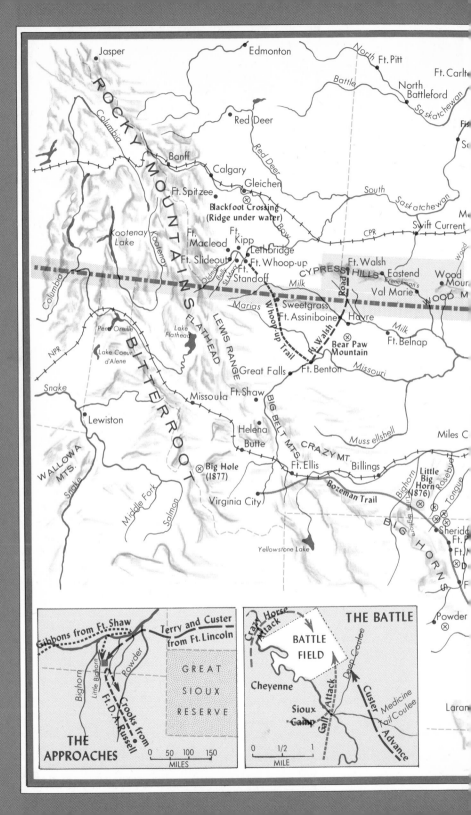